Arif Hassan

ISLAM & MUSLIMS
Transcending Context & Culture

BLUEROSE PUBLISHERS
India | U.K.

Copyright © Arif Hassan 2025

All rights reserved by author. No part of this publication may be reproduced, stored in a retrieval system or transmitted in any form or by any means, electronic, mechanical, photocopying, recording or otherwise, without the prior permission of the author. Although every precaution has been taken to verify the accuracy of the information contained herein, the publisher assume no responsibility for any errors or omissions. No liability is assumed for damages that may result from the use of information contained within.

BlueRose Publishers takes no responsibility for any damages, losses, or liabilities that may arise from the use or misuse of the information, products, or services provided in this publication.

For permissions requests or inquiries regarding this publication, please contact:

BLUEROSE PUBLISHERS
www.BlueRoseONE.com
info@bluerosepublishers.com
+91 8882 898 898
+4407342408967

ISBN: 978-93-7018-445-9

Cover design: Daksh
Typesetting: Tanya Raj Upadhyay

First Edition: April 2025

Dedicated to my father who nurtured in me an open mind and the spirit of enquiry

ACKNOWLEDGEMENT

This book fulfills my long-cherished desire to write about Islam and Muslims exploring their cultural expression, variation across time and context, and, the issues and challenges that people of this faith are facing today. The motivation to work on this book came from the knowledge and understanding that I got while working at the International Islamic University of Malaysia. Many thanks to all the scholars of Islamic studies who enriched my knowledge and provided me with opportunities to deliberate on the role of religion in society as it evolved over time.

I am a student of Social Psychology and have spent years conducting research studies on behavioral issues in management. I did not publish anything of this genre before. I started working on this book when I had more time from academic duties at the university. Thanks to the leisurely life that I am fortunate to have after retirement.

Special thanks to my good friend Dr. Razi Azmi for having a lively conversation with me on Islam, Muslims, current affairs, and challenges faced by the followers of religions in the modern world. He inspired and encouraged me to write this book. I am also indebted to my old friend Dr. Qamar Ahsan for reviewing the manuscript and writing foreword of this book.

I am grateful to my wife for taking care of me while I am busy writing. My life couldn't have been more pleasant without the love and care that my two children and the two grandkids provide.

I would like to extend my thanks to Bluerose publishers who worked hard at different stages of the book production. Special thanks to Ms. Ria Singh and Ms. Sakshi, the publication manager. Last but not least, thanks to Sri Satish Girija jee for introducing me to the Bluerose publishers.

FOREWORD

Islam, as a global faith, has transcended time, culture, and geography, uniting diverse peoples under the banner of its teachings. Yet, as it has expanded across continents and civilizations, its interpretation and practice have inevitably been shaped by the cultural and historical contexts in which it has taken root. This interplay between the universality of Islam and its contextual adaptations forms the core theme of *Islam and Muslims: Transcending Culture and Context*.

This book is a timely and necessary exploration of Islam beyond its commonly perceived monolithic identity. It provides a nuanced discussion of how Muslims around the world have upheld their faith while adapting to the social, political, and cultural realities of their respective environments. By examining these dynamic interactions, it challenges simplistic portrayals and deepens our understanding of Islam as both a universal faith and a lived tradition.

At a time when discourse surrounding Islam is often shaped by stereotypes or misconceptions, this work offers a much-needed perspective rooted in scholarship and lived experience. It highlights the diversity within the Muslim community and demonstrates that cultural differences do not negate the unity of Islamic belief. Instead, they enrich its practice and offer invaluable insights into the ways in which faith, identity, and culture intersect.

The author of this book has meticulously analyzed the historical and contemporary manifestations of Islam across regions, shedding light on the adaptability and resilience of Muslim communities. Their work stands as an invitation to engage in informed and respectful dialogue, to appreciate the plurality within the faith, and to recognize the shared values that connect Muslims across the globe.

It is my sincere hope that *Islam and Muslims: Transcending Culture and Context* will serve as a bridge of understanding, fostering meaningful conversations and inspiring readers to look beyond cultural boundaries in their engagement with Islam and its followers. This book is not only for scholars and students but for anyone seeking a deeper appreciation of the richness and diversity of the Islamic tradition.

Dr. Qamar Ahsan
Professor of Economics & Former Vice-Chancellor
Magadh University
February 10, 2025

PREFACE

The Muslim world, with its origins in the Arabian Peninsula in the 7th century CE, grew rapidly under the teachings of the Prophet Muhammad. The establishment of Islam brought about a profound transformation, creating a religious, political, and social order that reshaped Arabian society. Today, Muslims, the adherents of this faith, form the world's second-largest religious community, with over 1.9 billion followers and 50+ Muslim countries.

Islam's rich history is intertwined with remarkable contributions to various fields of human knowledge, including science, technology, mathematics, medicine, astronomy, and literature. Over centuries, the religion expanded across continents, profoundly influencing civilizations. The Muslim world has witnessed the rise and fall of great empires, most notably the Ottomans and Mughals, whose legacy still resonates in global history. The enduring legacy of Islamic civilization is etched into the very fabric of history, reflected in the remarkable monuments it has left behind. These architectural marvels—found in regions as diverse as the Indian subcontinent, Spain, Turkey, and Uzbekistan—stand as a testament to the ingenuity, creativity, and scientific achievements of Muslim architects, engineers, and artisans.

However, the story of Islam and Muslims transcends these visible landmarks. It is a narrative of faith, resilience, and adaptation, spanning centuries and continents. From its origins in the Arabian Peninsula to its flourishing presence in societies around the globe, Islam has been both a unifying spiritual force and a dynamic cultural phenomenon, shaping and being shaped by the contexts in which it exists.

This book, *Islam and Muslims: Transcending Context and Culture*, delves into the intricate tapestry of Islam's principles and its diverse expressions. It seeks to bridge the gap between historical achievements and contemporary challenges, providing a nuanced exploration of a faith practiced by nearly two billion people worldwide.

The Muslim world's contributions to fields such as science, technology, literature, and governance are well-documented. Yet, these accomplishments are often overshadowed by modern challenges, including Islamophobia, political conflicts, and the socio-economic struggles facing many Muslim countries. The portrayal of Muslims in global media, the ongoing crises in regions such as Palestine, and the tensions between tradition and modernity further complicate the narrative.

As a Muslim who has lived and engaged with communities across India, Malaysia, Australia, and beyond, I have witnessed the diversity and richness of Muslim societies. At the same time, I have been deeply moved by the stories of suffering faced by Muslims in many places. These experiences have inspired me to reflect on the complexities of Islam and its adherents, not just from a religious perspective but through the lens of shared humanity.

This book explores pivotal questions and issues confronting Muslims globally, including the role of religion in politics, the intersection of Islam with democracy, gender dynamics, the aspirations of Muslim youth, and the impact of globalization. It also examines the ongoing dialogue between faith and culture, tradition and modernity, religion and science, and the possibilities for fostering interfaith harmony and pluralism.

In today's interconnected world, understanding one another is not just a moral imperative but a practical necessity. Through this work, I hope to encourage readers—whether scholars, students, or the curious—to move beyond stereotypes and engage with Islam as both a faith and a lived reality. By exploring its historical achievements and contemporary challenges, this book aims to contribute to a deeper appreciation of Islam's universal values, such as compassion, justice, and unity, and to foster meaningful dialogue about coexistence in an increasingly complex world.

It is my sincere hope that *Islam and Muslims: Transcending Context and Culture* will inspire readers to embrace curiosity and empathy while appreciating the remarkable contributions and ongoing struggles of Muslim communities worldwide. May it serve as a reminder of the shared humanity that unites us all and the enduring potential for understanding and harmony in our global society.

Arif Hassan

TABLE OF CONTENTS

ACKNOWLEDGEMENT v

FOREWORD vii

PREFACE ix

CHAPTER 1 THE ORIGIN AND SPREAD OF THE MUSLIM WORLD 1

CHAPTER 2 FAITH, IDENTITY, AND BELONGING IN A GLOBALIZED WORLD 25

CHAPTER 3 ISLAMIC PRINCIPLES: INTERPRETATIONS ACROSS REGIONS 35

CHAPTER 4 WESTERN PERCEPTIONS AND STEREOTYPES OF MUSLIMS 48

CHAPTER 5 MUSLIM MINDSET: NAVIGATING THE CONFLICT BETWEEN TRADITION AND MODERNITY 62

CHAPTER 6 EMERGING A WESTERN ISLAM: BRIDGING CULTURES AND FAITHS 76

CHAPTER 7 EDUCATION, LITERACY, AND INTELLECTUAL TRADITIONS 91

CHAPTER 8 ROLE OF RELIGION IN POLITICAL SYSTEM AND GOVERNANCE 104

CHAPTER 9 ISLAM AND SCIENCE 113

CHAPTER 10 ISLAMIC VS. MUSLIM VALUES 144

CHAPTER 11 ECONOMIC DEVELOPMENT 164

CHAPTER 12 MUSLIM YOUTHS: CHALLENGES AND ASPIRATIONS 181

CHAPTER 13 INTERFAITH DIALOGUE AND CO-EXISTENCE 192

CHAPTER 14 GLOBALISATION AND FUTURE OF MUSLIM SOCIETIES 201

CHAPTER 15 ISLAM AND DEMOCRACY 211

CHAPTER 16 ISLAM AND GENDER EQUITY 228

CHAPTER 17 HUMAN DEVELOPMENT IN MUSLIM COUNTRIES 246

CHAPTER 18 THE GEOPOLITICS: CAUSES AND CONSEQUENCES 260

ANNOTATED BIBLIOGRAPHY 270

CHAPTER 1
THE ORIGIN AND SPREAD OF THE MUSLIM WORLD

Introduction

The Muslim world, with origins in the Arabian Peninsula in the 7th century CE, grew rapidly under the teachings of the Prophet Muhammad. With the establishment of Islam, a religious, political, and social order began to take shape, marking a profound transformation in Arabian society. This early Islamic community soon expanded, stretching from Spain in the west to the Indus Valley in the east within a century of Muhammad's death. Today, Muslims are spread over the globe.

Population[1]

According to a survey conducted by Pew Research Centre (2017), adherents of Islam represent the world's second-largest religion. As of 2020, Pew Research Centre projections suggested a total population of 1.9 billion Muslims worldwide. According to an estimate, there are 50 Muslim countries. Islam is the majority religion in Central Asia, Western Asia, North Africa, West Africa, the Sahel, and the Middle East (Wikipedia).

The diverse Asia-Pacific region contains the highest number of Muslims in the world, surpassing the combined

---

[1] Latest available country-wide data of Muslim population can be accessed on:https://worldpopulationreview.com/country-rankings/muslim-population-by-country

Middle East and North Africa. Around 62% of the world's Muslims live in the Asia-Pacific region (from Turkey to Indonesia), with over one billion adherents. Asia hosts the world's top 4 largest domestic populations, starting with Indonesia at 12.7% of the world, followed by Pakistan—11.1%, then India—10.9%, and Bangladesh—9.2%. Africa has the 5th and 6th largest populations in Nigeria—5.3%, and Egypt—4.9%. The Middle East hosts 7th and 8th with both Iran and Turkey holding an estimated 4.6%. Only about 20% of Muslims live in the Arab world (Wikipedia).

Islam is the dominant religion in the Maldives, Afghanistan, Pakistan, and Bangladesh. India is the country with the largest Muslim population outside Muslim countries with more than 200 million adherents.

The Middle East-North Africa (MENA) region hosts 23% of the world's Muslims, and Islam is the dominant religion in every country in the region other than Israel. The country with the single largest population of Muslims is Indonesia in Southeast Asia, which on its own hosts 13% of the world's Muslims. Together, Muslims in the countries of Southeast Asia constitute the world's third-largest population of Muslims. In the countries of the Malay Archipelago, Muslims are in the majority in Brunei, Indonesia, and Malaysia. About 15% of Muslims reside in Sub-Saharan Africa, and sizeable Muslim communities are also found in the Americas, Russia, China and Europe. Western Europe hosts many Muslim immigrant communities where Islam is the second-largest religion after Christianity (Wikipedia).

The Origin of Islam and the Life of Prophet Muhammad

Islam originated in the Arabian Peninsula in the 7th century CE. It was founded by Prophet Muhammad, whose teachings and revelations form the core of Islamic belief. Before the advent of Islam, the Arabian Peninsula was a land of diverse tribes, each with its customs and deities. The region's dominant social structure was tribal, with loyalty to one's tribe surpassing other affiliations. Mecca, a prominent city, was a religious and commercial hub, home to the Kaaba, a sanctuary housing idol of various tribal gods.

The pre-Islamic period, often referred to as *Jahiliyyah* ("Age of Ignorance"), was marked by polytheism, social inequality, and frequent tribal conflicts. However, Mecca's economic prosperity and cultural exchanges with neighboring Byzantine and Sassanian empires created a fertile ground for new ideas and beliefs. Amidst this backdrop, Islam emerged as a unifying and transformative force.

Muhammad was born in Mecca around 570 CE into the Quraysh tribe, a respected clan known for its guardianship of the Kaaba. His father, Abdullah, died before his birth, and his mother, Amina, passed away when he was six years old. Orphaned at an early age, Muhammad was cared for by his grandfather, Abdul Muttalib, and later by his uncle, Abu Talib.

Despite his humble beginnings, Muhammad gained a reputation for honesty and trustworthiness, earning the title "Al-Amin" (the Trustworthy). As a young man, he worked as a merchant and managed caravans for Khadijah, a wealthy widow. Their professional relationship blossomed into marriage, and Khadijah became his most steadfast supporter.

At the age of 40 Muhammad experienced his first revelation through the Angel Jibreel (Gabriel). This event marked the beginning of his prophethood. The revelation commanded him to "Recite" (Iqra), and subsequent messages emphasized monotheism, social justice, and submission to Allah (God). Initially, he shared his message privately with close family and friends. His wife, Khadijah, and his cousin, Ali, were among the first converts. Over time, his teachings attracted a small but dedicated group of followers, emphasizing moral conduct, charity, and worship of the one true God.

Muhammad's monotheistic message challenged the Quraysh's polytheistic traditions and economic interests tied to idol worship. As his following grew, so did the opposition from the Meccan elites. Muhammad and his followers faced persecution, social ostracism, and economic boycotts. Despite these hardships, Muhammad continued to preach, gaining converts from various strata of society. In 622 CE, faced with escalating hostility, Muhammad and his followers emigrated to Yathrib (later renamed Medina) in an event known as the Hijra. This migration marks the beginning of the Islamic calendar.

In Medina, Muhammad assumed the role of a statesman and spiritual leader, uniting warring tribes under the Constitution of Medina, which established a multi-religious, cooperative community. The document set forth principles of mutual respect and governance, ensuring the rights of Muslims, Jews, and other groups. During this period, Muhammad's role expanded to include military leadership. Several battles, including Badr, Uhud, and the Battle of the Trench, tested the resilience of the Muslim community. Despite setbacks, Muhammad's leadership solidified the Muslim position in the region.

In 630 CE, Muhammad and his followers peacefully entered Mecca, reclaiming the city and purging the Kaaba of its idols. This event marked the triumph of Islam in Arabia. Muhammad's forgiveness of his former adversaries exemplified his principles of mercy and reconciliation. In the following years, Islam spread rapidly across the Arabian Peninsula as tribes embraced the new faith. Muhammad delivered his Farewell Sermon in 632 CE, emphasizing equality, justice, and adherence to Islamic principles. Shortly after, he passed away in Medina, leaving behind a unified and vibrant community of believers.

Prophet Muhammad's life and teachings profoundly shaped the course of history. As the final prophet in Islamic tradition, he is revered for his exemplary character, leadership, and devotion. His revelations, compiled into the Qu'ran, and his sayings and actions (Hadith) serve as foundational texts for Muslims worldwide. The emergence of Islam brought significant social, political, and spiritual changes, uniting diverse peoples under a shared faith and ethical framework. Muhammad's legacy endures not only in the hearts of Muslims but also in the broader historical narrative as a transformative figure who reshaped the Arabian Peninsula and beyond.

Michael Cook (2024) in his book 'A History of the Muslim World: From Its Origins to the Dawn of Modernity' offers a comprehensive survey of Islamic history from its beginnings in the 7th century to the period preceding modernity. In this extensive work, Cook examines the formation, evolution, and cultural impact of the Islamic world, providing a deep and nuanced understanding of a vast and diverse civilization.

The book begins by recounting the life of Prophet Muhammad, focusing on his religious message, political strategies, and the socio-political climate of the Arabian Peninsula. Muhammad's emergence as a religious leader, military figure, and state builder is contextualized within the late Antique period[2], highlighting the transformative impact of Islam on Arabian society and beyond. Cook portrays Muhammad as both a reformer and a state founder whose message rapidly reshaped the region's religious and political dynamics.

Cook then delves into the period of the Rashidun (Rightly Guided) Caliphs and the subsequent Umayyad and Abbasid Caliphates, exploring their expansionist endeavors and administrative innovations. He emphasizes the significance of Islamic conquests and how these political entities integrated diverse cultures, languages, and legal systems within a broad imperial framework. The Caliphate's successes are explored, as well as internal tensions, including debates over succession, sectarian divides, and socio-economic challenges. The schism between Sunni and Shia Islam receives detailed attention, illustrating its deep-rooted impact on Islamic history and politics.

As Cook proceeds through subsequent centuries, he highlights the rise and fall of various Muslim empires and states across the Middle East, North Africa, South Asia, and

---

[2] The Antique Period of Islam refers to the early centuries of Islamic civilization, starting from the advent of Islam in the 7th century CE and extending into the early Abbasid era (approximately the 7th to 9th centuries CE). The term "Antique" is not commonly used in Islamic historiography but might be employed to signify the "formative" or "classical" era of Islam. It underscores the foundational nature of this period for Islamic religion, governance, culture, and scholarship.

parts of Europe. He explains the evolution of Islamic institutions, including the complex development of jurisprudence, educational structures, and Sufi mysticism. This diversity, Cook argues, underscored the adaptability and reach of Islamic civilization while producing distinctive regional expressions of faith and governance.

Particularly notable in Cook's account is his treatment of the intellectual and cultural flourishing that accompanied the so-called Golden Age of Islam. He illustrates how advancements in science, philosophy, medicine, and literature made the Muslim world a vibrant center of learning, with scholars like Avicenna (Ibn Sina), Al-Farabi, and Alhazen making lasting contributions to global knowledge. However, he also analyzes periods of stagnation, conflict, and political fragmentation that followed, with external pressures from the Crusades and Mongol invasions reshaping the Muslim world's boundaries and identities.

Cook later addresses the Ottoman, Safavid, and Mughal empires as powerful manifestations of Islamicate.[3] Rule. He underscores the complexities of these empires, noting their religious policies, cultural achievements, and adaptability in a changing world. The arrival of European colonial influence

---

[3] The term "Islamicate" was coined by historian Marshall Hodgson and is used to describe aspects of culture, society, or politics that, while related to Islamic civilization, are not strictly religious or tied solely to Islamic beliefs and practices. It encompasses the broader cultural expressions and influences that emerged within societies historically shaped by Islam, including art, architecture, literature, science, and social norms that extend beyond the religious sphere. For example, Islamic art, music, or scientific achievements that were developed in predominantly Muslim regions but which could also involve non-Muslim participants or influences would be considered "Islamicate." The term allows scholars to distinguish between religious Islam (which pertains directly to faith, practice, and doctrine) and the wider cultural context that developed around Islamic civilization.

and the beginnings of modernity that would reshape Muslim societies are touched upon as a lead-in to more recent history.

Schism Between Sunni and Shia Interpretations

The schism between Sunni and Shia Islam originated from a disagreement over the rightful successor to Prophet Muhammad after his death in 632 CE. This division is both political and theological, and it has shaped the history of Islam profoundly.

The Sunni-Shia schism is rooted in historical disputes but has evolved into a complex interplay of theological, political, and cultural differences. This begins with the succession dispute. Sunnis believe that the Prophet did not explicitly appoint a successor and that the Muslim community should choose their leader through consensus. This led to the selection of Abu Bakr, a close companion of Muhammad, as the first Caliph (leader). Shias hold that Prophet Muhammad had designated his cousin and son-in-law, Ali ibn Abi Talib, as his rightful successor. They argue that leadership should remain within the Prophet's family (Ahl al-Bayt).

The murder of the third Caliph, Uthman, and the subsequent leadership of Ali (the fourth Caliph) deepened the divisions. Ali faced opposition from factions within the Muslim community, particularly in the Battle of Siffin and the Battle of the Camel. After Ali's assassination, his son, Hasan, briefly assumed leadership but abdicated to avoid further conflict. However, the martyrdom of his younger son, Hussain, at the Battle of Karbala in 680 CE became a defining moment for Shia identity.

There are theological and ritual differences between the two. Sunni's believe that leadership (Caliphate) is a political role chosen by the community. There is no divine authority tied to leaders. For Shias leadership (Imamate) is a divine institution. Imams, descendants of Ali, are considered infallible and divinely guided.

Sunnis emphasize the Qu'ran and Hadith as primary sources of Islamic law, alongside consensus and analogy. In addition to the Qu'ran and Hadith, Shia places significant weight on the teachings and interpretations of the Imams.

Sunnis constitute approximately 85–90% of the Muslim population. Shias make up about 10–15%, with significant populations in Iran, Iraq, Lebanon, Bahrain, and parts of Pakistan and India. Historically, Sunni and Shia relations have oscillated between coexistence and conflict, often influenced by political power struggles and external factors. In modern times, geopolitical rivalries (e.g., between Sunni-majority Saudi Arabia and Shia-majority Iran) have exacerbated sectarian tensions. Despite these divisions, both groups share foundational beliefs in Islam, including the Qu'ran as the holy book, the Five Pillars of Islam, and reverence for the Prophet Muhammad.

Diverse Caliphates and Early Cultural Exchange

The early Muslim community developed under successive caliphates, including the Rashidun, Umayyad, Abbasid, and Ottoman caliphates. Each era left a unique cultural and intellectual imprint. The Umayyads, for example, expanded the empire into Europe and North Africa and introduced Islamic governance, law, and language across diverse cultures.

The Abbasid Caliphate, often called the "Golden Age of Islam," fostered an era of unprecedented intellectual growth. This era, centered in Baghdad, was marked by scholarship in fields like medicine, mathematics, astronomy, and philosophy. Through the translation movement, scholars translated Greek, Persian, and Indian texts into Arabic, creating a cultural synthesis that enriched Islamic civilization and influenced the development of knowledge worldwide.

The Rashidun, Umayyad, Abbasid, and Ottoman caliphates are significant Islamic empires that played crucial roles in the history of the Muslim world. Here is an overview of each:

***Rashidun Caliphate* (632–661 CE):** This caliphate was established after the death of Prophet Muhammad in 632 CE and lasted until 661 CE. It was led by the first four "Rightly Guided" caliphs (Arabic: al-Khulafā' al-Rāshidūn): Abu Bakr, Umar ibn al-Khattab, Uthman ibn Affan, and Ali ibn Abi Talib. This period was marked by rapid military expansion and the spread of Islam across the Arabian Peninsula, Levant, Persia (modern-day Iran), Egypt, and North Africa. The administrative framework for governance, such as a centralized treasury and judicial system, was established. Later, internal disputes emerged, culminating in a civil war (the First Fitna), which ended with the assassination of Caliph Ali and the rise of the Umayyad dynasty.

***Umayyad Caliphate* (661–750 CE; Córdoba branch until 1031 CE):** The Umayyad dynasty ruled from Damascus and later in Al-Andalus (modern Spain) through the Córdoba Caliphate. The caliphate was founded by Mu'awiya I, who moved the capital to Damascus. The

Umayyads expanded the Islamic Empire to its greatest territorial extent, including regions of North Africa, Spain, Central Asia, and parts of the Indian subcontinent. The significant conquests included the Iberian Peninsula (Spain) and expansion eastward into Central Asia. Their achievements included the development of Arabic as the administrative language, the establishment of the Dome of the Rock in Jerusalem, introduction of a centralized bureaucratic administration, with a focus on trade and infrastructure like roads.

The dynasty faced growing discontent over favoritism shown to Arab Muslims, leading to revolts by non-Arab converts (*Mawali*) and Shia Muslims, culminating in their overthrow by the Abbasids in 750 CE, except for their hold in Al-Andalus.

***Abbasid Caliphate* (750–1258 CE; 1261–1517 in Cairo):** The Abbasids overthrew the Umayyad dynasty and moved the capital to Baghdad. A branch continued to hold symbolic power in Cairo after the Mongol sack of Baghdad in 1258. The Abbasid period, especially under Caliphs like Harun al-Rashid and al-Ma'mun, is considered a golden age of Islamic culture, science, literature, and philosophy. It was marked by the establishment of the House of Wisdom (Bayt al-Hikma) in Baghdad, promoting translations of Greek, Persian, and Indian texts. Their rule marked a shift towards a more inclusive and multicultural approach, reflecting the empire's diversity. Their power began to wane due to internal divisions, regional autonomy, and external pressures like the Crusades and Mongol invasions. In 1258, the Mongols sacked Baghdad, ending the main Abbasid Caliphate's authority, but a remnant continued under Mamluk patronage in Cairo until the Ottoman takeover.

***Ottoman Caliphate* (1517–1924 CE):** The Ottomans claimed the caliphate after the conquest of Mamluk Egypt and the capture of the last Abbasid caliph in Cairo. Initially based in Istanbul (formerly Constantinople) following its conquest in 1453. At its height, the Ottoman Empire spanned Southeast Europe, Western Asia, and North Africa. Their governance model included a combination of Islamic tradition and a sophisticated administration and military power. They introduced the millet system[4] to manage religious minorities within its territory. Ottomans are known for architectural, artistic, and cultural achievements, like the construction of grand mosques (e.g., Hagia Sophia's transformation). By the 19th and early 20th centuries, the empire weakened due to internal decay, nationalist movements, and European pressures. The caliphate was formally abolished in 1924 by Mustafa Kemal Atatürk, founding the modern Republic of Turkey.

These caliphates significantly influenced political, cultural, religious, and intellectual developments in the Muslim world, shaping a legacy that endures to this day.

The Mughal Empire and The Spread of Islam

The Mughal Empire, one of the most influential and enduring dynasties in Indian history, was established in 1526 by Babur, a descendant of Timur and Genghis Khan. Over

---

[4] The Millet System was an administrative framework used by the Ottoman Empire to govern its religiously diverse population. It was a form of legal and cultural pluralism that allowed non-Muslim religious communities to govern themselves in matters of personal law and religion, while remaining loyal subjects of the Ottoman state.

the course of its nearly three-century reign, the empire not only shaped the political and cultural landscape of South Asia but also played a significant role in the spread of Islam in the region. The Mughals were instrumental in blending Islamic principles with indigenous traditions, fostering an environment of cultural synthesis and religious dialogue.

Babur founded the Mughal Empire in India after the battle of Panipat in 1526. Over successive generations, rulers such as Akbar, Jahangir, Shah Jahan, and Aurangzeb consolidated and expanded the empire, stretching it across much of the Indian subcontinent. While the empire was primarily Islamic in governance and culture, it ruled over a predominantly Hindu population. This dynamic required the Mughal emperors to adopt policies that would maintain stability while promoting their religious and cultural ideals.

One of the most remarkable aspects of the Mughal Empire was its approach to religious tolerance, particularly under Emperor Akbar (1556–1605). Akbar's policies, such as the abolition of the jizya tax on non-Muslims and the establishment of the Din-i-Ilahi, sought to foster harmony among diverse religious communities. Akbar's court was a hub of cultural and intellectual exchange, where Islamic, Hindu, Jain, and Christian scholars engaged in dialogue. This environment not only strengthened the empire's political foundation but also facilitated the spread of Islamic culture and ideas in a non-coercive manner.

The Mughal Empire is renowned for its architectural achievements, many of which reflect Islamic principles. Monuments such as the Taj Mahal, Humayun's Tomb, and the Jama Masjid stand as enduring symbols of the Mughal aesthetic, characterized by intricate calligraphy, geometric patterns, and expansive gardens. These structures were not merely expressions of imperial power but also served as centers of Islamic learning and worship, thereby reinforcing the faith's presence in the region.

Spread of Islamic Culture: The Mughals significantly contributed to the dissemination of Islamic culture through patronage of art, literature, and education. Persian became the court language, and a synthesis of Persian, Arabic, and local traditions gave rise to a rich literary and artistic heritage. Works like the *Akbarnama* and the *Ain-i-Akbari* provide detailed accounts of the empire's administration and cultural life, showcasing the integration of Islamic principles with indigenous practices. Additionally, the establishment of madrasas and Sufi shrines under the Mughals facilitated the spread of Islamic teachings among the local population.

Sufism played a vital role in the Mughal Empire's religious landscape. The Sufi saints, with their emphasis on spirituality and devotion, were instrumental in spreading Islam among the masses. The Mughals actively supported Sufi orders, constructing dargahs (shrines) and promoting festivals that drew people from diverse backgrounds. This inclusive approach made Islam accessible and appealing to a wide audience, contributing to its gradual proliferation across the subcontinent.

While the Mughal Empire initially thrived on its policies of inclusivity, its later years were marked by challenges. Aurangzeb's reign (1658–1707), for example, saw a shift towards more orthodox Islamic policies, including the reimposition of the jizya tax. These measures alienated segments of the population and weakened the empire's foundations. By the 18th century, the empire faced fragmentation due to internal dissent and external invasions, eventually succumbing to British colonial rule.

The Mughal Empire's legacy in spreading Islam is multifaceted. While it established Islam as a prominent cultural and religious force in South Asia, its most enduring contribution lies in its ability to harmonize diverse traditions. The Mughals demonstrated that the spread of Islam could be achieved not through force but through cultural engagement, intellectual exchange, and artistic patronage. Their era remains a testament to the possibilities of coexistence and mutual enrichment among different faiths.

The Crisis Within Empires and the Reforms

In the 19th century, the Mughal Empire fell to British colonial rule, Iran came under the weak Qajar dynasty influenced by Britain and Russia, and the Ottoman Empire remained the only significant Muslim power while most Muslim lands faced European colonization. Ottoman Sultan Selim III (1789–1807) attempted reforms to modernize the military but was opposed and overthrown by the Janissaries[5]. His successor, Mahmud II (1808–1839), abolished the Janissaries in 1826, diminishing the power of the ulema[6] and

---

[5] The Janissaries were an elite military corps in the Ottoman Empire, established in the late 14th century by Sultan Murad I. They were originally composed of young Christian boys taken from the Balkans through the devshirme system, converted to Islam, and trained as loyal soldiers for the Ottoman sultan. Over time, the Janissaries became one of the most powerful and influential groups in the empire, serving as the sultan's personal guard and the backbone of the Ottoman military.

[6] The ulema (also spelled *ulama*) are Islamic scholars, theologians, and jurists who are highly trained in Islamic law (*Shariah*), theology (*aqeedah*), and other religious sciences. The term comes from the Arabic word *'ulama'*, meaning "those who possess knowledge." The ulema play a central role in interpreting Islamic principles and guiding the Muslim community in religious, legal, and sometimes political matters.

enabling reforms like the establishment of Western-style military colleges and the Tanzimat reforms, which granted legal protections and religious equality to all subjects.

In Egypt, Mehmed Ali Pasha (1805–1848) eliminated the Mamluks and curtailed the influence of the ulema, introducing Western-style reforms in governance, education, and the military. Initially loyal to the Ottoman sultan, Mehmed Ali later turned against him and established a semi-independent dynasty in Egypt.

Both the Ottoman Empire and Egypt produced Western-educated intellectuals, such as the Young Ottomans, who advocated for constitutional monarchy. Sultan Abdulhamid II (1876–1909) initially supported these reforms but later dissolved the parliament and ruled as an autocrat for over three decades (Kuru, 2021).

The Role of Trade in the Spread of Islam

Islam's reach into new regions brought it into contact with various cultures, each of which left its mark on Islamic tradition. Key trade routes, such as the Silk Road, facilitated this expansion, enabling interactions with Persian, Indian, African, and European societies. As Islam spread across regions like Central Asia, West Africa, and Southeast Asia, it adapted to local customs and traditions, resulting in a mosaic of cultural practices and expressions.

For instance, in Persia, Islamic art and literature fused with pre-existing Persian traditions, contributing to a unique Persian Islamic identity seen in calligraphy, architecture, and Sufi mysticism. In Southeast Asia, Islamic beliefs integrated with existing Hindu-Buddhist influences, as seen in Javanese

Islam, where rituals often blended local and Islamic practices.

Linguistic Diversity and Cultural Pluralism

The Islamic civilization became home to a vast array of languages, including Arabic, Persian, Turkish, Urdu, and Malay. Arabic, as the language of the Qur'an, served as a unifying element, yet regional languages flourished and became vehicles for Islamic expression. Persian literature and poetry, for instance, became central to Islamic culture, with works like Rumi's poetry gaining immense influence.

This linguistic diversity was reflected in Islamic governance as well. The Ottomans, Safavids, and Mughals, who ruled Muslim empires spanning the Middle East, Persia, and South Asia, respected local languages and cultural practices while promoting Islamic values. This inclusivity underpinned a complex cultural tapestry where different traditions could coexist.

The Emergence of Regional Islamic Schools of Thought

Islamic jurisprudence (*fiqh*) developed diverse schools of thought reflecting the cultural and intellectual diversity within the Muslim world. Four primary Sunni schools (*Hanafi, Maliki, Shafi'i, and Hanbali*) and the *Ja'fari* school within Shia Islam became widespread across different regions, influenced by local customs and scholarly traditions. For example, the Hanafi school, prominent in Central Asia and South Asia, is known for its flexibility and incorporation of local customs, reflecting the adaptation of Islam to varied contexts.

Sufism also played a significant role in spreading Islam and shaping Muslim cultural life. Sufi orders or "tariqas" became a channel through which Islam was introduced to non-Arab cultures, especially in Sub-Saharan Africa and South Asia. Sufi practices incorporated music, dance, and poetry, such as the whirling dervishes of the Mevlevi order in Turkey or the qawwali music of South Asia, creating unique spiritual expressions within Islam.

Sufi Islam

Sufi Islam, often referred to simply as Sufism, is a mystical branch of Islam that emphasizes the inward search for God and the cultivation of a deep, personal relationship with the Divine. Sufism seeks to transcend the formal aspects of religion, focusing instead on spiritual purity, self-discipline, and the direct experience of God's presence. The core elements of Sufism are unity with God (*Tawhid*), love for God, and inner purification (*Tazkiyah*) which is the purification of the soul to remove ego (*nafs*) and worldly attachments, allowing the individual to become closer to God.

Sufi practices consist of (a) *Dhikr* (Remembrance) which consists of repetition of God's names or phrases like *La ilaha illallah* (There is no god but God) in a rhythmic, meditative manner to focus the mind and heart on God, (b) *Muraqaba* (Meditation) which is Contemplative practices where Sufis meditate on God's presence and reflect on their inner state, (c) *Sama* (Listening) which is musical and poetic gatherings, often featuring the recitation of mystical poetry and music, to inspire divine connection. The whirling dance of the Mevlevi order (commonly known as "whirling dervishes") is a famous example and, (d) Service and Humility including detachment from material possessions.

Sufi teachings are often organized into orders or brotherhoods (called *Tariqas*), each led by a spiritual guide (*Shaikh or Pir*). Some prominent orders include: *Qadiriyya* (One of the oldest and most widespread), *Naqshbandiyya* (Known for silent meditation and inner awareness), *Chishtiyya*, (Popular in South Asia, emphasizing love and tolerance), and *Mevlevi* (Associated with Rumi and the practice of Sama).

Sufi poets like Rumi, Hafiz, and Ibn Arabi have profoundly influenced Islamic thought and culture. Their works often convey themes of divine love, union with God, and the spiritual journey.

Sufism exists within both Sunni and Shia traditions but is not a separate sect. Many Sufis follow traditional Islamic jurisprudence (Shariah) while adding a mystical dimension to their practices. Some orthodox Islamic scholars criticize certain Sufi practices, such as shrine veneration, as deviations from Islamic teachings. However, Sufis argue that their practices are deeply rooted in the Qur'an and the Prophet Muhammad's teachings. The ultimate goal of Sufism is to achieve *fana* (annihilation of the self in God) and *baqa* (eternal abiding with God), leading to the realization of the Divine within oneself and the world.

Despite modern challenges like political opposition and misconceptions, Sufi orders remain influential worldwide. They continue to adapt, offering spiritual guidance to those seeking a deeper connection with their faith.

An Architectural Mélange: The Cultural Fusion

Islamic architecture offers a vivid illustration of cultural diversity. While early Islamic architecture was influenced by pre-Islamic Arabian styles, later expansions adopted and adapted local architectural traditions. The Great Mosque of Córdoba in Spain, the Blue Mosque in Istanbul, and the Taj Mahal in India each reflect the local aesthetic and architectural innovations while embodying Islamic principles.

Mosques often served as cultural hubs and reflected regional artistic tastes. North African mosques, for example, showcase intricate geometric tilework (zellige), while mosques in Persia and Central Asia are adorned with distinctive blue tile mosaics. These architectural achievements underscore the adaptation of Islam to different cultural settings and the integration of Islamic values with local artistic forms.

Role of the Muslim Diaspora

Over centuries, migration, trade, and conquest led to the establishment of Muslim communities far from the historic centers of Islam. This diaspora continued to enrich the cultural diversity of the Muslim world, as these communities preserved Islamic beliefs while embracing local practices.

The Indian Ocean trade routes, for instance, led to the establishment of Muslim communities in East Africa and Southeast Asia, where Islam became an integral part of local society. Swahili culture along the East African coast is a blend of Arab, Persian, and African influences, reflecting centuries of cross-cultural exchange facilitated by trade and Islam.

Globalization of Muslim Culture

Today, the Muslim world spans nearly every continent and reflects a remarkable variety of cultural, linguistic, and ethnic backgrounds. Muslim countries and diasporic communities contribute to a diverse and evolving global Islamic identity. Modern media, migration, and globalization have further enriched this diversity, as Muslims from different cultures interact, influence each other, and navigate the challenges of preserving identity in a rapidly changing world.

Historically, Muslim culture has been characterized by its rich diversity, with various regions developing unique interpretations and practices of Islam. The spread of Islam from its origins in the Arabian Peninsula to regions such as Southeast Asia, Africa, and Europe led to the formation of distinct cultural and religious traditions. The concept of the "ummah," or global Muslim community, has been a unifying force, despite the cultural and regional differences (Hassan, 2003).

Globalization has played a crucial role in shaping modern Muslim culture. The advent of satellite television, the internet, and social media has facilitated the exchange of ideas and information, allowing Muslims from different parts of the world to connect and share their experiences. This interconnectedness has led to a greater awareness of the diversity within the Muslim world and has challenged the traditional notion of a monolithic Islamic culture.

The globalization of Muslim culture has resulted in a vibrant exchange of cultural practices and ideas. Muslims in different regions have adapted Islamic teachings to their local contexts, creating a rich tapestry of cultural expressions. For example, the fusion of traditional Islamic art with contemporary styles in countries like Indonesia and

Malaysia has produced unique and innovative forms of artistic expression (Meuleman, 2002).

While globalization has brought about many positive changes, it has also presented challenges for Muslim communities. The rise of extremist ideologies and the politicization of Islam have created tensions within and between Muslim countries. Additionally, the rapid pace of globalization has led to concerns about the erosion of traditional cultural values and practices.

However, globalization also offers opportunities for Muslim communities to engage in dialogue, promote mutual understanding, and address common challenges. The increased visibility of Muslim voices in global forums and the growing recognition of the contributions of Muslim scholars, artists, and activists have helped to counter negative stereotypes and foster a more inclusive and diverse understanding of Islam.

Contemporary Muslim cultures encompass varied lifestyles, from conservative to progressive, with ongoing dialogues around the role of religion in society, education, and governance. The shared beliefs and principles of Islam serve as a unifying force, yet the global Muslim community embraces a mosaic of traditions that continue to evolve and adapt in response to social, political, and cultural shifts.

Scholarly research on the historical roots and cultural diversity of the Muslim world highlights its complex evolution and regional distinctions shaped by political, social, and religious dynamics. Key publications explore this diversity through themes such as the impact of Islamic empires, the role of Sufi movements, and the intersections of Islam with local cultures and pre-Islamic traditions.

One major area of study is the historical influence of the Ottoman Empire and other Islamic empires like the Safavid and Mughal, which helped spread Islam's legal, philosophical, and cultural frameworks across Asia, the Middle East, and parts of Europe. The Ottoman Empire's structure of power and administration, for instance, fostered cultural integration and diversity within its territories, creating a mosaic of Islamic traditions that varied from one region to another. Meanwhile, the Mughals promoted Persianate culture and architecture, influencing South Asian identity within an Islamic context.

The diversity of Islamic culture is also reflected in the distinct practices and beliefs within Sunni and Shia communities, as well as among various Sufi orders. Research has shown that different branches and sects of Islam maintain unique practices and interpretations, which can reflect local customs as well as theological differences. For instance, Sufi orders like the *Naqshbandiyya* and *Qadiriyya* played significant roles in Africa, South Asia, and the Middle East, blending Islamic spirituality with local rituals and folk traditions.

In modern contexts, studies examine how Islamic societies navigate contemporary issues of pluralism and secularism. For instance, some research points to generational differences in religious practices, with younger Muslims in certain regions exhibiting either more or less adherence to religious norms compared to older generations, depending on local political and social pressures (Pew Research Center, The World's Muslims: Unity and Diversity). Furthermore, the adaptation of Islamic principles within nation-states has sparked debates over the compatibility of Islam with modern governance structures, with various Islamic movements attempting to reconcile religious and national identities in the postcolonial period.

The historical roots and cultural diversity of the Muslim world showcase Islam's ability to adapt, integrate, and thrive in a variety of cultural contexts. This diversity is a testament to Islam's universality and flexibility, offering a rich tapestry that reflects the global nature of the Muslim experience. Today, as the Muslim world continues to grow and change, this cultural diversity remains a defining characteristic, embodying the balance between unity in faith and diversity in expression.

References

Ahmet, T. Kuru. (2021). *The Ulema-State Alliance: A Barrier to Democracy and Development in the Muslim World.* Institute for Global Change.

Berkey, J. I. (2010). In Irwin, R. (Ed.), *The New Cambridge History of Islam.* The New Cambridge University Press.

Cook, M. A. (2024). *A History of the Muslim World: From Its Origins to the Dawn of Modernity.* Princeton University Press.

Hassan, R. (2003). *Globalization's Challenge to Islam.* YaleGlobal Online.

Meuleman, J. (2002). *Islam in the Era of Globalization.* UK: Routledge Curzon.

Pew Research Centre. (2013). *The World's Muslims: Religion, Politics and Society.*

Siddiqui, A. H. (1999). *The Life of Muhammad.* Kuala Lumpur: Islamic Book Trust.

Wikipedia. (n.d.). *Islam by country.* Retrieved from https://en.wikipedia.org/wiki/Islam_by_country

CHAPTER 2
FAITH, IDENTITY, AND BELONGING IN A GLOBALIZED WORLD

The reconciliation of faith with national and cultural identities among Muslims worldwide is a dynamic process that reflects both shared beliefs and diverse cultural contexts. This balance is influenced by factors like regional traditions, political environments, historical contexts, and social dynamics, leading to unique expressions of Islamic identity across the Muslim world and within diaspora communities.

The Foundations of Islamic Identity

For many Muslims, faith is central to their identity, providing a spiritual framework that shapes their worldview and daily life. Key Islamic principles, like the belief in one God (*Tawhid*), following the teachings of the Prophet Muhammad, and adhering to practices like prayer and fasting, create a shared foundation for Muslims everywhere. However, how these beliefs are integrated with national and cultural identities varies significantly across different societies.

Islam emphasizes both a universal brotherhood and respect for cultural diversity, as reflected in verses of the Qur'an, such as, *"We have created you from male and female and made you peoples and tribes so that you may know one another"* (Qur'an 49:13). This foundational acceptance of diversity has enabled Muslims to embrace local traditions while maintaining their faith.

Islamic Identity Across Regions

Across the Muslim world, the interplay between Islam and cultural identity is complex and varies widely.

In the Middle East and North Africa (MENA) Islam is deeply intertwined with national identity, and cultural practices often reflect Islamic principles. For example, public observance of Islamic rituals, such as Ramadan fasting and Eid celebrations, is common and widely recognized as part of national heritage. However, countries like Egypt and Morocco have distinct local customs, cuisines, and dialects that reflect their ancient cultures and coexist alongside Islamic practices.

In South Asia (India, Pakistan, Bangladesh) Islamic identity is layered with centuries of cultural syncretism and adaptation. For instance, South Asian Muslims often celebrate the *urs* (death anniversary) of Sufi saints, a tradition that has roots in pre-Islamic customs and reflects the strong influence of Sufism. In countries like India, Muslims also participate in Hindu-majority cultural practices, such as Diwali and Holi, while still observing Islamic rituals. This balance reflects the interwoven cultural and religious identities in a pluralistic society.

In Southeast Asia (Indonesia, Malaysia) which is home to the largest Muslim population, yet Islamic identity here is marked by a unique blend of Indigenous and Islamic traditions. Indonesian Muslims, for example, have integrated pre-Islamic Javanese cultural elements into their religious practices, and Islam is often practiced with local adaptations. Similarly, Malaysia combines Malay identity with Islamic governance in ways that shape public life, from family laws to cultural celebrations.

National Identity and State Policies on Religion

The role of Islam in national identity is also shaped by state policies and the degree to which Islam is integrated into governance. Countries like Turkey, with its secular republic, and Indonesia, with its official "Pancasila" philosophy that recognizes religious pluralism, approach Islam as part of personal rather than official identity. Turkey's secularism, for example, has historically restricted visible expressions of religion in state institutions, though recent decades have seen a shift towards greater public visibility of Islamic practices. In Indonesia, the majority Muslim population practices Islam alongside traditional customs, and there is a broader acceptance of diverse Islamic expressions.

In countries like Iran and Saudi Arabia, Islam is deeply embedded within national law and governance, creating a more unified Islamic identity. In these contexts, national laws often mandate certain Islamic practices and moral standards, and there is less room for secular or pluralistic identity frameworks. Consequently, religious identity often aligns closely with national identity, though subcultures within these societies may express diversity in subtle ways, such as through art, dress, and localized customs. Iran and Pakistan present two extreme cases where an attempt to enforce strict Islamic rules by the State is made.

In Iran, for example, Khomeini initially argued that jurists, not human agents, have the authority to implement Shariah, with governance limited to enforcing divine law. However, after becoming Iran's Supreme Leader, he prioritized the needs of the Islamic Republic over strict adherence to Shariah, even allowing for the suspension of religious practices.

In Pakistan, General Zia-ul-Haq, after taking power in 1978, pursued the *Islamicization* of laws[7], education, and the economy. He formed an alliance with the Islamist Jamaat-e-Islami party and empowered the ulema by establishing a Federal Shariaht Court to ensure legislation complied with Shariah. Zia manipulated the court to uphold conservative interpretations, curbing progressive reforms. His policies have influenced ongoing authoritarianism, restrictions on religious freedom for minorities, and limitations on women's rights in Pakistan.

It is also to be noted that religion cannot always be the only basis of Muslim national identity. It is very well exemplified when Bangladesh was separated from Pakistan as an independent nation. During freedom struggle from British rule Muslims were aware of their identity differences from other religious groups. However, it was much stronger at the level of the elite than at the level of the masses (Islam, 1981). While it manifested in the creation of Pakistan as an Islamic state it also led to the emergence of the reformist movement, and the establishment of Aligarh Muslim University to provide modern education.

Diaspora Communities and Hybrid Identities

Muslim diaspora communities, particularly in Western countries, experience unique challenges and opportunities in balancing Islamic identity with cultural and national integration. These communities often develop "hybrid

---

[7] Islamicization of laws refers to the process of aligning a country's legal framework with Islamic principles and jurisprudence (Shariah). This involves the incorporation of Islamic values, teachings, and legal precepts into the laws governing various aspects of life, such as criminal justice, family matters, finance, and public morality.

identities" that merge faith with aspects of the host country's culture.

In North America, Muslims are a highly diverse group, with communities from South Asia, the Middle East, and Africa bringing varied cultural practices. Many Muslim Americans and Canadians adapt Islamic practices to Western cultural norms, creating a unique expression of Islam that might include community-based iftar events during Ramadan or celebrating American holidays like Thanksgiving alongside Islamic festivals. This flexibility reflects an adaptation to the multicultural and secular environment of North America.

In Europe, where many Muslim communities have long-established roots (such as Turkish communities in Germany or North African communities in France), Islamic identity often intersects with immigrant identity. European Muslims face distinct challenges, such as Islamophobia, which can intensify their attachment to Islamic identity as a source of resilience. However, younger generations frequently embrace both their European and Muslim identities, creating a sense of "European Islam" that values democratic principles alongside Islamic teachings.

In Australia and New Zealand's multi-cultural societies, Muslims often participate actively in civic life and engage in interfaith dialogues, balancing their Islamic identity with strong ties to their cultural and national identity. Eid festivals and mosque open days are common community events that allow Muslims to share their faith and traditions with the broader population, fostering a unique Australian or Kiwi Muslim identity that embraces openness and diversity.

Islam, Globalization, and the Media

Globalization and media have accelerated cross-cultural exchange and introduced Muslims worldwide to varied interpretations of Islam. Online platforms enable Muslims to engage in religious discussions, learn from different scholars, and connect with others who share similar experiences, fostering a "global ummah" (community).

In some cases, Muslims have adopted elements of global youth culture, and incorporated Western fashion, music, and media aligning them with Islamic principles. For instance, modest fashion, influenced by Western and Eastern aesthetics, has become a popular way for Muslim women to express their identity in both Islamic and cultural terms.

From the traditional abayas and thobes to contemporary designs, Islamic fashion offers a wide range of options for those seeking stylish and modest clothing. Various types of Muslim dress are worn by men and women around the world, reflecting both cultural and religious influences. Islamic fashion encompasses a diverse range of styles and designs that vary depending on the cultural context and geographic region. Here are some examples of Islamic fashion from across the globe:

Abaya: A loose-fitting, full-length outer garment worn by women in the Arab world, including Saudi Arabia, the United Arab Emirates, and Kuwait. It is typically black and covers the entire body except for the face, hands, and feet.

Hijab: A headscarf worn by Muslim women to cover their hair and neck. It is common in many Muslim countries, including Iran, Indonesia, and Malaysia. Hijabs come in various styles, including the traditional rectangular shape, and the more modern, fashionable styles.

Thobe: A traditional long robe worn by men in the Arab world, especially in Saudi Arabia and the Gulf States. It is usually made of lightweight fabric and comes in different colors and styles.

Kurta: A long shirt or tunic worn by men and women in South Asia, including India, Pakistan, and Bangladesh. It is typically made of cotton or silk and comes in different colors and styles.

Jilbab: A loose-fitting, full-length outer garment worn by Muslim women in Indonesia, Malaysia, and Brunei. It covers the entire body except for the face, hands, and feet.

Kaftan: A loose-fitting, long-sleeved garment worn by women in the Middle East and North Africa. It is usually made of lightweight fabric and comes in different color and designs.

Shalwar Kameez: A traditional outfit worn by men and women in South Asia, including India, Pakistan, and Bangladesh. It consists of a long tunic (kameez) worn over loose pants (shalwar).

Baju Kurung: A traditional outfit worn by women in Malaysia, Singapore, and Indonesia. It consists of a long, loose-fitting blouse (baju) worn over a long skirt (kain).

Dashiki: A loose-fitting shirt worn by men and women in West Africa, especially in Nigeria and Ghana. It is usually made of colorful, patterned fabric and can be worn with pants or a skirt.

Djellaba: A long, loose-fitting robe worn by men and women in North Africa, especially in Morocco and Algeria. It is usually made of wool or cotton and comes in different colors and designs.

These are just a few examples of the types of Muslim dress that are worn around the world, each with its own cultural and religious significance. Islamic fashion is a beautiful fusion of modesty and style that has become a popular choice among Muslim men and women worldwide. Whether traditional or contemporary, Islamic fashion offers a wide range of options for those seeking fashionable and modest clothing that adheres to their religious beliefs. (Source: https://www.muslimhut.com/islamic-fashion).

Reconciling Faith with Modern Challenges and Ideals

Muslims are increasingly engaging with questions of gender equality, social justice, and human rights within an Islamic framework. Some young Muslims are championing these causes, using both their faith and cultural background to advocate for reforms and to challenge stereotypes.

Muslims reconcile faith with national and cultural identities in varied ways. Some focus on preserving traditional practices, while others reinterpret Islamic principles in light of contemporary realities. This diversity highlights Islam's adaptability and the flexibility Muslims exercise in harmonizing faith with the complex layers of national, cultural, and social identities.

Hassan (2003) explores the multifaceted impact of globalization on Islam, particularly in light of the events following the September 11 attacks. He examines how globalization has influenced the concept of the *ummah* (the universal Muslim community) based on a shared faith and legal framework). Hassan argues that while globalization has strengthened a collective Muslim identity, it has also led to increased awareness of the diversity within the Islamic world, fostering both unity and division.

Historically, the *ummah* provided a sense of religious unity and helped shape the Islamic civilization. However, technological advancements such as satellite television, the internet, and increased travel have exposed Muslims worldwide to their vast cultural and social differences. This exposure, combined with the legacy of colonialism and the rise of nationalist movements, has fragmented the Islamic world into over 50 nations with varying political and economic interests. Despite this fragmentation, new communication technologies have facilitated a renewed awareness of a shared global Muslim identity.

In earlier times, the cohesion of the *ummah* was primarily maintained through adherence to the 'five pillars' of Islam and a perception that all Islamic societies should mirror the Arabian Islamic culture where Islam originated. Hassan suggests that globalization has challenged this view by revealing the cultural diversity among Muslims, as evident in differing gender roles, dress codes, and religious practices across countries like Indonesia, Saudi Arabia, and Turkey. This realization has led to tension between proponents of 'hybrid' (culturally diverse) Islam and advocates for 'authentic' Islam, who seek to impose a stricter, more uniform interpretation of Islamic principles.

The rise of fundamentalist movements, such as those inspired by figures like Maududi and Ayatollah Khomeini, is seen as a reaction to globalization's cultural and religious hybridity. These movements aim to reassert a 'pure' form of Islam by selectively interpreting religious doctrines from the past. However, modernity, characterized by the separation of societal institutions from religious influence, has intensified this tension.

Hassan posits the possibility of the *ummah* becoming a "decentered" community with multiple cultural centers, including Arabic Middle Eastern Islam, African Islam, Central Asian Islam, Southeast Asian Islam, and Islam in the West. This transformation could grant regional *ummahs* legitimacy to chart their own distinct social, political, and cultural paths while remaining part of the broader Muslim community. Such differentiation might challenge the central authority of the traditional holy sites in Mecca and Medina, sparking calls for reform in their governance.

References

Ahmed, R., & Johnson, L. (Eds.). (2020). *Studies on Muslim belonging and identity in Western nations.* Springer.

Esposito, J. (2003). *Globalization's challenge to Islam.* YaleGlobal Online. https://yaleglobal.yale.edu

Hassan, H. (1995). *Reading the Muslim mind.* American Trust Publication.

Hassan, R. (2003). *Globalization's challenge to Islam: How to create one Islamic community in a diverse world.* Yale University Press.

Islam, N. (1981). *Islam and national identity: The case of Pakistan and Bangladesh. International Journal of Middle East Studies, 13,* 55-72.

CHAPTER 3
ISLAMIC PRINCIPLES: INTERPRETATIONS ACROSS REGIONS

The foundational beliefs of Islam—known as the "Five Pillars" and core articles of faith—form the bedrock of Muslim spirituality and practice. However, the way these beliefs are interpreted and practiced varies across regions, schools of thought, and cultural contexts. Let's delve into these core beliefs, followed by an exploration of regional and doctrinal interpretations.

Foundational Beliefs of Islam

The foundational beliefs in Islam encompass the following.

A. The Five Pillars of Islam

The Five Pillars of Islam are core practices that every Muslim is encouraged to observe:

1. Shahada (Faith): The declaration of faith, "There is no god but Allah, and Muhammad is His messenger," is the foundation of Islam. This proclamation unites all Muslims and marks the entry into the faith.

2. Salah (Prayer): Muslims are required to pray five times a day facing Mecca. These prayers emphasize discipline, spirituality, and a direct connection with God.

3. Zakat (Charity): Muslims are instructed to give a portion of their wealth (typically 2.5% of savings annually) to the needy. This principle reflects Islam's emphasis on social welfare and compassion.

4. Sawm (Fasting): During the month of Ramadan, Muslims fast from dawn to sunset, fostering self-discipline, empathy, and spiritual growth.

5. Hajj (Pilgrimage): Muslims who are physically and financially able are required to make a pilgrimage to Mecca once in their lifetime. Hajj represents unity and equality as pilgrims gather regardless of status or nationality.

B. Articles of Faith

Beyond the Five Pillars, Muslims also adhere to six Articles of Faith:

1. Belief in Allah: Muslims believe in the oneness and supremacy of God (Allah).

2. Belief in Angels: Muslims believe in angels, who serve as messengers and servants of God.

3. Belief in the Prophets: Muslims respect a line of prophets, with Muhammad as the final prophet.

4. Belief in the Scriptures: The Qur'an is regarded as the final, unaltered revelation of God. Other scriptures, such as the Torah and Gospel, are respected but considered altered over time.

5. Belief in the Day of Judgment: Muslims believe in an afterlife where everyone will be held accountable for their actions.

6. Belief in Divine Decree: Muslims accept that all events unfold by God's will, yet human free will remains a central concept.

These beliefs provide a universal foundation, but their interpretation is shaped by different schools of thought, cultural influences, and historical contexts.

Interpretations by Islamic Schools of Thought

Islamic jurisprudence, theology, and philosophy vary across several main schools of thought, with regional and cultural factors shaping how beliefs and practices are understood.

Sunni Schools of Thought: Within Sunni Islam, there are four primary schools (*madhabs*) of jurisprudence, each with distinct interpretive methods. While they all share core beliefs, their rulings on certain issues may vary, especially in social and legal matters:

1. **Hanafi**: Known for its flexibility and reasoning (*qiyas*), the Hanafi school is prevalent in South Asia, Central Asia, and parts of the Middle East. Its rulings are often influenced by local customs, allowing for more contextual adaptations.

2. **Maliki**: Emphasizing the practices of the people of Medina, the Maliki school is predominant in North and West Africa. This school is somewhat traditionalist and considers community customs in its rulings.

3. **Shafi'i**: The Shafi'i school, prominent in East Africa, Southeast Asia, and parts of the Middle East, relies on the Qur'an and Hadith and is strict in its interpretations, though it permits the use of reason where scripture is silent.

4. **Hanbali**: Known for its literal interpretations, the Hanbali school, followed primarily in Saudi Arabia and parts

of the Gulf, strictly adhere to the Qur'an and Hadith. This school's rulings are generally more conservative.

These Sunni schools agree on essential beliefs but differ on finer points, such as specific rituals in prayer, marriage laws, and social customs.

Shia Schools of Thought: Shia Islam has its own jurisprudential system, with the *Ja'fari* school as the primary school of thought. Predominant in Iran, Iraq, and parts of Lebanon and Pakistan, Ja'fari jurisprudence places a strong emphasis on reasoning and interpretations by the Imams, particularly the twelve Imams recognized in Twelver Shia Islam.

Shia theology often emphasizes themes of justice and martyrdom, particularly associated with the Battle of Karbala and the martyrdom of Husayn, the Prophet Muhammad's grandson. The concept of *taqiyya* (religious dissimulation) is also present in Shia thought, allowing believers to conceal their faith in cases of persecution, reflecting a unique approach to faith in adverse cultural and political settings.

Cultural Variations and Regional Influences

Across regions, cultural practices shape how Islamic beliefs are incorporated into daily life, resulting in a rich diversity of expressions within the global Muslim community.

Middle East and North Africa (MENA): In the MENA region, Islam is deeply interwoven with culture and politics. The Five Pillars are widely observed, and Islamic festivals, like Ramadan and Eid, are central to public life. Traditional customs, such as Arab hospitality and respect for elders, align with Islamic teachings, reinforcing a cohesive cultural and religious identity. However, political differences have led to variations in practice; for example, Egypt's approach to Islamic law differs from Saudi Arabia's.

Central Asia: Islam remains the dominant religion in countries like Uzbekistan, Kazakhstan, Kyrgyzstan, Tajikistan, and Turkmenistan. The region is predominantly Sunni, following the Hanafi school of Islamic jurisprudence, although there are small Shia communities. The role of Islam varies across these states, with some governments imposing tight control over religious institutions to maintain secular governance, while others are more accommodating of religious practices. Islam in Central Asia reflects the region's complex history, marked by periods of cultural flourishing, political turbulence, and modern-day state regulation.

South Asia: South Asian Muslims", including Pakistan, India, and Bangladesh, often practice Islam within a cultural context that incorporates Sufi influences and syncretic practices[8]. Sufi shrines and the celebration of saints' anniversaries (*urs*) are widespread and reflect an interpretation of Islam focused on spirituality and personal devotion. These practices are seen alongside the stricter observances of South Asia's Deobandi and Barelvi movements, which influence different approaches to Islamic practice in the region.

Southeast Asia: In countries like Indonesia and Malaysia, local customs and Islam blend harmoniously. Islamic practices coexist with indigenous traditions, like

---

[8] Syncretic practices refer to the blending of different religious, cultural, or philosophical beliefs and practices into a new, cohesive system, often emerging in regions with diverse populations.

Javanese shadow puppetry (*wayang kulit*), which incorporates Islamic narratives. Similarly, Indonesian Muslims may hold elaborate ceremonies for the birth or death of loved ones, influenced by pre-Islamic practices yet aligned with Islamic values on community and respect.

Sub-Saharan Africa: In West and East Africa, Islam was spread largely through Sufi orders, and Sufi practices have left a significant impact. African Muslims often participate in rituals like *dhikr* (remembrance of God through chanting or music) and celebrate Islamic holidays in ways that incorporate traditional music and dance. Islam in this region is strongly influenced by community and family structures, with an emphasis on collective worship and social welfare.

The practice of Islam exhibits significant cultural variation across the world, reflecting the influence of local traditions, historical contexts, social norms, and regional customs. While Islam as a faith has core beliefs and practices, its interpretation and practice often adapt to the cultural realities of different Muslim communities. Here are some ways these variations manifest across different regions:

Regional and Cultural Variations

Diverse Legal Schools and Interpretations: Islam's two main branches, Sunni and Shia, differ in some beliefs, rituals, and legal practices. Within Sunni Islam, there are four main schools of jurisprudence (Hanafi, Maliki, Shafi'i, and Hanbali), each with its own interpretations on matters of worship, law, and daily life. Islamic jurisprudence (*fiqh*) often incorporates local customs that do not contradict Islamic principles, allowing for adaptations in areas like marriage, inheritance, and dispute resolution.

Religious Festivals and Celebrations: While the core rituals of the festivals are largely the same, the ways in which they are celebrated vary widely. For example, in Indonesia, Eid al-Fitr is marked by *mudik,* where people return to their hometowns to celebrate with their families, while in Egypt, the holiday might feature different local dishes and communal events. Mawlid al-Nabi (Prophet Muhammad's Birthday holiday) is observed differently across the Islamic world. In many countries, there are processions, recitations of poetry, and special prayers, while some communities see the celebration of the Prophet's birthday as an innovation not practiced by early Muslims.

Regional Dress Codes: Modesty in dress is emphasized, but the specific attire varies. Women in the Gulf countries may wear an *abaya* and *niqab*; in Iran, the *chador* is common; and in parts of Southeast Asia, women may wear a *baju kurung* or a headscarf (hijab) styled differently. Men may wear regional variations like the *thobe* in the Arab world or *shalwar kameez* in South Asia.

Sufi Practices and Rituals: Sufi practices emphasize the inner, spiritual aspects of Islam and often incorporate unique rituals, music, and dance. In Turkey, the Whirling Dervishes perform the *Sema* ceremony as a form of remembrance (dhikr) of God. In West Africa, Sufi orders (tariqas) engage in communal chanting and drumming as part of their rituals.

In many Muslim societies, especially in South Asia and North Africa, visiting the shrines of Sufi saints and engaging in *urs* (death anniversary commemorations) are common practices, despite differing opinions among Muslim scholars about their appropriateness.

Marriage and Family Customs: Islamic marriage (*nikah*) ceremonies have culturally specific elements. In South Asia, elaborate wedding celebrations spanning several days are common, with distinct traditions like the *mehndi* (henna) ceremony. In contrast, in the Middle East, weddings may have fewer pre-wedding rituals but emphasize traditional dances and songs.

While Islamic teachings emphasize family ties and responsibilities, how these are practiced can differ based on cultural norms. For example, extended family structures and collective decision-making are prevalent in many Middle Eastern and South Asian societies, while more nuclear family setups are common among Muslims in Western countries.

Food and Cuisine: While Muslims worldwide observe dietary rules, including halal meat, the specific cuisine reflects regional cultures. For example, North African Muslims may serve couscous dishes, while Indonesian Muslims have their own renditions of halal street food. In several countries, *Biryani, Pulao, and Kebab* dishes are popular, and are enjoyed by even non-Muslims.

In the observance of Ramadan's fast and the breaking of the fast (iftar), there are marked diverse culinary traditions. In many parts of the Arab world, dates and specific soups are used to break the fast, while South Asian Muslims enjoy a variety of fried snacks.

Islamic Art and Architecture: Regional architectural styles influence mosque design. The domed mosques of Turkey and Central Asia differ from the mosques in Sub-Saharan Africa, which often incorporate local materials and design techniques, such as the use of mud brick for the Grand

Mosque of Djenné in Mali. Similarly, the use of calligraphy to express Qur'anic verses is widespread but varies in style—ranging from the intricate Arabic calligraphy in the Arab world to Persian and Ottoman decorative elements and patterns.

Language and Rituals: While all Muslims recite the Qur'an in Arabic, the ways in which they do so, including their intonation, reflect regional accents and traditions. Islamic prayers and sermons are often delivered in the local language to help the community understand religious teachings better.

Community Roles and Gender Norms: Cultural practices influence the way gender norms are observed in different Muslim societies. Some communities allow for more visible roles for women in public and religious spaces, while others may emphasize stricter interpretations of gender separation.

Political Expressions: Countries like Saudi Arabia implement a stricter interpretation of Islamic law, while others, such as Indonesia and Turkey, have incorporated more localized and modern approaches to governance, blending Islamic and secular elements.

Modern Movements and Interpretive Variations

Contemporary movements within Islam further shape interpretations. Modernists attempt to reinterpret Islamic teachings in line with contemporary principles of democracy, gender equality, and science. Reformists in Turkey, Egypt, and Iran, for example, have debated notions of women's rights and secular governance in an Islamic context. On the other hand, revivalist movements stress a return to what they consider to be the "pure" form of Islam as practiced during the time of the Prophet. This attitude can be seen in movements such as Wahhabism in Saudi Arabia and Salafism, which consider cultural adaptations to Islam to be innovations that dilute the faith.

Progressive Muslims promote interpretations that focus on inclusivity, social justice, and relevance. They advocate for a rethinking of Islamic law in the context of modern human rights — in particular, gender and minority rights — and often work in Western countries at the juncture of Islam and liberal values.

Cultural variation in the practice of Islam demonstrates its adaptability and resilience across diverse contexts. While Islamic teachings provide a shared foundation, the lived expression of faith is deeply influenced by the historical, social, and cultural landscapes of each Muslim community. This diversity enriches the global Islamic experience, showcasing both unity and diversity within the faith.

Influence of Cultural Contexts in Diaspora Communities

Muslim communities in non-Muslim countries, particularly in the West, often practice Islam in ways that reconcile their faith with their new cultural surroundings.

United States and Canada: In North America, Muslims navigate a multicultural landscape, and there is a greater emphasis on individual spirituality, interfaith engagement, and adapting Islamic practices to a secular environment. Many North American Muslims celebrate holidays like Thanksgiving alongside Eid, blending Islamic and local traditions.

Europe: European Muslims, including those in France and Germany, face specific challenges due to secular state policies. In France, for instance, Islamic attire is sometimes restricted in public institutions, which affects how Muslims outwardly express their faith. Consequently, European Muslims often reinterpret aspects of their practice to balance integration with religious observance.

Australia and New Zealand: In Australia and New Zealand, Muslim communities tend to maintain cultural practices from their countries of origin while adapting to local customs. Mosques often serve as community hubs, where Muslims gather to celebrate religious and cultural events, fostering a unique fusion of Australian or Kiwi values with Islamic beliefs.

Diversity and Integration: Key Challenges

In an increasingly globalized world, the diversity of religious minorities in Western societies has become more pronounced. This diversity brings both opportunities and challenges for social integration and cohesion. One of the primary challenges for religious minorities is maintaining their unique cultural and religious identities while integrating into the broader society. This duality often creates a sense of belonging to two worlds, which can lead to internal and external conflicts. For example, young Muslims in Western countries may struggle with balancing their religious beliefs with the secular norms of their host countries. Yet another problem faced by religious minorities including Muslims is discrimination and prejudice, which can manifest in various forms, including hate crimes, social exclusion, and institutional biases. Islamophobia, anti-Semitism, and other forms of religious intolerance are prevalent in many Western societies. Such discrimination not only affects the mental and emotional well-being of individuals but also hinders their ability to fully participate in social and economic activities. There are instances where Muslims face discrimination in accessing employment, education, and housing. These economic challenges are often compounded by discrimination and biases in the labor market.

In a recent publication on religious diversity, Islam and integration in Western Europe Koening (2023) provided a good analysis of the situation. Koening noted that there are unique integration challenges faced by Muslims in Europe, where secularism and religious neutrality are often foundational societal values. This can create tension around visible religious practices, such as wearing the hijab, and debates around accommodations for religious observances. Western European countries have varied in their approaches to religious integration, with some adopting multicultural policies that promote cultural pluralism, while others advocate for assimilation into a secular national identity. Islamophobia is a significant obstacle to integration. Negative perceptions of Islam contribute to social exclusion, reinforcing stereotypes and potentially influencing public policy. Koening explores the role of national and international legal frameworks in protecting religious freedom. He analyzes cases where laws meant to ensure secularism conflict with the religious rights of Muslims, sparking debates over how best to balance secular values with religious freedoms.

The integration of religious minorities in Western societies is a multifaceted challenge that requires concerted efforts from governments, communities, and individuals.

Addressing issues of identity, discrimination, policy inconsistencies, and social cohesion is crucial for building inclusive societies that respect and celebrate diversity. By fostering mutual understanding and providing equal opportunities, Western societies can create environments where religious minorities can thrive and contribute positively to the broader community.

References

Armstrong, K. (2000). *Islam: A short history.* New York: Modern Library.

Aslan, R. (2005). *No god but God: The origins, evolution, and future of Islam.* New York: Random House.

Koenig, M. (2023). *Religious diversity, Islam, and integration in Western Europe—Dissecting symbolic, social, and institutional boundary dynamics.*

Köln Z Soziol, 75(Suppl 1), 121–147. https://doi.org/10.1007/s11577-023-00911-5

Nasr, S. H. (2002). *The heart of Islam: Enduring values for humanity.* New York: Harper One.

Schimmel, A. (1992). *Islam: An introduction.* NY: SUNY Press.

CHAPTER 4
WESTERN PERCEPTIONS AND STEREOTYPES OF MUSLIMS

The portrayal of Muslims in Western media has often been shaped by stereotypes and misrepresentations, which can have significant social, cultural, and political impacts. These portrayals are frequently narrow and focus on themes of violence, extremism, and cultural backwardness, reinforcing misconceptions about Muslims and Islam. Understanding these stereotypes and their broader implications is essential to addressing their influence on global perspectives and policies.

Common Stereotypes and Misrepresentations

Muslims as "Inherently Violent" or "Extremist": One of the most pervasive stereotypes in Western media is the association of Muslims with violence or terrorism. Media coverage often disproportionately focuses on extremist groups, framing them as representative of Islam. This creates a misleading narrative that Islam itself is inherently violent, which fails to reflect the beliefs or actions of the vast majority of Muslims. Examples: News outlets often highlight incidents involving Muslim extremists while providing less coverage of similar acts by non-Muslims. This selective portrayal reinforces a perception that violence is uniquely "Islamic." In a meta-analysis of 345 studies Ahmed, & Matthes (2017) found among other things that Muslims tend to be negatively framed, while Islam is dominantly portrayed as a violent religion.

In a more recent work, Erik Bleich & A. Maurits van der Veen (2022) reviewed 2,50000 articles on Islam and Muslims and reported articles that mentioned Muslims were more likely to be negative than stories touching on any other group. For Catholics, Jews and Hindus, the proportion of positive and negative articles was close to 50-50. By contrast, 80% of all articles related to Muslims were negative. They found overwhelmingly negative coverage, not only in the United States but also in the United Kingdom, Canada and Australia.

Coverage of extremism sometimes overlooks or minimizes the socio-political contexts that contribute to violence, such as foreign interventions, occupation, discrimination, and economic hardship. Instead, the narrative may imply a direct and inherent link between Islam itself and violent behavior, which misrepresents the beliefs of over a billion peaceful practitioners worldwide.

Some narratives may emphasize so-called "clashes of civilizations" and suggest an intrinsic opposition between "Islamic values" and "Western values," framing Muslims as outsiders and potential threats. This narrative fails to capture the lived realities of millions of Muslims who are active, contributing members of Western societies and dismisses the diversity of thought and practice within Islam.

This has come to the forefront during the ongoing conflict between Israel and Palestinians in Gaza. A notable criticism of Western media, particularly in the U.S. and U.K., is its tendency to prioritize Israeli government and military narratives. Coverage frequently emphasizes Israel's right to defend itself and gives substantial airtime to Israeli spokespeople, while comparatively fewer Palestinian voices are highlighted. This imbalance can lead to framing that portrays Palestinians predominantly in a defensive or reactive context, with limited exploration of their historical grievances and lived realities under prolonged occupation. Instances of dehumanization or reductionist language when referring to Palestinians have also been cited as problematic

Muslims as "Oppressive" or "Backwards": Another common stereotype is the portrayal of Muslim societies as oppressive, particularly toward women. Images of veiled women, discussions of restrictive gender roles, and the assumption that all Muslim countries are governed by strict interpretations of Islamic law contribute to the perception of Islam as monolithic and regressive. Examples: Media often focus on topics like mandatory veiling or honor-based practices without context or distinction between cultural traditions and Islamic teachings. This tends to obscure the diversity within Muslim communities, where beliefs and practices vary widely. While dress codes and the treatment of women vary greatly across different Muslim countries, media portrayals often focus on restrictive dress practices as evidence of broader gender-based repression. Such depictions tend to simplify complex cultural and religious practices, ignoring contexts where women choose to wear specific clothing out of personal or religious conviction. Case in point, India's legislative focus on issues associated with its Muslim community, such as the ban on *triple talaq* (instant divorce in Islamic law) (rare in modern times), highlights a complex interplay of social reform and political strategy. While such measures are often presented as progressive reforms, they are also viewed as tools for political gains and promoting negative stereotypes. This has broader social implications.

Similarly, coverage of women's issues in Muslim societies frequently highlights practices like forced marriages, honor killings, and gender segregation, often without similar scrutiny of domestic violence, gender inequality, or reproductive rights issues in non-Muslim contexts.

In much of Western media, Muslim women are often depicted as a homogenous group of victims who have no freedom, and whose primary existence revolves around oppression by male figures and repressive laws. This ignores the diversity of experiences among Muslim women globally, from those in leadership roles in countries like Indonesia, Malaysia, Pakistan, and Bangladesh to women actively challenging patriarchal norms in their communities. By focusing predominantly on stories of repression, a nuanced and accurate depiction is lost.

Muslims as "The Other" or "Foreign": In Western media, Muslims are frequently portrayed as foreign or alien, even when they are Western citizens. This perception, known as the "othering" of Muslims, suggests that Muslims cannot integrate into Western society, which contributes to stereotypes of Muslims as resistant to Western values or unwilling to assimilate. This narrative is often seen in coverage of Muslim immigrants or refugees, where emphasis is placed on cultural differences rather than shared values. Muslims in Western countries may be described with phrases like "the Muslim community," subtly implying separateness from the larger society.

Reductionist Portrayals of Islamic Culture: Western media often depict Islamic culture as simplistic, ignoring its depth and diversity. Complex beliefs, artistic traditions, and intellectual achievements of Muslim civilizations are often reduced to surface-level stereotypes. This overlooks the rich contributions of Muslim cultures to art, science, philosophy, and literature. Islamic art, music, and literature are rarely covered in mainstream Western media, reinforcing a one-dimensional view of Muslim identity that overlooks cultural and intellectual contributions.

The Clash of Civilizations Theory

This theory was proposed by political scientist Samuel P. Huntington (1996). Huntington argued that the primary source of conflict in the post-Cold War world would be cultural and religious identities, rather than ideological or economic differences. He identified several major civilizations, including Western, Islamic, and Confucian, and predicted that future conflicts would occur along the cultural fault lines between these civilizations. Huntington's theory has been criticized for reinforcing stereotypes about Islamic civilization being inherently in conflict with the West. This has contributed to a narrative that views Muslims as "the other," fostering suspicion and fear. The idea of a clash between civilizations has been used in political and media discourse to justify policies and rhetoric that target Muslim communities. This has led to increased Islamophobia and the portrayal of Muslims as a monolithic group opposed to Western values. The theory has exacerbated social tensions by framing interactions between Muslims and non-Muslims as inherently conflictual. This has hindered efforts at integration and mutual understanding, contributing to social fragmentation and prejudice. The global spread of the clash of civilizations narrative has influenced attitudes towards

Muslims in various countries, leading to a rise in hate crimes, discrimination, and exclusion from mainstream society.

Historical Roots and Motivations

The origins of these stereotypes are rooted in a mix of historical, political, and cultural factors, many of which date back to colonial times and Cold War politics.

Colonialism: During colonial rule in Asia, Africa, and the Middle East, Western powers often depicted Muslims as barbaric or uncivilized to justify occupation and control. This contributed to a long-standing narrative of cultural superiority over Muslim societies.

Orientalism: In the 19th and 20th centuries, the academic field of Orientalism framed Eastern societies, particularly Islamic ones, as exotic, mysterious, and inferior to Western civilization. Edward Said's book 'Orientalism' published in 1978 details how Western art and literature played a role in creating distorted images of Muslims as irrational or despotic. Orientalism is the framework through which Western writers, policymakers, and the general public have interpreted and defined the Islamic societies of the Middle East as "the Orient." The central premise of Orientalism is that the Orient is a fundamentally different, exotic, dangerous, unchanging, and "other" place. This concept of a foreign and strange East form a set of cultural, political, religious, and linguistic contrasts which, in turn, has enabled the "West" to think of itself as a distinct—and superior—entity. Orientalism served as a key ideological lynchpin of European colonialism; fundamentally, it is a discourse of dominance, superiority, and control that continues to have profound implications on today's geopolitical landscape

Political Motivations: Stereotyping of Muslims also gained traction during the Cold War, as Western media often depicted Muslim nations as hotbeds of anti-Western sentiment. After the 9/11 attacks, this narrative shifted to frame Muslims more directly as a security threat, further solidifying negative perceptions in the public consciousness.

Impact on Global Perspectives

The stereotypes perpetuated by Western media have a profound impact on how Muslims are perceived globally, reinforcing biases that affect both Muslim and non-Muslim societies.

Social Polarization and Islamophobia*:* Media-driven stereotypes contribute to Islamophobia in Western societies, often leading to increased suspicion, discrimination, and hostility toward Muslim individuals and communities. Social polarization intensifies as Muslims are subjected to prejudice in employment, education, and public life. Negative media portrayals lead to a sense of alienation and marginalization for Muslims, particularly for younger generations seeking acceptance in Western societies. Furthermore, fear-based portrayals of Islam reinforce public support for discriminatory policies, surveillance, or restrictive immigration laws, as well as suspicions toward Muslim charities or businesses.

Several studies have reported discrimination against Muslims in job recruitment. In a report (Sarah Green Carmichael, 2017), published in Harvard Business Review, job applicants in Germany who wore headscarves in their photos and had Turkish-sounding names, had to send 4.5 times more applications than those without headscarves and sounding German names. For example, an applicant named

"Meryem Öztürk" with a headscarf had to send 4.5 times as many applications as an applicant named "Sandra Bauer" to receive the same number of callbacks. Discrimination was even more pronounced in high-status and high-qualification occupations, despite the difficulty employers face in filling these positions. Yet another report published by the Women and Equalities Committee (2016) indicated that Muslim women were three times as likely as women in other social groups in the UK to be unemployed. Evidence of such discrimination was also reported in India. In a study two identical resumes were prepared, one bearing a Muslim woman and the other a Hindu woman's name. Over a period of ten months, 1,000 job applications were uploaded from each profile to 1,000 online job portals such as LinkedIn and Naukri. It was found that for every two callbacks that a Hindu woman received from job applications, a Muslim woman got only one (thediplomat.com, 2021).

Influence on Foreign Policy and Military Actions: Media representations also influence foreign policy by creating a framework where interventions in Muslim countries are justified through stereotypes. This "civilizing mission" approach can lead to policies that frame Western nations as protectors of freedom or democracy. Stereotypes were leveraged to justify the U.S.-led invasions of Iraq and Afghanistan. Similar portrayals have been used to rationalize involvement in Syria and other conflict zones, presenting Western actions as essential for stability in "violent" or "unstable" Muslim regions. More recently it is seen in the blind support offered to Israel by some western countries and especially the US in the ongoing war in Gaza, despite mass killings of innocent civilians.

Impact on Refugee and Immigration Policy: Negative portrayals of Muslims as a cultural threat or as incapable of assimilation have had significant effects on immigration policies, particularly regarding Muslim refugees. The 2017 U.S. travel ban targeting several Muslim countries is one example where media-driven fears influenced policy. In Europe, concerns over "Muslim integration" have been cited in debates over refugee quotas, asylum policies, and border control measures.

Impact on Muslim Societies: Western media portrayals also impact Muslims in Muslim societies, influencing how they view themselves and their place in the global community. Many Muslims may feel pressure to distance themselves from "extremist" depictions or to prove their alignment with Western values. This dynamic can create identity crises among young Muslims who feel compelled to either defend their beliefs or adopt secular identities that fit Western norms.

Implications for Policy, Intercultural Relations, and Global Security

The reinforcement of stereotypes has had a range of broader consequences for global politics, security, and intercultural relations:

Security Policies and Civil Liberties: Media stereotypes contribute to the normalization of policies that subject Muslims to heightened security measures. Profiling at airports, surveillance of Muslim neighborhoods, and controversial practices like secret evidence and indefinite detention are justified as necessary for "national security." Surveillance programs, like NYPD's "Demographics Unit," which monitored Muslim communities, were implemented following media portrayals that conflated Muslims with potential security threats. Such policies harm civil liberties, disproportionately targeting Muslims and stigmatizing entire communities.

Strained Intercultural Relations and Rise of Populism: Misrepresentations of Muslims contribute to misunderstandings and cultural friction. Populist leaders in Europe and North America have harnessed anti-Muslim rhetoric for political gain, creating a "clash of civilizations" narrative that undermines social cohesion. Examples: The rise of populist parties in countries like France, the Netherlands, and the U.S. has been fueled by Islamophobic rhetoric, which is often reinforced by media stories linking Muslims to societal decline, cultural incompatibility, or threats to national values.

Radicalization and Extremism: While media narratives often emphasize the threat of "Islamic extremism," such coverage can itself contribute to radicalization by alienating Muslims. Feelings of marginalization, particularly among younger Muslims, may lead some to radical views as a form of identity assertion. Studies have shown that alienation and stereotyping contribute to radicalization in marginalized communities. Policies based on misrepresentations reinforce grievances that extremist groups exploit, using them to recruit and radicalize disaffected individuals.

Marginalization and Identity Assertion: While most Muslims today, regardless of country or cultural context, recognize the challenge of religious identity among youth, their understanding of the nature of the problem and the best ways to address it differ. Some Muslims frame this challenge in terms of the urgent need to help Muslim youth today to remain faithful to Islamic teachings and to practice their religion in an otherwise secular and distracting world. Other Muslims criticize an over-emphasis on exclusivism or rigid interpretations of Islamic law, fearing they lead to isolationism and even extremism; and they understand the challenge of lying in encouraging Muslim youth to strive to be better contributors to a pluralistic global community while drawing on their Islamic heritage and its teachings (Marcia Hermansen, 2012).

Erosion of Soft Power and Diplomatic Relations: Stereotypes that cast Muslims as oppositional or incompatible with Western values strain diplomatic relations with Muslim countries, potentially undermining soft power. When Western governments adopt policies that target Muslims based on media stereotypes, it weakens alliances and complicates cooperation on issues like climate change, trade, and counterterrorism.

Correcting the Mischaracterizations

In the minds of many particularly in the Western world, Islam is synonymous with the Middle East, Muslim men with violence, and Muslim women with oppression. In the post-9/11 world, a clash of civilizations appears to be increasingly manifest and the War on Terror seems a struggle against Islam. These are symptoms of Islamophobia. The term "Islamophobia" accurately reflects the largely unexamined and deeply ingrained anxiety in many when considering Islam and Muslim cultures. Islamophobia also discusses the misunderstanding of the Muslim world more generally, such as the assumption that Islam is primarily a Middle Eastern religion, whereas the majority of Muslims live in South and Southeast Asia, and the misperception that a significant portion of Muslims are militant fundamentalists, whereas only a small proportion are.

Efforts to address stereotypes and misrepresentations in media are critical for fostering more informed perspectives and healthier global relations. Steps toward achieving this include (a) promoting Muslim voices in media. Muslim journalists, academics, and public figures can offer nuanced insights that challenge simplistic portrayals, (b) Media organizations can implement training programs that help journalists avoid stereotypical narratives, focusing instead on accurate, culturally sensitive coverage of Muslim societies, (c) Expanding media coverage to showcase the cultural, intellectual, and humanitarian contributions of Muslims can build a more balanced view. This includes reporting on Muslim achievements, art, social justice work, and positive social contributions.

By addressing these issues, the media can help reduce the negative stereotypes and biases that currently influence global perspectives and policy. A more nuanced understanding can support peacebuilding, mutual respect, and effective policies that reflect the complexity and diversity of the Muslim world.

In the words of Ali (2020) "Islam in different parts of the world … is more than just a religion, a cultural system or a social structure, but is a complex composite of diverse institutional processes and functions, social routines and norms, and sacred rituals and practices responsible for shaping the lives of Muslims."

References

Ahmed, S., & Matthes, J. (2017). *Media representation of Muslims and Islam from 2000 to 2015: A meta-analysis. International Communication Gazette, 79*(3), 219-244.

Ali, M. (2018). *The "identity crisis" of younger Muslims: Younger Muslim America, faith, community, and belonging.* NY: Oxford University Press.

Bertrand, M., Chugh, D., & Mullainathan, S. (2005). *Implicit discrimination. American Economic Review, 95*(2), 94-98.

Carmichael, S. G. (2017, May 26). *Employers are less likely to hire a woman who wears a headscarf. Harvard Business Review.*

Gottschalk, P., & Greenberg, G. (2007). *Islamophobia: Making Muslims the enemy.* Lanham: Rowman & Littlefield.

Huntington, S. P. (1993). *The clash of civilizations? Vol.72*(3), 22-49.

Marcia, H. (2012). *Muslim youth and religious identity.* In M. J. Bunge (Ed.), *Children, adults, and shared responsibilities: Jewish, Christian, and Muslim perspectives* (pp. 19-134). Cambridge University Press.

Said, W. E. (1980). *Islam through Western eyes. The Nation.* Retrieved November 4, 2024, from https://www.thenation.com/article/archive/islam-through-western-eyes/

Said, W. E. (2019). *Orientalism.* Penguin Books.

Online Sources

The Conversation. (n.d.). *The Riz Test: How Muslims are misrepresented in film and TV.* Retrieved from https://theconversation.com/the-riz-test-how-muslims-are-misrepresented-in-film-and-tv-110213

The Conversation. (n.d.). *Yes, Muslims are portrayed negatively in American media: 2 political scientists reviewed over 250,000 articles to find conclusive evidence.* Retrieved from https://theconversation.com/yes-muslims-are-portrayed-negatively-in-american-media-2-political-scientists-reviewed-over-250-000-articles-to-find-conclusive-evidence-183327

The Diplomat. (2022, July). *Islamophobia exists in India's private sector.* Retrieved from https://thediplomat.com/2022/07/islamophobia-exists-in-indias-private-sector

CHAPTER 5
MUSLIM MINDSET: NAVIGATING THE CONFLICT BETWEEN TRADITION AND MODERNITY

The complex interplay between tradition and modernity within Muslim societies is a subject of significant academic, political, and cultural inquiry. Spanning diverse geographical regions and cultures, the Muslim experience is far from monolithic. While tradition is anchored in the tenets of Islam and centuries-old practices, modernity brings with it new social norms, technological advances, and globalized cultural influences. The resulting tension is multifaceted, touching on religious beliefs, gender roles, education, governance, and identity.

Historical Backdrop

The rise of modern Europe in the 18th century coincided with what many scholars refer to as the decline of the Ottoman Empire. Prior to that the Ottomans had regarded themselves to be superior by the end of this period the power relationship between the Ottoman Empire and Europe began to shift in Europe's favor. The decline of the Ottoman Empire and the rise of Europe led to a soul-searching and an urge for modernization. Thus, the Ottoman government began to open embassies and send officials to study in Europe. This created conditions for the "gradual formation of a group of reformers with a certain knowledge of the modern world and a conviction that the empire must belong to it or perish" (Hourani, 1983, p.43).

In the period between 1839 and 1876, the Ottoman government began instituting large-scale reforms as a way to modernize and strengthen the empire. Many of these reforms involved adopting successful European practices that were considered antithetical to conservative Muslims. In addition to military and administrative reforms, Ottoman rulers implemented reforms in the sphere of education, law, and the economy. This included new universities and changes in curricula, as well as new economic systems and institutions. There were also European-inspired changes to the law that restricted Islamic law to family affairs such as marriage and inheritance. (Wikipedia).

The influence of modernism in the Muslim world resulted in a cultural revival. Legal reform was attempted in Egypt, Tunisia, the Ottoman Empire, and Iran, and in some cases, these reforms were adopted. At the recommendations of reform-minded Islamic scholars, western sciences were taught in new schools. Much of this had to do with the intellectual appeal of social Darwinism[9], since it led to the conclusion that an old-fashioned Muslim society could not compete in the modern world. Thus, what could be called "Islamic modernism" emerged as a movement that aimed to reconcile the Islamic faith with some modern values and trends such as democracy, rights, nationalism, rationality, science, equality, and progress (https://www.islamicity.org/ 9110/islam-and-modernity). Some of the prominent names spearheading the movement of modernization were Jamal al-

---

[9] Social Darwinism is a socio-political theory that applies the concept of "survival of the fittest" from Charles Darwin's theory of evolution to human societies. The term is often associated with the late 19th and early 20th centuries, when some thinkers and political leaders used it to justify a range of social, political, and economic practices.

Din al-Afghani, Muhammad Abduh, Muhammad Rashid Rida, Qasim Amin, Sir Sayyid Ahmad Khan, & Sir Muhammad Iqbal (Wikipedia).

Almost all Muslim countries in modern times have an embarrassed modern outlook based on a distinction between positive and negative modernity applying ethical standards. For example, no issue is seen in the modern banking system based on Islamic finance principles.

Nonetheless, there are several instances when conservative Muslims opposed scientific theories, discoveries, and technology. Here are a few examples.

Printing Press: When the printing press was introduced to the Ottoman Empire (**15th-18th Centuries**), there was significant resistance from conservative religious scholars. They feared it would lead to the spread of heretical ideas and undermine the role of traditional calligraphers and religious scribes. As a result, printing in Arabic script was prohibited for religious texts until the early 18th century, delaying the spread of printed books in the Islamic world.

Copernican Astronomy (16th-17th Centuries): The heliocentric model of the solar system, introduced by Copernicus and later supported by Galileo, faced resistance in some parts of the Islamic world. Conservative scholars opposed it on the grounds that it contradicted the geocentric model mentioned in traditional interpretations of Islamic cosmology. The heliocentric theory was slow to gain acceptance, though it was eventually incorporated into Islamic astronomical studies.

Theory of Evolution (19th-20th Centuries): Charles Darwin's theory of evolution has been widely opposed by conservative Muslims, who argue that it conflicts with the Qu'ranic account of creation. Some have viewed it as incompatible with the belief in Adam as the first human. Evolution remains controversial in many Muslim countries, with calls to exclude it from school curriculums or to teach it alongside religious creationism.

Women's Education and Modern Medicine (19th-20th Centuries): In the 19th and early 20th centuries, conservative Muslims in some regions opposed the education of women and the adoption of modern medical practices, such as vaccinations. These were seen as violations of traditional gender roles or as Western impositions. Over time, many of these practices were embraced, but initial resistance slowed progress in some areas.

Television and Cinema (20th Century): In the mid-20th century, conservative Muslim groups in countries like Saudi Arabia and Iran criticized television and cinema, claiming they promoted un-Islamic values and indecency. Restrictions were imposed on media content, and the introduction of these technologies was delayed in some regions. However, Islamic programming eventually became widespread.

Stem Cell Research and Organ Transplants (21st Century): Certain conservative Islamic scholars initially opposed stem cell research and organ transplantation, fearing they could lead to violations of Islamic ethics, particularly concerning the sanctity of the human body. Over time, many scholars issued fatwas (religious rulings) in favor of these technologies, provided they adhered to ethical guidelines.

Social media and the Internet (21st Century): Social media platforms and the internet have faced criticism from conservative Muslims for facilitating access to unregulated content, including material seen as immoral or anti-Islamic. Some countries have implemented censorship or restrictions on internet use, though social media is now widely used for both personal and religious purposes.

Tradition and Its Roots in Islam

Islam, as a religion and way of life, has profoundly shaped Muslim societies. Rooted in the Qur'an and the Hadith (sayings and actions of the Prophet Muhammad), Islam provides guidance on virtually all aspects of life. The core tenets of Islam—such as prayer, fasting, charity, and the pilgrimage to Mecca—serve as spiritual anchors for over a billion Muslims worldwide. Tradition often represents the continuity of these religious and cultural practices, serving as a link to heritage and a source of identity, stability, and community cohesion.

However, the adherence to tradition varies across Muslim countries and communities. In some cases, Islamic law (Shariah) has been institutionalized and used as the basis for legal and social norms, while in others, cultural practices, regional customs, and political dynamics shape the expression of Islam. Tradition, therefore, serves not just as a set of rituals but as a broader worldview.

Modernity: Definition and Challenges

Modernity represents a broad set of transformations, encompassing secular governance, scientific progress, technological development, gender equality, human rights, and individual freedoms. It is often perceived as a break from the past and a shift toward rationalism, innovation, and global integration. The conflict between tradition and modernity in the Muslim mindset emerges from the challenge of balancing centuries-old religious norms with the rapid and often disruptive changes of the modern world.

For many Muslims, modernity offers opportunities and new horizons—access to education, technological connectivity, economic progress, and civil rights movements. Yet, it also provokes a sense of vulnerability and cultural erosion, as Western secular ideals may seem at odds with Islamic values. This dilemma poses a central question: Can Muslim societies modernize without losing their cultural and religious roots?

Education and Knowledge

The pursuit of knowledge is a fundamental tenet of Islam, as evidenced by the historical contributions of Muslim scholars to science, medicine, mathematics, and philosophy during the "Golden Age" of Islam. However, the struggle to reconcile traditional religious education with modern, secular curricula has been a point of contention.

In many Muslim countries, religious schools (madrasas) have traditionally focused on teaching the Qur'an, Arabic grammar, and Islamic jurisprudence. While these schools preserve Islamic tradition, critics argue that they sometimes fail to equip students with the skills needed for success in modern, secular economies. Conversely, Western-style education systems can be viewed as neglecting religious values or promoting secularism.

An integrated approach, which incorporates both religious and secular knowledge, represents a possible path forward. Several countries, such as Malaysia and Indonesia, have attempted to balance these two domains to varying degrees of success. However, resistance from traditionalist factions remains, often rooted in fear of Western cultural imperialism.

Islamization of Knowledge

In the late 20th century, scholars such as Ismail Al-Faruqi articulated the concept of the "Islamization of knowledge" concept. It focuses on the mastery of modern sciences, understanding Islamic knowledge in various fields, and establishing the relevance of Islamic values to contemporary academic disciplines. Ismail al-Faruqi's work plan systematically integrates Islamic principles with modern disciplines. This movement sought to reclaim the integrationist ethos of the Golden Age, emphasizing compatibility between Islam and contemporary disciplines.

The Islamization of knowledge is an intellectual and educational project aimed at integrating Islamic principles and values with modern knowledge, including science, philosophy, and the humanities. The concept emerged in the late 20th century, primarily as a response to the perceived secularization and Western dominance of contemporary academic disciplines. The aim is to produce knowledge that is ethically grounded in Islamic teachings while being relevant and beneficial to contemporary society.

The Islamization of knowledge can complement reason, analytical thinking, and the scientific mindset through the promotion of ethical inquiry, support for empiricism, and addressing moral questions. However, the process needs to avoid overly rigid interpretations of Islamic texts or limit scientific exploration. It should also avoid dismissing widely accepted scientific theories (e.g., evolution) if they seem incompatible with traditional understandings of Islam. If the process becomes overly dogmatic, prioritizing ideology over evidence, it risks undermining the objective and open nature of scientific inquiry.

Supporters argue that the Islamization of Knowledge enables Muslims to maintain their religious identity in a secular world while benefiting from modern advancements. Critics, however, highlight potential risks, such as conflating religion with science, restricting academic freedom, and imposing a single interpretation of Islam on diverse Muslim societies.

A balanced approach to Islamization of knowledge encourages dialogue between faith and reason. By emphasizing critical thinking, contextualization, and ethical boundaries, it can enrich both Islamic scholarship and global scientific discourse. However, for this integration to be effective, it requires mutual respect between religious traditions and secular academic methods, avoiding extremes on either side.

Gender Roles and Women's Rights

The issue of gender roles in Muslim societies exemplifies the tension between tradition and modernity. Traditionalists often interpret Islamic teachings to justify strict gender roles and limit women's public participation, viewing these roles as divinely ordained. On the other hand, many modernists and feminists within Muslim societies argue for gender equality, drawing on Islamic principles of justice and compassion.

The rise of female political leaders, activists, scholars, and businesswomen in Muslim countries highlights the evolving landscape. Female enrollment in universities now outnumber their male counterpart in several Muslim countries. Yet, efforts to promote gender equality frequently encounter resistance from conservative elements who perceive such changes as a threat to societal stability and religious identity. This conflict illustrates the challenges of reinterpreting religious teachings to accommodate changing social norms.

Governance and Political Systems

The relationship between Islam and the state is another point of tension. In some countries, Islamic law forms the basis of the legal system, while others adopt secular models. The rise of political Islam, particularly in the 20th and 21st centuries, demonstrates a response to both colonial legacies and modern political failures.

Political movements such as the Muslim Brotherhood in Egypt and Ennahda in Tunisia have sought to balance Islamic values with modern political structures. However, their efforts have often been met with skepticism, both domestically and internationally, as some fear that "Islamic democracy" may infringe on minority rights or fail to respect pluralism. Striking the balance between tradition and democratic governance remains a key challenge.

The Role of Technology and Social Media

The rapid proliferation of technology and social media has created new avenues for connecting with global culture and ideas. For many Muslims, access to technology has allowed for new interpretations of Islam, as online forums, apps, and influencers disseminate diverse viewpoints. Traditional religious authorities, however, may struggle to maintain their influence in this decentralized, digital environment.

On one hand, social media empowers reform-minded individuals to advocate for change, challenge oppressive norms, and engage in interfaith dialogue. On the other, extremist groups have also leveraged technology to promote radical ideologies, further complicating the discourse on tradition and modernity.

Identity and Belonging

Navigating the tension between tradition and modernity often comes down to questions of identity. For many Muslims living in Western societies, the challenge is not only to maintain religious and cultural traditions but to adapt to multicultural and secular environments. Islamophobia and discrimination exacerbate this struggle, leading some to adopt more assertive forms of identity while others seek greater integration.

In Muslim countries, the clash between modernity and tradition is often framed as a struggle for authenticity. Nationalist movements may seek to redefine what it means to be "Muslim" in a modern context, either by embracing or resisting global influences.

Bridging the Divide

Emin Poljarevic (nd) in his paper 'Islamic Tradition and the Meanings of Modernity' explores the complex interaction between Islamic traditions and modernity, examining how various Islamic actors and movements have navigated the challenges and opportunities presented by contemporary global dynamics. Poljarevic analyzes diverse interpretations and strategies employed by Muslim communities and leaders to reconcile or resist aspects of modernity, addressing themes like secularism, political authority, cultural identity, and globalization.

The author delves into the ways modernity is perceived within Islamic thought, reflecting on its impact on political, social, and personal spheres. He highlights the spectrum of responses—from reformist, moderate engagements to more conservative or radical stances—demonstrating the plurality of voices within the Muslim world. His work contributes to a nuanced understanding of how tradition and modernity are negotiated and redefined within Islamic contexts.

The debate surrounding the compatibility of modernity and Islamic tradition has persisted for centuries. There is a common perception that Islamic tradition is particularly unsuited to incorporate or benefit from modernity's conceptual tools and its purported liberating potential. Consequently, it is often assumed that advocates of Islam and liberalism are fundamentally opposed, stemming from the belief that they operate within distinct paradigms of understanding, knowledge, and even their goals and aspirations. To resolve this tension, dialogue and adaptability are key. Many Muslim scholars and leaders emphasize "*ijtihad*" (independent reasoning) as a way to reinterpret Islamic teachings in light of modern challenges. This process, however, requires flexibility and an openness to change, which can be difficult to achieve in conservative contexts.

Moderation (Wasatiyyah): The Core Islamic Value

Wasatiyyah is an Arabic term in Islam that means moderation, balance, or being in the middle path. It is derived from the root word "wasat", which means "middle" or "central." Wasatiyyah represents a core Islamic value advocating for a balanced approach in all aspects of life, avoiding extremes on either side. The principle of wasatiyyah is emphasized in the Qu'ran, where Allah says:

"And thus, We have made you a just community (ummatan wasatan) that you will be witnesses over the people and the Messenger will be a witness over you." (Surah Al-Baqarah, 2:143)

Here, *"ummatan wasatan"* (a just or balanced community) signifies that Muslims are called to embody moderation, justice, and fairness in their beliefs, actions, and dealings. The key aspects of Wasatiyah include avoiding extremism in worship or neglecting religious obligations. Following the Prophet's example of balanced worship, family life, and social engagement. Promoting justice, equity, and compassion and treating others with kindness and fairness, regardless of their background or beliefs. It also includes practicing moderation in spending, avoiding extravagance or miserliness, and encouraging lawful earning and ethical trade. Interpersonal relationships, demand maintaining a balance between individual rights and communal responsibilities and advocating for dialogue, tolerance, and peaceful coexistence. At the global level, it means encouraging mutual understanding and respect among different cultures and religions and rejecting violence and extremism as means of achieving goals.

Wasatiyah requires striking a balance in life by avoiding two extremes: excessiveness (*ghuluw*) and negligence (*tafrīt*). It encourages Muslims to embody a middle path that is practical, inclusive, and adaptable to changing circumstances, always guided by Islamic principles. This concept serves as a reminder that Islam promotes a harmonious way of life, where justice, mercy, and balance are central values for individuals and communities. Referring to extremism Hassan (2014) emphasized that "Muslims who use violence in promoting the cause of Islam are in fact violating the teachings of Islam and do great disservice to it". Hassan emphasizes that extremism in religion is strongly prohibited by Prophet Muhammad.

The tension between tradition and modernity in Muslim societies is not simply a binary conflict but rather a fluid and evolving process. By thoughtfully engaging with both their cultural heritage and the challenges of the modern world, Muslims worldwide strive to find ways that uphold their faith while welcoming progress. In this ongoing conversation, tradition and modernity do not have to be at odds; instead, they can complement and strengthen one another in the quest for a just and inclusive future.

References

Ahmed, M. K. (2014). *Perspectives on the discourse of Islamization of education. American Journal of Humanities and Social Sciences, 2*(1).

al-Faruqi, I. R. (1982). *Islam: Source and purpose of knowledge: Proceedings and selected papers of second conference on Islamization of knowledge.* IIIT.

al-Faruqi, I. R. (1982). *Islamization of knowledge: General principles and work plan.* IIIT.

Emin, P. (n.d.). *Islamic tradition and meanings of modernity. International Journal for History, Culture and Modernity, 3*(1), 29–57.

Hassan, M. H. (2014). *Wasatiyyah as explained by Prof. Muhammad Kamal Hassan: Justice, excellence and balance. Counter Terrorist Trends and Analyses, 6*(2), 24–30.

Hassan, M. K. (2013). *The need to understand Al-Wasatiyyah.* Kuala Lumpur: IIUM Press.

Hefner, R. (2010). *Introduction: Muslims and modernity: Culture and society in an age of contest and plurality.* In R. W. Hefner (Ed.), *The New Cambridge History of Islam* (pp. 1-36). Cambridge University Press.

Hourani, A. (1983). *Arabic thought in the liberal age: 1798–1939.* New York: Cambridge University Press. Retrieved November 24, 2024.

Iqbal, M. A., & Mabud, S. A. (2019). *Challenge of globalization to the Muslim Ummah: Religious extremism and the need for middle path (Wasat). Strategic Studies, 39*(3), 73–88.

Maiwada, D. A. (1997). *Islamization of knowledge: Background and scope. The American Journal of Islamic Social Sciences, 14*(2).

Wikipedia. (n.d.). *Modernity.* Retrieved November 20, 2024, from http://en.wikipedia.org/wiki/Modernity

CHAPTER 6
EMERGING A WESTERN ISLAM: BRIDGING CULTURES AND FAITHS

The term Western Islam typically refers to the practice and interpretation of Islam by Muslims living in predominantly non-Muslim, Western countries, such as Europe, North America, and Australia. It is not a separate form of Islam but reflects the unique dynamics, challenges, and adaptations of Muslim communities in these regions.

Islam, one of the world's major religions, has a long history of cultural adaptation and diversity, thriving in varied societies across the globe. In recent decades, as Muslim communities have grown and established roots in the Western world, the emergence of a "Western Islam" has become a significant phenomenon. This development reflects not just a demographic shift but also a deeper integration of Islamic principles with the cultural, social, and political frameworks of Western societies. The concept of Western Islam embodies a synthesis of faith and context, striving to remain true to Islamic values while addressing the challenges and opportunities of living in the West.

Islam's ability to adapt to different cultural, social, and political contexts is one of its most remarkable features. From its earliest days, Islam encountered diverse societies, each with unique customs, languages, and traditions. Rather than imposing uniformity, Islam integrated with local cultures, resulting in rich and varied expressions of faith across the globe.

Historical Roots of Adaptation

Islam has always been a dynamic faith, adapting to the cultures and traditions of the regions it spread to. From the architectural splendor of Moorish Spain to the philosophical advancements in the Abbasid Caliphate, Islam's presence has historically been shaped by the cultural norms of its environment. The emergence of Western Islam is no different. It reflects a broader historical pattern of Muslims contextualizing their faith while maintaining core religious tenets.

When Islam emerged in 7th-century Arabia, it began as a unifying force among the diverse tribes of the Arabian Peninsula. The Qur'an and the teachings of Prophet Muhammad emphasized values like justice, compassion, and equality, while also addressing specific local issues such as tribal rivalries and social hierarchies. As Islam spread beyond Arabia, its core principles remained intact, but its practices and cultural expressions began to reflect the new environments in which it took root.

During the Rashidun, Umayyad, and Abbasid Caliphates, Islam encountered the civilizations of Persia, Byzantium, and South Asia. These interactions profoundly influenced Islamic culture, governance, and scholarship. When Islam spread to Persia, it absorbed elements of Persian art, administration, and literature. Concepts like the Persian court system influenced the governance of Islamic empires, while Persian architecture inspired Islamic designs.

In regions influenced by the Byzantine Empire, Islamic architecture and art adopted elements such as domes, mosaics, and intricate ornamentation, evident in landmarks like the Dome of the Rock in Jerusalem.

In South Asia, Islam coexisted with Hindu and Buddhist traditions, giving rise to unique cultural blends. Sufi traditions, for instance, incorporated local music, dance, and spiritual practices to connect with diverse communities.

Perhaps one of the most striking examples of Islamic adaptation is found in Al-Andalus (Muslim Spain), where Muslims ruled for nearly 800 years. This period saw a vibrant coexistence of Muslims, Christians, and Jews, fostering a golden age of intellectual and cultural exchange. Contributions from Andalusian Islam included:

Philosophy: Thinkers like Ibn Rushd (Averroes) synthesized Greek philosophy with Islamic theology, influencing European thought.

Science and Medicine: Advances in medicine, astronomy, and mathematics flourished in institutions like the University of Cordoba.

Art and Architecture: The Alhambra Palace in Granada stands as a testament to the unique architectural style that blended Islamic, Christian, and local Spanish elements.

The Ottoman Empire further demonstrated Islam's adaptability, encompassing diverse cultures across Europe, the Middle East, and North Africa. The Ottomans allowed for religious pluralism under the millet system, enabling various communities to govern themselves under their own religious laws. Ottoman art, literature, and cuisine reflected the fusion of these diverse cultural influences.

In Southeast Asia, particularly in Indonesia and Malaysia, Islam spread primarily through trade rather than conquest. Here, Islamic teachings blended with local traditions, resulting in distinctive practices such as the celebration of Islamic holidays with regional customs. The syncretic approach made Islam accessible and appealing to local populations.

The historical roots of Islamic adaptation underscore the religion's inherent flexibility and openness to cultural diversity. These examples demonstrate that the essence of Islam lies not in rigid uniformity but in the universal values it promotes, which can be expressed through a variety of cultural lenses. As Western Islam emerges, it follows in this rich tradition of contextualization. The experiences of previous generations of Muslims adapting to new contexts provide a valuable blueprint for how Islam can integrate with Western cultures while remaining true to its core teachings. This historical perspective not only enriches our understanding of Islam's global legacy but also inspires hope for its future as a force for unity and coexistence.

Characteristics of Western Islam

Integration of Values: One defining characteristic of Western Islam is its alignment with the universal values of human rights, democracy, and gender equality that are widely upheld in the West. While traditional Islamic teachings often support these values, Western Muslim communities have emphasized reinterpretations of Islamic jurisprudence to better reflect contemporary societal norms. This reinterpretation has been particularly visible in debates on women's roles, freedom of expression, and interfaith dialogue.

Pluralism and Diversity: Western Islam celebrates pluralism. Muslims in the West come from diverse cultural and ethnic backgrounds, creating a melting pot of traditions and practices. This diversity fosters dialogue and cooperation within the Muslim community, as well as with non-Muslims. Mosques and Islamic centers in the West often serve as hubs for multicultural activities, highlighting Islam's adaptability to diverse settings.

Youth and Identity: Second- and third-generation Muslims in the West have played a pivotal role in shaping Western Islam. Balancing dual identities, they seek to remain devout while participating fully in their societies. This has led to the rise of Western Muslim thinkers, artists, and activists who are redefining what it means to be both Western and Muslim. From fashion to music to political activism, young Muslims are forging new pathways for self-expression that resonate with their unique experiences.

Reclaiming the Narrative: In the face of rising Islamophobia and media misrepresentation, Western Muslims have also been at the forefront of efforts to reclaim Islam's image. Grassroots initiatives, interfaith programs, and social media campaigns aim to challenge stereotypes and showcase Islam as a religion of peace, compassion, and social justice. Western Muslims have undertaken numerous efforts to counter Islamophobia and reclaim Islam's image. Organizations like CAIR (Council on American-Islamic Relations) in the U.S. actively engage in education, advocacy, and interfaith collaboration to dispel misconceptions about Islam. Muslim leaders and activists, such as Imam Omar Suleiman, participate in interfaith events to promote understanding between Muslims and other religious communities.

VisitMyMosque Campaign in the UK is the initiative that invites non-Muslims to visit mosques, interact with

Muslim communities, and learn about Islam directly. Many Muslim women in the West use social media to challenge stereotypes about the hijab and assert their right to wear it as a personal and empowered choice.

Muslim organizations like *Islamic Relief* and *Penny Appeal* not only assist Muslim communities but also extend their aid to people of all backgrounds, demonstrating Islamic values of compassion and service. During crises, Muslim communities in the West often spearhead relief efforts, such as organizing food drives or raising funds for disaster-stricken areas.

These efforts showcase how Western Muslims are creatively and courageously reclaiming their narrative, fighting prejudice, and contributing positively to society.

Challenges and Criticisms

Despite its promise, the emergence of Western Islam is not without challenges. Conservative voices within the global Muslim community may view these developments as diluting Islamic principles. On the other hand, certain Western political and social movements may resist the integration of Islam, seeing it as incompatible with Western values. Navigating these tensions requires open dialogue, education, and mutual respect.

Internal challenges within Muslim communities consist of diverging interpretations of Islam. Muslim communities worldwide have diverse cultural, theological, and sectarian traditions. Western Islam, with its efforts to reinterpret Islamic teachings in line with Western values, is often viewed with skepticism by more conservative or traditionalist segments of the Muslim world. Critics argue that adapting Islam to Western contexts risks compromising core Islamic values and practices. Sunni-Shia dynamics, as well as debates among smaller sects like Sufis or Salafis, can create fragmentation within Western Muslim communities. Moreover, second and third-generation Muslims often face identity crises, torn between their cultural heritage and Western societal norms. This duality leads to alienation from both their religious roots and Western peers. Radicalization emerges among a small minority, driven by a desire to assert a "pure" form of Islam in reaction to perceived cultural dilution.

In many Western Muslim communities, there is a shortage of locally trained Islamic scholars and leaders who understand the Western context. As a result, imported imams from non-Western countries may struggle to address the unique challenges of Western Muslims. Younger generations may feel disconnected from religious authorities who cannot relate to their lived experiences.

External Challenges from Western Societies

The rise of Islamophobia in many Western countries is one of the most significant challenges for Western Islam. Prejudices are fueled by misrepresentations of Islam in the media, often associating the religion with extremism. Political rhetoric that portrays Muslims as a monolithic "other" incompatible with Western values. Discriminatory policies and hate crimes create a hostile environment for Muslims.

Western societies often struggle to differentiate between integration (maintaining cultural identity while participating in broader society) and assimilation (erasing cultural differences). This creates tension when Muslims seek to preserve their religious practices, such as wearing the hijab or observing dietary restrictions. Advocate for spaces like Islamic schools or prayer facilities, which are sometimes viewed as segregationist. In some Western countries, especially in Europe, rigid interpretations of secularism can conflict with the public expression of religion. For instance, bans on religious symbols, such as the hijab in public institutions in France, disproportionately affect Muslims. Policies targeting Muslim communities, such as surveillance programs, perpetuate feelings of mistrust and marginalization.

The Role of Western Governments and Societies. Western governments and societies have a vital role to play in fostering an environment where Western Islam can thrive. Policies that promote inclusivity, combat discrimination, and protect religious freedoms are essential. Likewise, efforts to understand and engage with Muslim communities as integral parts of Western society, rather than as "outsiders," will contribute to this process.

The emergence of Western Islam is not merely a response to migration but a testament to the adaptability and universality of the Islamic faith. It represents a bridge between cultures, offering a model of coexistence where faith and modernity enrich one another. In an increasingly globalized world, Western Islam stands as a powerful example of how diverse identities can coexist and thrive within a shared framework of values and aspirations.

Global Geopolitical Implications. Western Islam is often overshadowed by global conflicts involving Muslim-majority countries. Events like terrorism, wars in the Middle East, or human rights issues in Islamic states shape negative perceptions of Islam as a whole. This creates a burden for Western Muslims to constantly defend their faith against stereotypes.

Muslims in the West frequently point to double standards, where Christian or Jewish religious practices are celebrated while Islamic practices are scrutinized. For example, Christmas and Hanukkah are widely recognized and accommodated, but Islamic holidays like Eid may not receive similar acknowledgment in workplaces or schools. Also, the construction of mosques often faces more opposition compared to churches or synagogues.

Reform vs. Orthodoxy. Some Muslims critique the very concept of Western Islam as unnecessary. They argue that Islam, as a universal religion, already accommodates any cultural context and does not require reinterpretation. Movements for Western Islam are sometimes seen as led by intellectual elites disconnected from the everyday struggles of ordinary Muslims. The idea of "Western Islam" risks creating a dichotomy between Muslims in the West and those in the rest of the world, potentially fracturing the global Muslim community (ummah).

Systemic Inequalities Faced by Muslim Communities in the West

Muslim communities in Western countries often experience systemic inequalities in areas such as employment, education, housing, and representation. These challenges are frequently linked to factors such as Islamophobia, discrimination, and socio-economic disadvantages. Below are specific examples, supported by data, that illustrate these systemic inequalities:

Employment Discrimination. Muslims in Western countries face significant barriers to employment due to biases based on their religion or ethnicity. A 2022 report by the House of Commons Library revealed that Muslim unemployment rates in the UK are almost twice as high as the national average. For example, Unemployment among Muslims stood at 6.7%, compared to the UK-wide rate of 3.9%. Similarly, Muslim women faced the highest levels of disadvantage, with 65% of Muslim women of working age being economically inactive.

In the United States, a 2017 study by the Institute for Social Policy and Understanding (ISPU) found that 42% of Muslims reported experiencing some form of religious-based discrimination at work. This is significantly higher than other religious groups.

In France, a study published in the *Proceedings of the National Academy of Sciences (PNAS)* (2019) found that job applicants with "Muslim-sounding" names were 2.5 times less likely to be called for an interview compared to applicants with "Christian-sounding" names, despite having identical qualifications.

Education Inequality. Muslim students in the West often face discrimination, lower academic expectations, and cultural alienation within educational systems. According to ISPU's 2022 report, 50% of Muslim students aged 11-18 in the US reported being bullied because of their religion, which is double the rate for other groups. Among bullied Muslim students, 1 in 3 said that teachers or school officials perpetrated the bullying.

A 2017 report published in the UK by the Social Mobility Commission highlighted disparities in education.

Only 6% of British Muslims are in higher managerial, administrative, or professional occupations compared to 10% of the overall population. The report also indicated that Muslim students, particularly those from Pakistani and Bangladeshi backgrounds, often face lower expectations from educators, leading to underachievement in higher education.

Housing and Neighborhood Segregation. Muslim communities often encounter challenges in accessing quality housing, frequently living in poorer neighborhoods with limited resources. For example, many Muslims in France, particularly those of North African descent, live in banlieues (suburban housing estates), which are often stigmatized and associated with poverty and social exclusion. According to a 2020 report by *Observatoire des Inegalités*, Muslim-majority areas experience higher rates of unemployment (up to 26%) and limited access to public services compared to wealthier, non-Muslim neighborhoods.

In the US the Pew Research Center (2021) found that 44% of American Muslims reported living in households earning less than $30,000 annually, compared to 24% of the general population. Many Muslim-majority communities in urban areas, such as Detroit and New York City, face higher rates of overcrowding and substandard housing conditions.

Political and Media Representation. Muslims are significantly underrepresented in political leadership and frequently misrepresented in media narratives. In the UK, Muslims make up approximately 6.5% of the population (2021 Census), yet they are underrepresented in Parliament, holding only 4.3% of seats (22 Muslim MPs as of 2023). In the US, Muslims constitute about 1.1% of the population, but only 3 Muslims currently serve in Congress (2025).

Media Representation. A 2021 study by the University of Southern California's Annenberg Inclusion Initiative analyzed 200 popular films and found that Muslims made up only 1.6% of all speaking characters, despite comprising over 24% of the global population. Moreover, over 90% of portrayals were negative, often depicting Muslims as violent or extremist.

Hate Crimes and Islamophobia. Muslims in Western societies are disproportionately targeted by hate crimes and discriminatory practices. In the US the FBI's 2022 Hate Crime Statistics revealed that anti-Muslim incidents accounted for 13% of religiously motivated hate crimes, despite Muslims being just 1.1% of the population. Incidents often included vandalism of mosques, physical assaults, and verbal harassment. In Canada, a 2022 Statistics Canada report showed a 71% increase in police-reported hate crimes targeting Muslims between 2020 and 2021.

In Europe, the European Islamophobia Report (2022) highlighted that in Germany, 901 anti-Muslim incidents were recorded in 2021, including mosque vandalism and assaults on visibly Muslim individuals. In France, Islamophobic acts increased by 52% between 2019 and 2021, with hijab-wearing women being frequent targets.

Health Disparities. Muslim communities often face inequitable access to healthcare due to socio-economic barriers and cultural insensitivity. In the US a 2022 report by the Muslim Wellness Foundation found Muslim Americans are more likely to experience mental health stigma, with only 36% seeking professional help for mental health issues compared to 67% of the general population. Discrimination in healthcare settings is a barrier, with 24% of Muslims reporting unfair treatment by healthcare providers. In the UK, a 2020 Public Health England report revealed that Pakistani and Bangladeshi Muslims had significantly higher rates of diabetes and cardiovascular disease compared to the general population, largely due to socio-economic disadvantages and lack of access to preventative care.

The systemic inequalities faced by Muslim communities in the West highlight the ongoing challenges of integration and inclusion. Addressing these disparities requires a concerted effort from governments, civil society, and Muslim communities themselves. By promoting equity in employment, education, housing, and representation, and combating Islamophobia, Western societies can foster environments where Muslim communities can thrive and contribute fully to the social, cultural, and economic fabric of their nations.

Strategies to Address Challenges

1. **Education and Dialogue**: Combat ignorance and prejudice through interfaith initiatives, community outreach, and educational programs that highlight Islam's positive contributions to Western societies.

2. **Empowering Youth**: Invest in programs that support Muslim youth in navigating identity challenges, providing mentorship, and promoting leadership development.

3. **Policy Advocacy**: Advocate for policies that ensure religious freedoms, combat discrimination, and promote equitable opportunities for Muslims.

4. **Developing Local Leadership**: Train imams and scholars who understand the unique needs of Western Muslims and can address issues like gender equality, pluralism, and modern ethics.

5. **Global and Local Collaboration**: Foster partnerships between Western Muslim communities and the broader Muslim world to bridge divides and promote mutual understanding.

The challenges and criticisms faced by Western Islam are complex, involving internal debates within Muslim communities and external pressures from Western societies. However, these hurdles are not insurmountable. With a focus on inclusivity, education, and mutual respect, Western Islam can continue to grow as a vibrant and enriching part of the global Islamic tradition and the multicultural fabric of Western societies. This evolution has the potential to challenge stereotypes, bridge cultural divides, and offer a compelling model of coexistence for the world.

References

Al-Sayyid, N. (2002). *Muslim Europe or Euro-Islam: On the discourses of identity and culture.* In N. Al-Sayyad & M. Castells (Eds.), *Muslim Europe or Euro-Islam* (pp. 9–29). Lanham: Lexington Books.

Alim, H. S. (2005). *A new research agenda: Exploring the trans-global hip-hop umma.* In M. Cooke & B. Lawrence (Eds.), *Muslim networks: From Hajj to hip-hop* (pp. 264–274). Chapel Hill: The University of North Carolina Press.

Allievi, S. (2002). *Converts and the making of European Islam. ISIM Newsletter, 11*, 1–7.

Baxter, K. (2008). *Contemporary Islamic discourse in Europe: The emergence of a 'Euro-Islam'?* In B. MacQueen, K. Baxter, & R. Barlow (Eds.), *Islam and the question of reform: Critical voices from Muslim communities* (pp. 94–113). Carlton: Melbourne University Publishing.

Cesari, J. (Ed.). (2014). *The Oxford handbook of European Islam.* Oxford: Oxford University Press.

Duderija, A. (2015). *The emerging of a Western Muslim identity.* In R. Tottoli (Ed.), *Routledge handbook of Islam in the West* (pp. 198–214). New York/London: Routledge.

Duderija, A., & Rane, H. (2019). *An emerging Western Islam.* In *Islam and Muslims in the West. New directions in Islam.* Palgrave Macmillan, Cham. https://doi.org/10.1007/978-3-319-92510-3_12

Roald, A. S. (2004). *Women in Islam: The Western experience.* London: Routledge.

CHAPTER 7
EDUCATION, LITERACY, AND INTELLECTUAL TRADITIONS

Education, literacy, and intellectual traditions hold a significant and deeply rooted place in Muslim societies. Historically, Islam emphasized the pursuit of knowledge and intellectual growth, which led to the establishment of educational systems and thriving intellectual traditions across the Muslim world. This emphasis on education and learning continues to influence contemporary Muslim societies, though there are challenges and variations in how educational goals are achieved across regions.

Let's examine the historical foundations, the role of education and literacy, and the impact of intellectual traditions on modern Muslim societies.

Historical Foundations

From the earliest days of Islam, the pursuit of knowledge has been strongly encouraged. Several Qu'ranic verses and hadith (sayings of the Prophet Muhammad) stress the importance of education, literacy, and intellectual growth. The first revelation of the Qur'an commands, "Read in the name of your Lord who created," highlighting the centrality of literacy and learning in Islam. The Qur'an also refers to God as "Al-Alim," or "The All-Knowing," and often encourages reflection, study, and understanding as acts of devotion.

The Prophet Muhammad emphasized education and the seeking of knowledge. Statements like, "Seeking knowledge is obligatory for every Muslim," have inspired generations to pursue education as both a religious and social duty. His endorsement of learning extended to both men and women, though how societies interpreted this ideal varied over time.

The Role of Madrasas and Educational Institutions

Muslim societies were early adopters of formal education systems, with the establishment of *madrasas* (schools) that focused on religious, scientific, and literary education. These institutions evolved to become some of the earliest universities and centers of learning in the world. Traditionally, madrasas were institutions that taught a broad curriculum including Qu'ranic studies, Hadith, jurisprudence (fiqh), mathematics, astronomy, medicine, philosophy, and literature. Students were taught to memorize the Qur'an and engage in discussions on various subjects, fostering analytical thinking and intellectual inquiry.

Famous centers of learning, such as *Al-Qarawiyyin* in Morocco (founded in 859 CE) and *Al-Azhar* in Cairo (founded in 972 CE), became pivotal to the development of Islamic scholarship. Baghdad's House of Wisdom (Bayt al-Hikma), founded in the 8th century, played a major role in translating Greek, Persian, and Indian works into Arabic, which preserved and expanded global knowledge on subjects like medicine, philosophy, mathematics, and astronomy.

These institutions encouraged the exchange of ideas and became models for later European universities. By establishing organized systems of education, early Muslim societies made knowledge accessible to a wider audience and contributed to intellectual advancements that impacted not only the Islamic world but also the West.

Literacy and the Spread of Knowledge

Literacy has long been considered a virtue in Muslim societies, particularly due to the central role of the Qur'an, which was to be read, recited, and studied. The spread of literacy was facilitated by several factors.

The Use of Arabic: As the language of the Qur'an, Arabic became a widely taught language, not only among Arabs but across Muslim regions. This facilitated the spread of a common written language that united diverse ethnic and linguistic groups.

Educational Initiatives: Islamic governments and rulers encouraged the development of schools and libraries, often funding them through *waqf* (charitable endowments). These endowments enabled scholars and students to study without financial burdens, supporting educational accessibility across socioeconomic backgrounds.

Role of Scholars and Scribes: Scholars and scribes contributed to the preservation and transmission of knowledge. Notable scholars, like Ibn Sina (Avicenna), Al-Ghazali, and Ibn Khaldun, wrote works that were widely copied, read, and shared, supporting an intellectual culture that valued literacy and scholarly debate. Here is a brief overview of these scholars.

Ibn Sina (Avicenna) (980–1037). He was born in Bukhara (modern-day Uzbekistan). Ibn Sina was a polymath during the Islamic Golden Age. He is widely regarded as one of the most influential thinkers and writers in the fields of medicine, philosophy, and science. His book, *Al-Qanun fi al-*

Tibb (The Canon of Medicine), became a standard medical text in both the Islamic world and Europe for centuries. It covered pharmacology, diseases, and anatomy. He was a key figure in integrating Aristotelian and Neoplatonic thought into Islamic philosophy, particularly through his works like *Kitab al-Shifa* (The Book of Healing), a vast philosophical and scientific encyclopedia. He made significant contributions to logic, mathematics, and astronomy. He developed the concept of the "Necessary Being," which influenced later Islamic and Western philosophers.

Al-Ghazali (1058–1111). He was born in Tus (modern-day Iran). Al-Ghazali was a theologian, jurist, philosopher, and mystic. He is considered one of the most important reformers in Islamic thought. His book, *Ihya' Ulum al-Din* (The Revival of the Religious Sciences), remains a seminal work in Islamic spirituality, covering theology, ethics, and Sufism. In his book *Tahafut al-Falasifa* (The Incoherence of the Philosophers), he critiqued Neoplatonic and Aristotelian philosophy, challenging philosophers like Ibn Sina. This work had profound implications for Islamic and Western philosophical traditions. He bridged Islamic orthodoxy and Sufism, advocating for a balance between outward religious practice and inner spirituality. Al-Ghazali's emphasis on the importance of integrating reason and faith influenced Islamic education and scholarship.

Ibn Khaldun (1332–1406). He was born in Tunis (modern-day Tunisia). Ibn Khaldun was a historian, sociologist, economist, and philosopher. He is considered the father of the social sciences and historiography. He is famous for his seminal work, *Muqaddimah* (Prolegomena), which laid the foundation for understanding history and society through systematic and scientific methods. Ibn Khaldun introduced concepts like *asabiyyah* (social cohesion) and cycles of civilizations, explaining the rise and fall of states. He emphasized the role of economic conditions, geography, and human behavior in shaping historical events. His insights into statecraft and governance were advanced for his time, influencing later political theorists.

These scholars profoundly impacted Islamic and global intellectual traditions, shaping fields ranging from philosophy and theology to sociology and medicine. Their works remain studied and respected across cultures and disciplines.

Intellectual Traditions and Achievements

The Islamic Golden Age (8th to 14th centuries) witnessed the flourishing of intellectual traditions, with Muslims making groundbreaking advancements across various fields.

Philosophy and Theology: Muslim philosophers, like Al-Farabi, Ibn Sina, and Ibn Rushd (Averroes), engaged with Greek philosophy and sought to reconcile it with Islamic teachings. They developed a tradition of rational inquiry that emphasized reason alongside faith, leading to debates on topics like metaphysics, ethics, and the nature of God.

Several schools of thought emerged, including *Ash'arism* and *Mu'tazilism,* which differed on interpretations of free will, divine attributes, and predestination. These discussions enriched Islamic thought and encouraged philosophical inquiry as a tool to understand both religious and scientific concepts.

Science and Medicine: The scientific achievements of Muslim scholars were significant and have had lasting impacts on global knowledge. Scholars like Al-Khwarizmi (father of algebra), Al-Razi (a pioneer in medicine), and Ibn Haytham (founder of optics) made foundational contributions to mathematics, medicine, astronomy, and chemistry. Islamic medical texts, such as Ibn Sina's Canon of Medicine and Al-Razi's writings on smallpox and measles, were used in European medical schools for centuries. These works emphasized observation, experimentation, and systematic study, laying early foundations for modern science.

Mathematics and Astronomy: Mathematics was particularly valued, with Muslim scholars refining and expanding upon earlier Greek and Indian mathematical systems. Al-Khwarizmi's work on algebra, for example, introduced systematic solutions for linear and quadratic equations. Muslim astronomers, like Al-Battani and Al-Tusi, made precise observations that contributed to a better understanding of planetary motions. Observatories were established in cities like Baghdad and Maragheh, fostering scientific study and experimentation.

Literature and the Arts: Islamic literature flourished, with a rich tradition of poetry, philosophy, and storytelling that drew from Arab, Persian, and Turkish influences. Epic works, such as Firdawsi's (Abu'l-Qâsem Ferdowsi Tusi) Shahnameh (Book of Kings) and Rumi's (Jalāl al-Dīn Muḥammad Rūmī) mystical poetry, continue to influence global literature. Islamic art and architecture reflected intellectual and spiritual values. Calligraphy, in particular, became a revered art form as Muslims sought to honor the

Qur'an's verses through visually captivating styles. Architectural achievements, such as the Alhambra and the Blue Mosque, reflect the integration of artistic expression with theological symbolism.

Contemporary Education and Literacy

Modern Muslim societies face challenges and variations in education and literacy levels, influenced by factors such as economic disparities, political structures, and regional conflicts. However, there is a strong commitment to education and literacy within these communities, often supported by national and international initiatives.

In many Muslim countries, national education systems incorporate both secular and religious studies. Some governments, such as those in Turkey, Malaysia, and the UAE, have invested heavily in education reform to improve literacy rates and create more equitable access to education.

Countries like Iran and Egypt have achieved high literacy rates through government initiatives, although disparities remain between urban and rural areas. Education reforms often emphasize STEM (Science, Technology, Engineering, Mathematics) fields, while also preserving traditional Islamic subjects.

There is a range of educational options, from state schools to Islamic schools, each with distinct curriculums. Many Muslim families also send their children to private or international schools that combine secular subjects with Islamic studies.

Despite stereotypes about Muslim women, many Muslim societies have prioritized women's education. Countries like Indonesia, Malaysia, and Tunisia have made significant strides in achieving gender parity in education, with women enrolling in universities at rates comparable to men. While some countries face cultural or economic barriers that limit women's educational opportunities, efforts by governments and NGOs are focused on empowering women through scholarships, vocational training, and literacy programs.

Nonetheless, there are challenges associated with Madrasa education. Some regions still rely heavily on madrasa education, where emphasis may be placed more on religious studies than on secular subjects. Efforts are being made to modernize madrasa curricula, integrating STEM subjects, social sciences, and language skills to better equip students for modern economies.

Countries like Pakistan, Bangladesh, and India have initiated reforms to broaden madrasa curriculums to include subjects that align with the national education framework.

Higher Education Institutions

Higher Education Institutions (HEIs) in Muslim countries encompass a wide range of universities, colleges, and other educational establishments that play an essential role in advancing education, research, and development across the Muslim world. Here are some notable features and institutions:

In many such countries, there is a unique integration of religious education and secular subjects. This allows for curricula that blend modern scientific learning with traditional Islamic teachings. International Islamic University Malaysia, for example, has faculty of Engineering, Medicine, Pharmacy, Science, Architecture,

Information Technology, Economics, Finance Accounting, Business Administration, Human Sciences and Islamic studies. The University motto reads as "Garden of knowledge and virtue." (Visit the university website www.iium.edu.my for details).

Similar Islamic Universities have been established in Pakistan, Bangladesh, Indonesia, and a few other countries. Besides, there are several other universities in these countries offering modern contemporary courses and state-of-the-art training and education to build human capital. However, while some countries, like Malaysia and Turkey, have invested heavily in higher education and research, others face limitations due to financial constraints, political instability, or conflict.

Many HEIs in Muslim countries are part of collaborations and networks, such as the Federation of the Universities of the Islamic World (FUIW), which works to improve educational standards and foster cooperation among member institutions. Moreover, initiatives like Malaysia's drive to become an international education hub and efforts by the Gulf countries to create state-of-the-art campuses highlight the varied and evolving landscape of higher education in these nations.

Muslims have made significant contributions to science and technology in modern times across various fields, building on the rich intellectual heritage of the Islamic Golden Age. These contributions reflect the creativity, innovation, and interdisciplinary approach of Muslim scientists, researchers, and technologists. Below are notable examples:

- Dr. Mehmet Öz (Turkey/USA): A leading cardiothoracic surgeon and television personality, he has contributed to public understanding of health and wellness.

– Dr. Huda Zoghbi (Lebanon/USA): A neuroscientist who discovered the genetic basis of Rett syndrome and contributed to understanding neurological disorders.

- Dr. Noureddine Melikechi (Algeria): A physicist and biomedical researcher working on laser diagnostics for cancer detection.

- Dr. Ahmed Zewail (Egypt): The 1999 Nobel Laureate in Chemistry for his pioneering work in femtochemistry, studying chemical reactions on the femtosecond timescale.

- Dr. Abdus Salam (Pakistan): The 1979 Nobel Laureate in Physics for his contributions to the electroweak unification theory, which is fundamental to particle physics.

- Dr. Fazlur Rahman Khan (Bangladesh): Known as the "father of modern skyscrapers," he pioneered structural systems like the tubular design used in buildings like the Willis Tower and the John Hancock Centre.

- Dr. Samir Arif (Iraq): A key figure in developing communication systems and artificial intelligence algorithms.

- Anousheh Ansari (Iran/USA): The first Muslim woman in space and an advocate for private space exploration. She co-founded the XPRIZE Foundation, which promotes innovation in space and other fields.

- Dr. Syed Ataur Rahman (Pakistan): Contributed to space science and satellite development in collaboration with international space agencies.

- Dr. Lotfi Zadeh (Iran): Creator of fuzzy logic, which has applications in artificial intelligence, robotics, and control systems.
- Dr. Umar Saif (Pakistan): Known for his work in IT innovation and digital governance, including initiatives for e-governance in Pakistan.
- Dr. Mohammad Younis (Jordan): An expert in solar energy systems and sustainable development technologies.
- Dr. Muhammad Yunus (Bangladesh): Founder of Grameen Bank and recipient of the Nobel Peace Prize for his work in microfinance, which has lifted millions out of poverty.
- Dr. Shinya Yamanaka (Japan, with Muslim collaborators): Developed induced pluripotent stem cells (iPSCs), with contributions from Muslim scientists working on bioethics in Islamic contexts.
- Dr. Farouk El-Baz (Egypt): Worked on desert research, water resource management, and space applications to understand Earth's geology.
- Dr. Pervez Hoodbhoy (Pakistan): A physicist and science communicator who advocates for science education and rational thought in the Muslim world.
- Dr. Hayat Sindi (Saudi Arabia): A leading advocate for STEM education among women in the Arab world and a co-developer of diagnostic tools for resource-poor settings.
- Dr. Alaa Murabit (Libya): A medical doctor and advocate for gender equality and peacebuilding, focusing on the intersection of health, technology, and policy.

Impact of Intellectual Traditions on Modern Muslim Identity

The intellectual heritage of Muslim societies continues to shape modern Muslim identity, contributing to a sense of pride in historical achievements. Educational initiatives are often inspired by this heritage, encouraging younger generations to pursue knowledge and innovation while remaining connected to Islamic values.

Muslim intellectual contributions are gaining renewed recognition in the global community, with efforts to incorporate Islamic scientific and cultural achievements into mainstream educational curricula. For many Muslims, intellectual traditions serve as a reminder of the potential for harmony between faith and reason. In a globalized world, where Muslims often grapple with balancing religious beliefs and modern values, these traditions offer a framework that is both adaptable and rooted in identity.

The emphasis on education, literacy, and intellectual growth in Muslim societies has fostered a rich legacy of knowledge and innovation. The intellectual traditions of the Islamic Golden Age are a testament to the foundational value placed on learning, and they continue to inspire contemporary Muslim societies. While modern challenges remain, the commitment to education endures, underscoring the diverse perspectives and needs of the community.

References

Abu-Rabi, I. M. (Ed.). (2006). *The Blackwell companion to contemporary Islamic thought.* Blackwell Publishing.

Ali, U. (2020). *A new approach to Islamic intellectual tradition.* In *Pathways to contemporary Islam* (pp. 77–98). Amsterdam University Press.

Fleischmann, F., & Verkuyten, M. (2021). *Being a Muslim in the Western world: A social identity perspective.* In B. G. Adams & F. J. R. van de Vijver (Eds.), *Non-Western identity. Identity in a changing world.* Springer, Cham.

Hughes, W. A. (2013). *Muslim identities: An introduction to Islam.* New York: Columbia University Press.

Robert, P. (2011). *The Islamic scholar who gave us modern philosophy. Humanities, 32*(6).

Wikipedia. (n.d.). *List of Muslim philosophers.* Retrieved from https://en.wikipedia.org/wiki/List_of_Muslim_philosophers

CHAPTER 8
ROLE OF RELIGION IN POLITICAL SYSTEM AND GOVERNANCE

Muslim countries vary widely in how they incorporate or separate Islamic principles within their political and legal systems. This diversity is influenced by factors like colonial history, the political influence of religious institutions, interpretations of Islamic law (Shariah), and social and cultural norms. While some countries implement Shariah as a central legal foundation, others maintain secular frameworks with limited or symbolic references to Islamic principles. Here's a look at different approaches:

Countries with Shariah as the Primary Legal Framework

Several Muslim countries use Shariah as the foundational legal system, applying Islamic principles comprehensively across legal and political spheres. These countries often implement Shariah directly through civil and criminal laws, which govern areas such as family law, criminal justice, and financial practices. Examples:

Saudi Arabia: Saudi Arabia's legal system is based entirely on Shariah, particularly the Hanbali school of Sunni Islamic jurisprudence. Its judicial system does not rely on a written constitution or codified laws, as it draws directly from the Qur'an, Hadith, and fatwas (rulings by Islamic scholars). Religious scholars have substantial influence in governance, though there have been some social reforms, like permitting women to drive and travel independently.

Iran: After the 1979 revolution, Iran adopted a theocratic governance model based on Shia Islamic principles, particularly the concept of *Vilayat-e Faqih* (Guardianship of the Jurist), which grants supreme power to a religious leader, or Supreme Leader. Iran's legal and political systems are heavily informed by Shia jurisprudence, blending Islamic law with a parliamentary structure, though religious leaders maintain significant control over political decisions and judiciary interpretations.[10]

Countries with Dual Legal Systems

Some Muslim countries employ a dual legal system where Shariah is applied in specific areas, such as personal status law (covering family matters, marriage, divorce,

---

[10] According to the latest survey of the Pew Research group (2022). More than 80 countries out of 198 included in the survey have either an official state religion or a clearly favored religion. And among the 43 countries with state religions, a majority – 27 (or 63%) – are Islamic, including a broad swath of countries stretching across North Africa, the Middle East and South Asia, from Morocco to Pakistan. For many people in these countries, religion can't be separated from the power of the state. In a series of surveys conducted from 2008 to 2012, nearly all Muslims in Afghanistan (99%), nine-in-ten in Iraq (91%) and large majorities elsewhere in sub-Saharan Africa, the Middle East and South Asia said Shariah – Islamic law – should be the official law of the land in their country. (The survey found much lower support for religious law among Muslims in the post-Soviet republics of Central Asia and in the Balkans.

On the other hand, Muslims around the world don't necessarily agree on what Shariah means in practice. Some say Shariah should be open to multiple interpretations. Many favors applying it in matters of family law, such as divorces and inheritances, but not in criminal cases. And even among Muslims supporting Shariah, majorities in many countries say it should apply only to Muslims, not to people of other faiths – although some of those countries enforce laws against blasphemy and apostasy (the act of leaving one's religion), limiting possibilities for secularization or religious change within their borders

(https://www.pewresearch.org/religion/2022/12/21/key-findings-from-the-global-religious-futures-project)

inheritance, etc.), while other areas of law are governed by secular legal codes. This approach allows a balance between Islamic values and modern legal principles, often accommodating the diverse beliefs within the population. Examples:

Malaysia: Malaysia has a dual legal system where Shariah law applies primarily to Muslims in areas like family law and inheritance. Each Malaysian state has its own Shariah courts, which operate parallel to civil courts that handle criminal law, contracts, and other civil matters. While civil laws are secular, the federal constitution recognizes Islam as the official religion, though it protects religious freedom for non-Muslims.

Indonesia: Indonesia is the world's most populous Muslim country and is officially secular, with a legal system influenced by Dutch colonial law, local customary law (*adat*), and Islamic principles. Shariah law is largely confined to personal matters and is only officially applied in Aceh, where local laws allow certain Islamic punishments (like flogging). Indonesia's constitution upholds the principle of *Pancasila*, which promotes a pluralistic society with room for all religions.

Secular States with Islamic Influences

In some Muslim countries, the state maintains a secular legal system, though Islamic principles may still inform social norms, political policies, or certain legal provisions. These countries may recognize Islam as the state religion, and while Islamic values influence public life, religious law does not govern the national legal system. Examples:

Turkey: Turkey is a secular republic, with a legal system based on European civil law, established under Mustafa Kemal Atatürk's secular reforms in the early 20th century. Although Turkey's constitution declares the country secular, Islam plays a symbolic role, and recent governments have pushed for policies that reflect conservative Islamic values. However, Shariah law is not part of the national legal framework.

Tunisia: Tunisia has a secular constitution, yet it acknowledges Islam as the state religion. The legal system is largely secular, but Islamic principles influence family law and personal status matters, with significant reform, such as laws that guarantee women's rights and permit civil marriages. Tunisia has a tradition of progressive social policies in areas of gender equality and civil liberties, distinguishing it as a blend of Islamic and secular principles.

Countries with Tokenistic Islamic References

Some Muslim nations retain Islamic references symbolically within their legal and political frameworks, often maintaining a secular legal system that is not governed by Shariah but is influenced by Islamic values. These countries usually endorse Islam culturally but rely on civil codes in legal matters, and religious law is not applied at the national level. Examples:

Senegal: Senegal's constitution is secular, and the country is known for its religious tolerance. While 95% of the population is Muslim, Senegal does not enforce Shariah in its legal system. However, Islamic values hold social significance, and religious leaders influence public opinion and cultural life, even though they do not have formal political power.

Albania: Albania is a secular country with a predominantly Muslim population, where religion plays a minimal role in political and legal systems. Albania's legal system is based on European models, and Islam is considered part of its heritage rather than a source of law or political influence.

Regional and Cultural Variations in Shariah Interpretation

Interpretations of Shariah vary widely across regions, reflecting the diversity of Islamic jurisprudence and cultural influences. Different schools of thought, such as the Hanafi, Maliki, Shafi'i, and Hanbali schools in Sunni Islam, and Ja'fari jurisprudence in Shia Islam, contribute to regional variations in how Islamic principles are applied in law and politics.

Sunni vs. Shia Approaches: Sunni-majority countries like Egypt and Saudi Arabia tend to follow Sunni schools of thought, whereas Iran, Iraq, and parts of Lebanon follow Shia jurisprudence. These differences affect interpretations of family law, criminal justice, and political governance.

Local Customary Laws: In regions like North Africa, Central Asia, and parts of Southeast Asia, local cultural practices (such as *adat* in Indonesia and Malaysia)[11] are

---

[11] Adat is a term used in Indonesia and Malaysia that broadly refers to traditional customs, norms, and practices that govern the behavior and social conduct within communities. While the specific practices and beliefs may vary by region and ethnic group, adat serves as a code of conduct rooted deeply in the cultural heritage, spirituality, and local wisdom of these societies. Here's an overview of how it functions in both countries:

incorporated into interpretations of Shariah, leading to a blend of Islamic and customary laws.

Legal Reforms and Adaptations: Countries like Morocco have implemented family code reforms that blend Islamic principles with gender equality and modern human rights standards. The Moroccan *Moudawana*, a progressive family law code introduced in 2004, addresses marriage, divorce, and child custody in ways that promote women's rights within an Islamic framework.

Contemporary Debates and Challenges

The role of Islamic principles in political and legal systems is often the subject of debate within Muslim countries, especially as they address modern human rights standards, women's rights, and democratic governance.

Many such countries are exploring ways to balance Islamic principles with gender equality. For instance, Tunisia and Morocco have implemented laws that grant women equal rights in marriage and inheritance, despite opposition from more conservative religious groups.

Some countries, such as Saudi Arabia and Iran, face international scrutiny over Shariah-based punishments like corporal and capital punishment, which conflict with international human rights standards. Balancing Islamic legal principles with global human rights frameworks remains a challenge for these nations.

In countries like Pakistan and Egypt, there is an ongoing debate over the role of Islam in democracy and governance.

Overall, adat is a living tradition that evolves while preserving cultural identity, often adapting to modern influences and blending with other legal or religious norms.

Some argue for an increased role of Islamic law in public life, while others advocate for a secular approach that accommodates religious diversity and democratic freedoms. Turkey is yet another case. In the early 20th century, Kemal Atatürk led Turkey through a process of rapid secularization and crushed Islamic opposition to his authoritarian rule. Since Atatürk's death in 1938, however, Turkey has been gradually moving away from his militant secularism and experiencing "a quiet Muslim reformation." Islamic political identity is not homogeneous but can be modern and progressive as well as conservative and potentially authoritarian. Yavuz (2005) argues that Islamic social movements can be important agents for promoting a democratic and pluralistic society, and that the Turkish example holds long term promise for the rest of the Muslim world.

Islamic Social Movements

Islamic social movements encompass a wide range of groups and ideologies aimed at social, political, and religious reform, often rooted in the principles and teachings of Islam. These movements have evolved over time, influenced by historical, cultural, and political contexts, and vary widely in their objectives, methods, and scope.

These movements today can be categorized into several types based on their goals and methodologies. They may be categorized as Reformist, Revivalist, Militant, Social welfare, and Political movements.

The reformists aim to adapt Islamic teachings in a modern context while preserving core principles. For example, the Progressive Muslim movements advocate for gender equality, human rights, and interfaith dialogue. On the other hand, the revivalists seek to revive and reinforce traditional Islamic practices and beliefs. Salafi movements such as Tablighi Jamat, and Salafi advocate for return to the practices of early Muslims. While Tablighi Jamaat focuses on individual and community piety the Salafi movements advocate a return to the practices of early Muslims. The Militant Movements use violence to achieve political or ideological goals, often framed as jihad. Organizations like Al-Qaeda and ISIS come under this category. These groups represent a minority but have disproportionately shaped global perceptions of Islamic movements. Social welfare movements focus on addressing societal needs like education, healthcare, and poverty alleviation through Islamic frameworks. Examples include Islamic charities like the Edhi Foundation (Pakistan) and various Zakat-based initiatives. Finally, political movements engage in political processes to implement Islamic principles in governance. The examples are the Muslim Brotherhood in Egypt which advocates for Islamic governance within a democratic framework and the Justice and Development Party in Turkey which aims to combine Islamic values with modern political practice with modern needs.

In recent years, several Islamic movements have embraced inclusivity, technological integration, and efforts to tackle global challenges such as poverty and climate change. These movements often merge traditional Islamic values with innovative approaches, reflecting an evolving understanding of Islam's role in addressing modern issues.

Muslim countries showcase a spectrum of approaches to incorporating (or separating) Islamic principles within their political and legal systems. While some countries fully integrate Shariah into all aspects of law, others maintain secular frameworks with limited religious influence, and many opt for a hybrid model that balances Islamic values with modern governance. These variations reflect the adaptability of Islamic principles to diverse cultural, political, and social contexts, underscoring the diversity within the global Muslim community.

References

Frederic, V. (Ed.). (2013). *Political Islam: A critical reader.* Routledge.

Nader, H. (2009). *Islam, secularism, and liberal democracy: Toward a democratic theory for Muslim societies.* Oxford University Press.

Norshahril, S. (Ed.). (2018). *Islam in Southeast Asia: Negotiating modernity.* Singapore: ISEAS-Yusof Ishak Institute.

Pew Forum. (2013). *The world's Muslims: Religion, politics, and society.* Retrieved from http://www.pewforum.org/Muslim/the-worlds-muslims-religion-politics-society.aspx

Yavuz, M. H. (2005). *Islamic political identity in Turkey.* Oxford University Press.

CHAPTER 9
ISLAM AND SCIENCE

Overview

Like most of the other faiths, Muslims too are increasingly exposed to the challenges coming from scientific knowledge and reasons. The tension has been there for a long time but has been exacerbated in recent times with the knowledge explosion especially through the Internet. The conflict between faith and science in the Muslim world is a multifaceted issue rooted in historical, cultural, religious, and political dynamics. During the Islamic Golden Age (8th to 13th centuries), Muslim scholars such as Al-Khwarizmi, Ibn Sina (Avicenna), and Al-Razi (Rhazes) were at the forefront of scientific discovery. Their contributions to mathematics, medicine, astronomy, and chemistry laid the groundwork for modern science. The Islamic world was then characterized by an openness to knowledge, a spirit of inquiry, and the integration of science and faith. However, this intellectual dynamism gradually waned due to political fragmentation, colonialism, and shifts in religious and social attitudes, leading to skepticism toward modern scientific discoveries in some regions.

While Islam itself is not inherently opposed to scientific inquiry, puritanical interpretations often view modern science as a challenge to religious beliefs. This is evident in the rejection of evolutionary theory in many Muslim countries. For example, in Pakistan, the teaching of evolutionary biology is often limited or omitted from school curricula due to opposition from religious groups who perceive it as contradictory to Islamic teachings about creation. Similarly, in the Middle East, countries like Saudi Arabia have struggled to reconcile Darwinian evolution with their religious beliefs. This rejection not only stifles biological sciences but also impacts related fields, such as genetics and biotechnology.

Puritan preaching sometimes promotes the idea that religious and worldly knowledge are separate domains, undermining the holistic approach to education that characterized the Islamic Golden Age. During that era, scholars integrated religious understanding with scientific inquiry, recognizing both as complementary paths to truth. However, puritanical interpretations often argue that worldly knowledge, particularly modern scientific advancements, distracts people from spiritual growth and obedience to religious law. This separation has led to an intellectual compartmentalization where religious studies are prioritized while science and philosophy are either marginalized or viewed with suspicion. The resulting mindset diminishes the value of interdisciplinary learning, which was a hallmark of the Golden Age. For example, scholars like Ibn Sina seamlessly combined medical research with theological reflection, fostering advancements that enriched both realms. In contrast, modern educational paradigms influenced by Puritan ideologies often discourage such integration, narrowing intellectual horizons and reducing innovation. Education systems in many Muslim countries prioritize religious studies over STEM subjects. While religious education may be important, an imbalance can limit exposure to critical thinking and scientific methods, perpetuating skepticism toward scientific advancements.

Some studies have compared the golden age of Islam with the European dark age (8-13 centuries). It is reported that while Muslim countries were open and maintained a clear boundary between religion and State it was just the opposite in Western Christian societies. There was a strong alliance between the Catholic church and royal authorities. Western Christian countries were places of religious orthodoxy and intolerance in comparison to their Muslim counterparts. These aspects of Western Europe are considered to be directly related to its scientific and socioeconomic backwardness between the eighth and 11th centuries. Western Europe had neither a philosopher like Ibn Sina, nor a city like Baghdad, nor its own gold coin (Daly, 2021).

Muslims during this period experienced significant agricultural growth and cultivated various new crops, many of which spread to Europe and whose English names (artichoke, cotton, lemon, orange, and spinach) originally came from Arabic. Scholars have emphasized that modern capitalism owes much to early Muslims' financial innovations, such as the cheque and the bill of exchange. In the words of Fernand Braudel: "Anything in Western capitalism of imported origin undoubtedly came from Islam." It was also Muslims who taught Western Europeans how to produce paper. In Baghdad and many other cities, Muslim polymaths such as Ibn Sina (often regarded as the father of early modern medicine) made groundbreaking scholarly contributions to mathematics, optics, and medicine (cf. Kurua, 2021).

Post-golden-age Muslim countries, political instability, and authoritarian governance further promoted skepticism toward science. Leaders often prioritize short-term political gains over long-term investments in scientific research and technological innovation. Government funding for scientific institutions was frequently inadequate, and bureaucratic inefficiencies stifled progress. In much of the Middle East, government spending on research and development (R&D) is still among the lowest in the world. For instance, Saudi Arabia allocates less than 1% of its GDP to R&D, compared to over 3% in technologically advanced nations like South Korea. This lack of investment reflects a broader skepticism toward the value of scientific research and its potential to drive economic and social development. Here is a chronology of the decline of scientific progress in the Islamic world after the 13th Century.

13th Century (The Mongol Invasions): The Mongol conquests devastated key Islamic centers, including the destruction of Baghdad in 1258. Baghdad, a hub of scientific knowledge and home to the House of Wisdom, was razed, and countless manuscripts were lost. This marked the symbolic end of the Islamic Golden Age. Political instability disrupted scholarly activities, and resources for scientific inquiry dwindled.

14th Century (Rise of Religious Orthodoxy): The theological dominance of scholars like Al-Ghazali (d. 1111) began to exert greater influence on intellectual thought. Al-Ghazali's critique of rationalism, particularly in *The Incoherence of the Philosophers*, challenged the primacy of reason and empirical observation, promoting a reliance on divine will. Philosophical and scientific inquiry increasingly came under suspicion, with orthodoxy discouraging speculative thinking.

15th–16th Centuries (Ottoman, Safavid, and Mughal Empires): The emergence of powerful Islamic empires shifted focus to military, administrative, and cultural consolidation rather than scientific advancement. While some scientific patronage persisted (e.g., observatories in the Ottoman Empire), it lacked the vibrancy of earlier centuries. The outcome was scholarly isolationism diminished cross-cultural exchange and increased focus on preserving traditional knowledge rather than fostering innovation.

17th Century (The Rejection of Modernity): Interaction with European powers intensified, but many Islamic scholars rejected European scientific advancements, associating them with colonialism or religious heresy. Educational institutions often emphasized religious studies over empirical sciences, leading to a stagnation in scientific output. A growing chasm between Islamic traditions and the rapidly advancing scientific revolution in Europe.

18th Century (Colonization and Economic Decline): European colonial expansion and the weakening of Islamic empires disrupted local economies and governance. Economic hardships reduced funding for scientific endeavors, and the imposition of colonial educational systems marginalized traditional Islamic knowledge systems. Colonial rule introduced Western scientific models but often suppressed local innovation and adaptation.

19th Century (The Advent of Modern Science): Islamic societies began importing Western technology and education during efforts to modernize. However, they were facing challenges from conservative religious authorities and a lack of integration between traditional Islamic knowledge and modern scientific methods. Science was viewed as a foreign import rather than an organic part of Islamic intellectual heritage.

20th Century (The Persistence of Structural Barriers): Post-colonial Islamic states invested in modernization, but efforts were uneven and often hindered by political instability. A few barriers to progress are underdeveloped educational systems with rote learning methods, limited investment in research and development, and continued tension between religious orthodoxy and secular scientific approaches. As a result, despite notable individual achievements, institutionalized science lagged behind global standards in most Islamic countries.

21st Century (Efforts to Reconnect): Some Islamic countries (e.g., Turkey, Malaysia, UAE) have made strides in investing in science and technology. However, challenges remain in overcoming entrenched attitudes that separate science from faith and building research institutions that can compete internationally.

Increased global collaboration and the rise of knowledge economies provide new pathways for progress. Now there are initiatives aimed at fostering scientific inquiry and overcoming skepticism in Muslim countries. Organizations and individuals are working to reconcile Islamic values with modern science and promote critical thinking. For example, Saudi Arabia's establishment of the King Abdullah University of Science & Technology (KAUST) in 2009 marked a significant step toward advancing scientific research in the region. The university aims to attract global talent and create a hub for innovation, particularly in energy, environmental sciences, and biotechnology. Such initiatives demonstrate the potential for change when skepticism toward science is addressed.

Pervez Hoodbhoy's (1991) book, 'Islam and Science: Religious Orthodoxy and the Battle for Rationality', provides a critical examination of the relationship between Islam and scientific inquiry. The book explores historical, cultural, and theological dimensions of how Islamic societies have engaged with science from the medieval period to the modern era. Hoodbhoy, a Pakistani physicist and intellectual, presents a nuanced argument that blends historical analysis with contemporary critique. Hoodbhoy concurs with what is discussed earlier that the Islamic Golden Age (8th to 13th centuries) was a period of remarkable scientific achievement. During this era, Muslim scholars made significant contributions to mathematics, astronomy, medicine, and other fields. These advancements were fueled by a culture of openness, intellectual curiosity, and the integration of knowledge from Greek, Indian, Persian, and other civilizations. Hoodbhoy notes the decline of scientific progress in the Islamic world after the 13th century. He attributes this to various factors, including the rise of religious orthodoxy, political instability, and a shift in focus away from rational inquiry toward dogmatic interpretations of religion. He critiques the rise of religious orthodoxy that stifled critical thinking and scientific exploration and argues that the theological dominance of scholars like Al-Ghazali, who emphasized divine will over rational causality, discouraged the pursuit of empirical science. Thus, it is wrong to blame religion as a barrier to scientific progress. First, the scientific and economic progress achieved by Muslim countries was superior to that of Western Europe from the eighth to the 12th centuries, proving that Islam and progress coexisted for many centuries. Actually, it was the holy nexus between the Islamic Ulema (scholars) and the rulers that stifled this progress.

During the fifteenth and sixteenth centuries, Kurua (2021) notes that Western Europe underwent multiple developmental revolutions by leveraging three key innovations: the printing press, the nautical compass, and gunpowder. In contrast, Muslim empires effectively utilized only gunpowder, owing to their military-centric priorities. It took these empires three centuries to adopt printing technology, as they lacked both an intellectual class to recognize its scholarly importance and a merchant class to grasp the financial potential of print capitalism. Military leaders in Muslim societies dismissed the printing press as irrelevant, while the ulema viewed it as a threat to their educational monopoly.

This delay in adopting the printing press led to a growing literacy gap between Western Europe and the Muslim world. During the eighth to twelfth centuries, the largest libraries in Muslim societies held hundreds of thousands of books, compared to fewer than a thousand in the largest European libraries. However, the printing revolution reversed these positions. European societies swiftly embraced the technology, while Muslim societies lagged behind. For example, during the entire 18th century, Ottoman printing presses produced only about 50,000 books, whereas European presses printed approximately one billion. By the time European colonization of Muslim lands began in the 18th century, the scientific and economic stagnation of the Muslim world was already well-established.

The impact of European colonialism on the Muslim world disrupted traditional institutions and introduced Western science and technology. While colonial powers brought technological advancements, they also created a sense of inferiority and dependence that hindered the development of indigenous scientific traditions. Yet, while Western colonialism was undoubtedly detrimental to the progress of science in Muslim countries, it did not start their problems. Solely blaming Western imperialism detracts from the domestic problems of Muslim countries.

Hoodbhoy critiques the current state of science in many Muslim countries, pointing to underfunding, lack of critical thinking in education, and the persistence of anti-scientific attitudes. He argues that religious orthodoxy continues to impede the growth of a scientific culture even today. He advocates for a reformation in how Islamic societies approach science and education. Hoodbhoy emphasizes the need for a rational and critical approach to knowledge that harmonizes faith with empirical inquiry and calls for educational reforms to foster creativity, innovation, and respect for scientific principles.

Hoodbhoy's analysis is both scholarly and polemical. He combines historical research with a passionate plea for rationality and modernization. His critique of religious orthodoxy and its impact on scientific progress is provocative and challenges traditional narratives within the Muslim world. At the same time, he acknowledges the complex interplay of historical, cultural, and political factors that have shaped the trajectory of science in Islamic societies.

Islam Agnosticism and Atheism

The term atheism refers to the belief that God does not exist, whereas agnosticism refers to the position that the existence or non-existence of God is uncertain or unknowable. In Islam, atheists are categorized as *kafir*, a term that is also used to describe *polytheists (shirk),* and that translates roughly as "denier" or "concealer". *Kafir* carries connotations of blasphemy and disconnection from the Islamic community. In Arabic, "atheism" is generally translated *ilhad*, although this also means "heresy". A person who denies the existence of a creator is called a *dahriya*. The Qu'ran speaks repeatedly of people going back to unbelief after believing, and gives advice on dealing with "hypocrites".

"O Prophet, just disregard the unbelievers and the hypocrites and be firm against them. Their abode is Hell, -- an evil refuge indeed. They swear by God that they said nothing [evil], but indeed they uttered blasphemy, and they did it after accepting Islam, and they meditated a plot which they were unable to carry out: this revenge of theirs was [their] only return for the bounty which God and His Apostle had enriched them! If they repent, it will be best for them; but if they turn back [to their evil ways], God will punish them with a grievous penalty in this life and in the Hereafter. They shall have none on this earth to protect or help them." (Sura 9:73,74).

Muslims are not at liberty to change their religion or become atheists. Atheists in Islamic countries and communities frequently conceal their non-belief. Religiosity in the Arab world is seen to be essential for morality and atheism is widely associated with immorality. Religious attitudes have grown more conservative since the 1980s, compared to the preceding decades when secular socialism was politically dominant. Nonetheless, atheism is tolerated if it is not conspicuous and a worldwide support network for ex-Muslims has existed since 2007. Some commentators believe that the number of undeclared atheists in the Arab world is substantial. According to a 2012 WIN/Gallup poll of Saudi citizens, 5 percent of Saudis identify as "convinced atheists", the same percentage as in the U.S. (Wikipedia).

Malik (2018) in his book 'Atheism and Islam: A Contemporary Discourse' offers a comprehensive examination of the interactions between contemporary atheism—particularly the New Atheism movement—and Islam. The term new atheism refers to the belief against Islam and the existence of God post 9/11. Malik begins by exploring the rise of new atheism, highlighting prominent figures such as Sam Harris, Daniel Dennett, Richard Dawkins, and Christopher Hitchens. He delves into their critiques of religion, with a particular emphasis on Islam, noting that their arguments often portray Islam as irrational and inherently violent. Additionally, the book examines the perspectives of ex-Muslim atheists like Ayaan Hirsi Ali, Ali Rizvi, Armin Navabi, and Ibn Warraq, who have been vocal in their criticism of Islamic doctrines based on personal experiences.

The core points of arguments presented by atheists against Islam are categorized into scientific, philosophical, theological, and sociological contentions.

Scientific Contentions: The debate over evolution is central, with atheists often citing it to challenge Islamic creation narratives. Malik discusses how Muslims can engage with evolutionary theory without compromising their faith.

The debate over the concept of evolution, particularly as it intersects with science, atheism, and agnosticism, revolves around philosophical, theological, and scientific perspectives. Evolution, grounded in Charles Darwin's theory of natural selection, is a scientific framework for understanding the diversity of life on Earth. It explains how species change over time through genetic variations and environmental pressures. Evolution theory is supported by substantial evidence from various fields, including fossil records, genetics, comparative anatomy, and biogeography. Scientists broadly accept evolution as a foundational biological principle. Atheists often embrace evolution because it provides a naturalistic explanation for the origin and development of life, eliminating the need for supernatural intervention. Some atheists, like Richard Dawkins in his book 'The God Delusion', argue that evolution undermines religious creation myths, challenging the necessity of a deity in explaining life's complexity. Agnostics typically maintain a position of uncertainty about the existence of a deity. They may accept evolution as a scientific explanation while remaining neutral about its implications for theology. They often highlight that evolution does not inherently confirm or deny the existence of God. They view the scientific theory as separate from metaphysical questions.

Some religious groups reject evolution in favor of creationism, which asserts that life was created by God as described in religious texts. This viewpoint accepts that life shows complexity but attributes it to a purposeful designer rather than undirected natural processes. This perspective argues that science addresses "how" questions about the mechanisms of life, while religion addresses "why" questions about meaning and purpose. The debate touches on existential questions about humanity's place in the universe, the meaning of life, and moral values.

The debate over evolution involves a complex interplay of science, philosophy, and theology. While science focuses on empirical evidence and natural processes, atheists and agnostics interpret these findings within broader worldviews. The discussion underscores the diverse ways humans grapple with understanding existence and the origins of life.

Philosophical Contentions: Some scholars critique the atheistic reliance on scientism—the belief that science is the ultimate path to knowledge—and examine arguments for God's existence, including discussions on quantum mechanics and occasionalism (Malik, 2018).

Scientism is a philosophical stance that elevates science as the ultimate or exclusive path to knowledge and truth. It often involves the belief that scientific methods and principles should be applied to all aspects of life, including fields traditionally outside science, such as ethics, religion, and metaphysics. The key characteristics include reductionism, exclusivity, and empirical bias.

Scientism is often invoked to critique religious views, including Islam, by dismissing religious claims as unscientific or unempirical. However, critics of scientism argue that this approach misunderstands the nature of religion and overextends the scope of science. Scientism often rejects religious texts, such as the Qu'ran, as unverifiable or non-empirical, arguing they lack scientific credibility. Religious miracles are often dismissed as scientifically implausible, with proponents of scientism demanding empirical evidence for supernatural occurrences. Scientism critiques creationist interpretations of religious texts, such as Islamic views of Adam and Eve, by emphasizing the evidence for evolution. Scientism also challenges religious moral frameworks, arguing that ethics can be derived from a scientific understanding of human behavior and social dynamics.

Religious thinkers often critique scientism for overstepping its bounds and failing to address the metaphysical and moral dimensions of human existence. They argue that science deals with the natural world and cannot address questions of purpose, meaning, or the existence of the divine. Islam, like other religions, emphasizes that revelation and spiritual insight provide knowledge beyond the empirical realm. Islamic theology views human beings as spiritual as well as physical entities. Scientism's materialistic reductionism overlooks the spiritual and moral dimensions of life. Furthermore, questions such as "Why does the universe exist?" or "What happens after death?" lie outside the scope of scientific inquiry. Islam offers answers to these existential questions through faith and theology.

When scientists or proponents of scientism critique religion based on their worldview, religious scholars and philosophers often respond by highlighting that scientism itself is not a scientific stance but a philosophical one, which cannot be proven scientifically. Secondly, science answers "how" questions but not "why" questions, leaving room for religious explanations.

Scientism represents a worldview that elevates science as the ultimate arbiter of truth but is often criticized for its inability to address metaphysical and existential questions. In the context of Islam, scientism's critiques are countered by emphasizing the complementary roles of science and religion, the limitations of empirical methods, and the richness of spiritual and moral dimensions that transcend scientific inquiry.

Theological Contentions: Malik (2018) explores issues related to Islamic hermeneutics, jurisprudence, and spirituality, addressing how atheists interpret Islamic texts and practices to support their critiques.

Hermeneutics refers to the principles and methodologies of interpreting texts, particularly sacred texts like the Qur'an. Many atheists criticize Islam by focusing on literal interpretations of Qur'anic verses or Hadiths (sayings of the Prophet). They often highlight verses related to violence, gender roles, or punishment, arguing that these promote backward or harmful values. Islamic scholars counter this by emphasizing the importance of contextual interpretation, which considers the historical, cultural, and linguistic background of the texts. Critics often select specific verses to paint Islam as intolerant or oppressive without considering the broader Qur'anic themes of mercy, justice, and compassion. Muslim scholars argue that such readings disregard principles of *intertextuality*, where verses must be understood in relation to the entire Qur'anic message. Contemporary Muslim thinkers apply frameworks like *maqasid al-Shariah* (objectives of Islamic law) to reinterpret texts in light of modern values like human rights and gender equality, challenging the rigid readings that atheists critique.

Islamic Jurisprudence (*Fiqh*) involves the interpretation and application of Islamic law (*Shariah*) to various aspects of life. Atheists often criticize the hudud punishments in Shariah (e.g., amputation for theft, stoning for adultery) as being barbaric and incompatible with modern ethical standards. Muslim scholars clarify that such laws are subject to strict conditions and serve as deterrents, not as commonly enforced practices. They also argue that these laws were progressive within their historical context

Atheists argue that Islamic jurisprudence is rigid and resistant to change. However, scholars highlight the tradition of *ijtihad* (independent reasoning) as a mechanism for reforming and adapting laws. The stagnation of ijtihad, they assert, reflects cultural and political factors rather than the religion itself.

Critics often focus on laws related to inheritance, polygamy, and testimony, claiming they institutionalize gender inequality. Islamic scholars defend these practices as context-specific and argue that modern reinterpretations align with contemporary understandings of equality.

Spirituality in Islam emphasizes the internal, transformative aspect of the faith, centered on developing a relationship with God. While many Muslims view Sufism as a profound spiritual tradition, some atheists dismiss it as superstition or irrational mysticism. They argue that its focus on divine experiences lacks empirical evidence. Proponents of Sufism counter that spirituality transcends materialist frameworks and offers a holistic understanding of human existence.

Atheists often critique the idea that morality requires a divine foundation, arguing that secular ethics can provide a robust moral framework. Islamic spirituality posits that faith in God provides a deeper purpose and grounding for ethical behavior, going beyond utilitarian or relativistic moral systems.

Rituals like prayer, fasting, and pilgrimage are sometimes dismissed as meaningless routines by atheists. Muslims argue that these practices cultivate discipline, gratitude, and mindfulness, contributing to personal and societal well-being.

Atheists approach Islamic texts and practices from a critical perspective, often based on historical analysis to argue that Islamic texts are products of their time, reflecting the socio-political realities of 7th-century Arabia rather than divine revelation. Critics evaluate Islam against modern secular values like human rights and gender equality, highlighting perceived shortcomings. Atheists frequently associate Islam with the actions of extremists, using selective interpretations of texts to argue that violence and intolerance are intrinsic to the religion.

Muslim scholars and thinkers emphasize the diversity and richness of Islamic traditions, countering reductionist critiques. Engaging in interfaith and atheist-Muslim dialogues to bridge misunderstandings and challenge stereotypes. Encouraging rigorous academic research in theology, history, and philosophy to address the intellectual challenges posed by atheism.

Sociological Concerns: Malik (2018) has discussed the societal implications of atheism in Muslim communities, including the challenges faced by individuals who leave Islam and the broader impact on Islamic society. The decision of Muslims to leave Islam in Islamic societies can have profound social implications. These implications vary significantly depending on the specific society, its cultural context, legal framework, and the prevalence of conservative or progressive values. Depending upon the context it may result in stigma and ostracism, community rejection, and isolation.

In some countries governed by Shariah law, apostasy is criminalized, potentially punishable by imprisonment or death. Apostates might face legal discrimination, including losing custody of children, inheritance rights, or the ability to marry legally within the community. Apostates may also face family rejection. Families may feel dishonored or betrayed, leading to strained relationships or even disownment. Women who leave Islam may face more severe consequences due to gender roles and expectations in patriarchal settings. They might encounter threats to their personal safety or forced marriage to "restore honor." Apostates might struggle with guilt, fear, or anxiety due to societal and familial pressures. The absence of support from their immediate community might lead them to seek solidarity in online forums or secular groups.

Malik emphasizes the need for Muslims to engage constructively with atheistic critiques. He advocates for the development of interdisciplinary platforms that integrate scientific, philosophical, and theological perspectives to address the challenges posed by atheism. Additionally, he underscores the importance of adhering to Qur'anic principles in fostering dialogue and understanding. Overall, Malik's views serve as a vital resource for understanding the complex relationship between modern atheistic movements and Islamic thought, offering insights into how Muslims can thoughtfully and effectively respond to contemporary critiques of their faith.

Evolution, Freewill, Randomness, and Transsexual Issues

The Islamic perspective on evolution, free will, randomness, and transsexual issues varies widely among scholars, theologians, and believers due to the diversity within Islamic traditions, schools of thought, and cultural contexts. Here's a broad overview of how these topics are approached in Islamic discourse.

Evolution. Many traditional Muslim scholars have rejected the concept of evolution, particularly human evolution, as it seems to contradict the Qur'anic narrative of Adam being created directly by Allah. However, some Muslim thinkers reconcile evolution with Islamic teachings by suggesting that evolution may explain the development of species but that humans were uniquely created by Allah. Nidhal Guessoum (2023) and other progressive scholars argue for a theistic evolution perspective, suggesting that Allah guided evolutionary processes. The Qur'an does not explicitly discuss biological evolution, leading some scholars to interpret relevant verses metaphorically or in ways compatible with scientific theories.

One of the very well-known Islamic scholars Javed Ahmad Ghamidi has a nuanced approach to topics like human evolution, free will, and randomness rooted in his interpretation of the Qur'an, reason, and science. Ghamidi does not reject scientific findings outright but insists that any scientific theory should not contradict the essential tenets of the Qur'an.

Regarding evolution, he asserts that the Qur'an explicitly states that Adam, the first human, was created directly by God and was not the product of evolution. Verses like *"Indeed, the example of Jesus to Allah is like that of Adam. He created Him from dust; then He said to him, 'Be,' and he was"* (Qur'an 3:59) emphasize this. However, Ghamidi does not entirely dismiss the possibility of evolution concerning other species. He allows room for the idea that life forms may have evolved over time but maintains that Adam's creation was a unique and divine act, independent of evolutionary processes. Ghamidi emphasizes that the Qur'an is not a book of science but of guidance. While it may allude to natural phenomena, it is not meant to provide detailed explanations of scientific processes. This means the Qur'an and science operate in different realms. He acknowledges the validity of scientific inquiry but underscores that science is based on observation and experimentation, which are subject to change. Therefore, scientific theories should not be used to reinterpret Qur'anic verses unless they are definitive.

According to Ghamidi, Adam was created as a being with intellect and free will, specifically chosen by God to be His vicegerent on Earth. This spiritual and moral distinction between Adam and his progeny is central in the Qur'anic narrative and is not addressed by evolutionary theory, which focuses solely on biological processes.

Ghamidi promotes the idea that faith and reason can coexist. He argues that Muslims should engage with scientific findings with an open mind but must differentiate between theories and established facts. He believes that if there seems to be a conflict between science and religion, either our understanding of the scripture is incomplete, or the scientific theory is not yet fully developed.

For Ghamidi, the Qur'anic narrative places significant emphasis on human dignity, morality, and the divine purpose of life. He contends that evolutionary theory, even if valid for biological development, cannot explain the metaphysical aspects of human life, such as the soul, morality, and consciousness. Ghamidi's interpretation carefully navigates between affirming the divine creation of Adam as described in the Qur'an and acknowledging the possibility of evolution in other aspects of creation. He emphasizes a harmonious relationship between science and faith, advocating for intellectual openness without compromising the foundational teachings of Islam.

Critiques of scholars like Javed Ahmad Ghamidi's interpretation of evolution often come from more traditional or conservative scholars and thinkers. They raise theological, scriptural, and epistemological concerns. Many traditional Islamic scholars argue that Ghamidi's approach, which allows room for evolution while affirming the special creation of Adam, may compromise the literal understanding of Qur'anic verses. For example, verses like *"He created him from clay and breathed into him His spirit"* (Qur'an 38:71-72) are interpreted by many scholars as clear evidence of Adam's direct creation by God, without any evolutionary process. Traditional scholars often caution against reinterpreting scripture based on contemporary scientific theories, as science is ever-changing and may lead to instability in religious interpretation. Ghamidi contends that while the Qur'an is timeless, its interpretation must consider the intellectual and scientific developments of the time.

Some Islamic scholars worry that integrating evolutionary theory into Islamic discourse risks opening the door to secular or materialist worldviews that exclude God entirely from the process of creation. They argue that evolution is often presented in ways that contradict theistic explanations, and accommodating it within Islam may inadvertently validate secular ideologies.

Ghamidi's framework explicitly incorporates God's role in creation, but critics argue that evolution's philosophical underpinnings are difficult to reconcile with Islamic theology without significant reinterpretation. Some argue that Ghamidi's willingness to engage with evolution reflects an overreliance on modern science as a framework for understanding the Qur'an. They believe that Islamic theology should remain distinct from scientific paradigms, as science deals with the observable world, while religion addresses metaphysical truths. However, Ghamidi sees no conflict between science and faith, provided that scientific theories are not misused to contradict clear religious teachings. However, critics believe that his approach risks blurring the boundaries between the two domains.

Free Will. Islamic theology traditionally grapples with the balance between human free will and divine predestination (*qadar*). Two main theological schools address this. The *Ash'arites* emphasize divine will and predestination while acknowledging limited human agency (*kasb*). Whereas, the *Mu'tazilites* advocate for human free will, arguing that Allah's justice requires that humans have the autonomy to choose between right and wrong. Modern discussions often explore how free will relates to neuroscience and psychology, emphasizing the moral responsibility inherent in Islamic teachings.

Ghamidi maintains that free will is a fundamental aspect of human existence, as it is tied directly to accountability, morality, and the purpose of life. He emphasizes that humans are created as moral agents with the ability to choose between right and wrong. This ability is what distinguishes humans from other creatures and makes them accountable for their actions. The Qur'an highlights this responsibility in verses like:

"Indeed, we guided him to the way, be he grateful or ungrateful." (Qur'an 76:3)

According to Ghamidi, this guidance refers to the internal and external faculties God has granted humans—reason, conscience, and divine revelation—to help them navigate moral choices. Ghamidi asserts that free will is the basis of human accountability in Islam. The concept of reward and punishment in the Hereafter only makes sense if humans have the ability to act freely. He often refers to verses that highlight individual accountability:

"Whoever does righteousness benefit his own soul, and whoever does evil harms it." (Qur'an 41:46)

This underscores that humans have the autonomy to choose their actions, and they bear the consequences of those choices.

On the complex topic of *qadr* (divine decree or predestination), Ghamidi reconciles it with free will by explaining that while God's knowledge is infinite, it does not negate human freedom. He explains that God, being omniscient, knows what choices humans will make. However, this foreknowledge does not compel humans to act in a particular way. It is like a teacher predicting a student's grade based on their performance—the prediction does not cause the outcome. Ghamidi rejects deterministic interpretations of *qadr* that negate human agency, as this would undermine the Qur'anic emphasis on personal accountability. According to Ghamidi, life is a test of free will. Humans are placed in situations where they must make moral and ethical choices, and their decisions reflect their character and faith. Without free will, the concept of testing would be meaningless. Ghamidi explains that while humans are free to choose their path, God provides guidance through prophets and revelations to ensure that they are not left without direction. However, accepting or rejecting this guidance remains the individual's choice:

"Indeed, we have shown him the way, whether he be grateful or ungrateful." (Qur'an 76:3)

Ghamidi maintains that God is sovereign and ultimately in control of everything in existence. However, He has granted humans limited autonomy within this divine framework. This balance ensures that while God's plan unfolds as intended, humans still have the freedom to shape their destiny within the parameters set by God. Ghamidi's view emphasizes that humans must take responsibility for their actions. Blaming external factors, destiny, or God for one's moral failings is not acceptable. He encourages believers to focus on making the best choices in accordance with God's guidance, rather than getting overly entangled in philosophical debates about predestination.

Randomness. Randomness in nature is often understood as part of Allah's plan, reflecting human limitations in perceiving order. In the Qur'an, Allah is described as having complete knowledge and control over all events. For example, the apparent randomness of natural phenomena, such as weather or mutations, can be seen as tools of divine will. Muslim scientists and scholars, like those in the theistic evolution camp, argue that randomness in processes like evolution does not negate divine control but rather demonstrates Allah's complexity and creativity.

Ghamidi asserts that nothing in the universe is truly random from God's perspective. Everything operates under God's will and wisdom, even if it appears chaotic or random to human beings. The Qur'an repeatedly emphasizes that God is the ultimate planner and that every event unfolds according to His knowledge and decree:

"Indeed, all things We created with predestination." (Qur'an 54:49)

This means that what humans perceive as "randomness" is, in reality, a manifestation of God's intricate and often incomprehensible plan. Ghamidi acknowledges that humans, with their limited understanding, may perceive certain events as random or accidental because they cannot comprehend the underlying causes or divine wisdom behind them. For example, natural phenomena like earthquakes or rain may seem random, but they are part of a system governed by divine laws. These laws operate with consistency and purpose, even if their immediate outcomes appear unpredictable.

From Ghamidi's perspective, the concept of randomness can intersect with human free will and accountability. While humans may experience seemingly random occurrences (e.g., being in the right or wrong place at the right or wrong time), they still retain moral agency in responding to such situations. This aligns with his broader belief that life is a test, where both planned and unexpected events serve to reveal the character and choices of individuals.

Ghamidi reconciles the idea of chance with God's omniscience. Events that seem to occur by chance are fully known to God and fall within His overall knowledge and control. For instance, a person winning a lottery or being saved from an accident may seem like a stroke of luck. Ghamidi would argue that these outcomes are part of God's preordained plan, even if the mechanisms (e.g., random draws, natural laws) appear chance-based.

Although Ghamidi does not explicitly discuss scientific randomness (e.g., in quantum mechanics or evolutionary theory), his general stance on science suggests that he would see randomness as a tool or mechanism within God's created system. For instance, mutations in evolution or the probabilistic nature of particles might be described as processes designed by God, operating within a framework of divine intent. Thus, according to him, everything in the universe serves a purpose, even if that purpose is not immediately apparent to humans. Apparent randomness might be a way to test human resilience, faith, or reliance on God. This aligns with the Qur'anic message that trials and tests, whether understood or not, are inherent to human life:

"Do you think that you will enter Paradise while such [trial] has not yet come to you as came to those who passed on before you?" (Qur'an 2:214)

Ghamidi strongly emphasizes God's justice. Apparent randomness in the distribution of wealth, opportunities, or suffering is not seen as unfair but rather as part of the divine test for both the individual and society. He would argue that these situations are ultimately balanced by divine justice in the Hereafter, where every inequity is addressed.

Some critics argue that Ghamidi's emphasis on divine control and the absence of true randomness might undermine the concept of free will. If everything is part of God's preordained plan, how can human choices truly be autonomous? Critics from a scientific perspective argue that Ghamidi's view on randomness does not adequately address the implications of empirical randomness observed in fields like quantum mechanics or evolutionary biology. For instance, quantum mechanics suggests intrinsic randomness at the subatomic level. Similarly, evolutionary theory relies on random mutations as a key mechanism for natural selection.

Ghamidi's distinction between "apparent randomness" (from a human perspective) and the absence of randomness (from God's perspective) may be viewed as a theological assertion rather than a logical or empirical argument. Critics argue that this approach sidesteps the philosophical problem of randomness entirely, reducing it to a matter of faith.

Some Critics point to the problem of evil as a challenge to Ghamidi's view of randomness. If God controls everything and randomness is only an illusion, why do seemingly random and unjust events (e.g., natural disasters, diseases) occur? Some might argue that such events appear truly random and without purpose, challenging the idea that they are part of a divine plan. Ghamidi frames these events as tests or trials in life, which are meaningful within the context of the larger divine plan. However, critics find this explanation unsatisfactory when applied to extreme cases of suffering. Ghamidi's argument that everything has a purpose within the divine plan is seen as overly teleological (purpose-driven). Critics argue that not all events or phenomena necessarily have an inherent purpose and that attributing purpose to all occurrences may be speculative. Ghamidi's position is deeply rooted in the Qur'anic worldview, where God's wisdom underpins all creation. Critics, especially those with secular perspectives, reject this as circular reasoning.

Some argue that Ghamidi's explanations about randomness lack specificity and are open to subjective interpretation. For instance, claiming that seemingly random events are tests or part of God's plan may not provide concrete answers for people grappling with existential questions. Ghamidi's approach encourages faith and trust in God's wisdom rather than providing empirical explanations. Critics, however, view this as insufficient for addressing intellectual doubts.

Ghamidi's view that randomness is part of a divinely orchestrated system may conflict with modern cosmological models that suggest randomness and chance played a significant role in the formation of the universe (e.g., the Big Bang and stochastic processes in star formation). Ghamidi argues that such processes are not truly random but part of God's laws governing the universe. Critics, however, see this as a theological overlay of scientific theories.

Transsexual Issues. Islamic jurisprudence traditionally recognizes clear gender roles and is based on a binary understanding of male and female as created by Allah. Many Islamic scholars acknowledge the existence of intersex individuals (*khuntha*) and provide guidelines for their inclusion in society, often making provisions for corrective procedures based on medical necessity. Opinions differ among scholars on the question of transgender identity as well. Some strictly oppose gender reassignment, viewing it as altering Allah's creation. Others, particularly in contexts like Iran, allow gender reassignment surgery if it aligns an individual's physical body with their perceived gender, arguing that this corrects a biological or psychological condition. The discourse on transgender issues is influenced by broader societal debates about identity, justice, and human dignity, with progressive Islamic voices advocating for compassion and understanding.

Progressive and conservative Islamic perspectives on transgender issues vary significantly due to differences in interpretation of Islamic texts, views on gender, and approaches to modernity.

Progressives often highlight values like justice, mercy, and individual dignity in Islamic teachings. They argue that Islam requires compassion for all, including transgender individuals, and that exclusion or discrimination contradicts these principles. They argue that gender diversity is part of Allah's creation, pointing to the concept of *fitra* (natural disposition) to support transgender identities.

Many progressive voices support gender-affirming medical care, viewing it as a way to alleviate suffering and align the body with a person's true self, which they argue aligns with Islamic values of seeking well-being. They often integrate human rights principles, advocating for the rights and dignity of transgender individuals as part of broader social justice efforts.

Conservative scholars often adhere to a literal understanding of Qu'ranic texts and Hadith, viewing gender as binary and assigned by Allah. They see a deviation from binary gender roles as contrary to the divine will. Conservatives often reject modern ideas of gender fluidity or transgender identity, considering them Western constructs incompatible with Islamic values. Some conservatives do acknowledge gender dysphoria but advocate for addressing it without transitioning, emphasizing patience and acceptance of one's birth-assigned sex. Gender-affirming surgeries or hormone therapies are often seen as impermissible attempts to alter Allah's creation, referencing Qu'ranic verses like 4:119, which warn against altering Allah's design.

Transgender issues are sometimes viewed as a threat to traditional gender roles and modesty codes. Conservatives emphasize maintaining distinct male and female roles to preserve societal order. Many conservative communities oppose granting legal recognition or rights to transgender individuals, arguing it could undermine Islamic morality or societal values.

Both progressives and conservatives often agree on the recognition and rights of *khunsa* (intersex individuals), as classical Islamic jurisprudence has provisions for intersex people. In some Muslim-majority countries, even conservative circles have varying stances based on local customs, such as Pakistan's recognition of *hijra* (a traditional third gender) while maintaining conservative views on gender roles.

Ultimately, the divide reflects broader tensions between adapting to contemporary understandings of identity and adhering to traditional interpretations of Islamic teachings.

References

Akyol, M. (2021). *Reopening Muslim minds: A return to reason, freedom, and tolerance.* New York: St. Martin.

Bessard, F. (2000). *Caliphs and merchants: Cities and economies of power in the Near East (700–950)* (pp. 241–264). Oxford University Press.

Braudel, F. (n.d.). *Civilization and capitalism, 15th–18th century. Vol. 2: The wheels of commerce* (S. Reynolds, Trans.). New York: Harper & Row.

Daly, J. (2021). *The rise of Western power: A comparative history of Western civilisation.* New York: Bloomsbury Academic.

Guessoum, N., & Bigliardi, S. (2023). *Islam and science: Past, present, and future debates.* Cambridge University Press.

Hoodbhoy, P. (1991). *Islam and science: Religious orthodoxy and the battle for rationality.* Zed Books.

Ibn Khaldun. (1967). *The Muqaddimah: An introduction to history* (Vol. III, F. Rosenthal, Trans.). New York: Pantheon Books.

Koehler, B. (2014). *Early Islam and the birth of capitalism.* New York: Lexington Books.

Malik, S. A. (2018). *Atheism and Islam: A contemporary discourse.* Abu Dhabi: Kalam Research & Media.

Watson, A. M. (1983). *Agricultural innovation in the early Islamic world: The diffusion of crops and farming techniques, 700–1100* (pp. 31–50, 62–65). New York: Cambridge University Press.

CHAPTER 10
ISLAMIC VS. MUSLIM VALUES

Introduction

Islamic values represent a comprehensive ethical and moral framework meant to guide Muslims in every aspect of their lives. Rooted in the Qu'ran, the sayings (hadith) and actions of Prophet Muhammad, and centuries of jurisprudential scholarship, these values form the cornerstone of individual and collective conduct in Islamic societies. They aim to foster a profound sense of responsibility to God (Taqwa), harmonious interpersonal relationships, and a just and equitable society. For Muslims, adherence to these values is not only an expression of faith but also a means of contributing positively to the broader human community.

The ideals of Islam, such as justice, compassion, humility, and honesty, are universal and timeless. They transcend cultural and geographical boundaries, offering a moral compass for Muslims in all situations. Justice ('Adl) is a divine command central to governance and social relations, while compassion (Rahmah) underscores the ethical treatment of all beings, including non-Muslims, animals, and the environment. Similarly, humility (Tawadu) is prescribed to counter arrogance and pride, and honesty (Sidq) is emphasized as a critical component of trustworthy relationships. These values collectively create an aspirational vision of a society founded on peace, mutual respect, and human dignity.

However, in practice, many Muslim communities today face challenges that hinder the full realization of these ideals. The disconnect between Islamic teachings and lived realities manifests in issues like corruption, social injustice, and sectarianism, which are inconsistent with the principles of Islam. These discrepancies often lead to critiques of Muslim societies, both from within and outside the Islamic world, questioning their adherence to the faith's ethical framework. Some call the discrepancy as Islamic vs Muslim values. Like people from many other faiths followers of Muslims engage in behaviors that are not ethical and moral. This gives a wrong message about the religion that they represent. There are several reasons for this divergence. Understanding the gap between Islamic and Muslim's day-to-day behavior requires an exploration of historical, cultural, and political factors. Historical contexts, such as colonial legacies have reshaped Islamic societies often prioritizing survival over adherence to values. Similarly, cultural traditions and tribal affiliations have sometimes overridden religious principles. Political exploitation of Islam and the challenges of globalization, including materialism and secular influences, further complicate the ability of Muslims to fully embody their values.

Equally important are psycho-social determinants of an individual's ethical conduct. Research studies have demonstrated the role of moral development, personality traits, and situational factors as important determinants. Thus, no matter what religious background an individual comes from his or her behavior is determined by these factors. For instance, Ashton & Lee (2008) reported that honesty and humility are personality traits that indicate the tendency to be fair and genuine while dealing with others. As such people who are high on these traits can be considered to have high morals as it involves balancing self-interest with the interest of others which is a pre-requisite for building positive social relationships.

Some other personality traits that contribute to moral behavior are conscientiousness, self-control, and consideration for future consequences. A person high on conscientiousness is dependable, self-disciplined, and careful. Those low on this trait are irresponsible, lazy, and disorganized. Several studies have established a strong positive relationship between this trait and ethical behavior (Berry et al, 2012; Cohen et al, 2014; Podsakoff et al, 2006). Self-control is yet another dominant personality trait which has a bearing on ethical behavior. It predisposes a person to inhibit immediate gratification for a long-term goal. Those having a low level of self-control display more aggressive and selfish behavior (Gino, Schwteitzer, Mead, & Ariely, 2011; Lian et al, 2014). Consideration for future consequences predisposes a person to engage in self-regulation, for example, not showing aggression towards others when they believe that such behavior could be costly in the future. They are thus less likely, for instance, to lie in business negotiations (Hersfield et al, 2012).

Yet another factor that determines an individual's moral or ethical conduct is moral identity. Moral identity refers to the way a person views himself or herself and the extent to which being moral is central to his or her identity. Internalization of moral identity becomes a driving force to stay away from unethical acts and encourages behavior such as helping and charitable giving. Individual life experiences, family upbringing, culture, and religion shape moral identity.

The Cherished Values

Islamic teachings articulate a robust set of ethical and moral ideals designed to foster spiritual development, social harmony, and justice. These values, derived primarily from the Qu'ran and the Sunnah (the sayings and practices of Prophet Muhammad), serve as a comprehensive guide for individual and collective conduct. Below are some of the core ideal values in Islam, which are meant to be reflected in the daily lives of Muslims:

Justice ('Adl): Justice is a cornerstone of Islamic ethics, emphasized repeatedly in the Qu'ran and the Sunnah. The Qu'ran explicitly commands fairness and impartiality, even in situations involving personal loss or discomfort:

"O you who believe! Stand out firmly for justice, as witnesses to Allah, even though it be against yourselves, your parents, or your kin..." (Qu'ran 4:135).

Justice in Islam encompasses all spheres of life, including legal, social, and economic realms. It calls for the fair treatment of individuals, equitable distribution of resources, and the establishment of systems that protect the rights of all, especially the vulnerable. Muslims are urged to uphold justice as an act of worship, reflecting their accountability to Allah.

Compassion and Mercy (Rahmah): Compassion is a defining trait of Islam, encapsulated in the names of Allah, *Ar-Rahman* (The Most Compassionate), and *Ar-Rahim* (The Most Merciful). The Qu'ran describes Prophet Muhammad as a mercy to all creation:

"And We have not sent you, [O Muhammad], except as a mercy to the worlds" (Qu'ran 21:107).

Compassion in Islam extends to all beings, including animals and the environment. Muslims are encouraged to assist those in need, forgive others, and show kindness in their interactions. This value is central to creating a harmonious society where empathy and solidarity are the norm.

Honesty and Truthfulness (Sidq): Honesty is one of the most emphasized virtues in Islam. Muslims are instructed to be truthful in speech and conduct, avoiding deceit, fraud, and hypocrisy. The Qu'ran states:

"O you who believe! Fear Allah and speak words of appropriate justice" (Qu'ran 33:70).

Prophet Muhammad was known as *Al-Amin* (The Trustworthy) even before his prophethood, exemplifying the importance of integrity. This value is vital in building trust within communities and ensuring fairness in personal and professional dealings.

Humility (Tawadu): *Tawadu* (modesty and humility) is the opposite of arrogance, pride, and haughtiness. It can also be interpreted as one's awareness of one's real position before God. Islam advocates humility as a means to counter arrogance and pride. The Qu'ran cautions against self-conceit and calls for modesty in behavior:

"And do not walk upon the earth exultantly. Indeed, you will never tear the earth [apart], and you will never reach the mountains in height" (Qu'ran 17:37).

Prophet Muhammad was a paragon of humility, often engaging in tasks such as mending his clothes, milking goats, and serving his companions. Humility fosters a sense of equality and mutual respect among individuals, promoting a sense of collective responsibility.

The Pursuit of Knowledge (Ilm): Knowledge is highly revered in Islam, with the first revelation of the Qu'ran urging the Prophet to "read" (*Iqra*). Seeking knowledge is considered an obligation for every Muslim, as highlighted in the well-known hadith:

"Seeking knowledge is an obligation upon every Muslim." (Sunan Ibn Majah, Hadith 224).

This value is not limited to religious studies but extends to all fields that contribute to human well-being. Islam encourages the pursuit of knowledge as a means to better understand creation, improve society, and fulfill one's responsibilities as a steward of the earth (*khalifah*).

Patience and Perseverance (Sabr): Patience is a recurring theme in the Qu'ran, described as a virtue necessary for enduring life's trials and striving towards righteousness. The Qu'ran states:

"Indeed, Allah is with the patient" (Qu'ran 2:153).

Muslims are encouraged to exercise patience in the face of adversity, maintain self-control in challenging situations, and persevere in fulfilling their duties to God and society.

Generosity and Charity (Infaq and Sadaqah): Generosity is a defining characteristic of a faithful Muslim. The Qu'ran repeatedly emphasizes the importance of giving in charity, both as a form of worship and a means of social equity:

"The example of those who spend their wealth in the way of Allah is like a seed [of grain]; it sprouts seven ears, and in every ear is a hundred grains" (Qu'ran 2:261).

Charitable acts include mandatory almsgiving (*zakat*), voluntary charity (*sadaqah*), and acts of kindness, such as feeding the poor or assisting a neighbor. These practices are meant to reduce inequality and foster a spirit of mutual support.

Gratitude (Shukr): Gratitude is central to the Islamic worldview, where Muslims are encouraged to acknowledge Allah's blessings and show appreciation through words and deeds:

"If you are grateful, I will surely increase you [in favor]" (Qu'ran 14:7).

Gratitude fosters contentment and a positive outlook, motivating individuals to contribute to society and assist others.

The Enacted Values

While the cherished values of Islam provide a lofty and comprehensive ethical framework, the lived realities of Muslims often reflect a significant gap between these ideals and their practical application. This divergence arises due to a variety of factors, including historical circumstances, socio-political dynamics, cultural influences, and individual shortcomings. The following are key areas where the actual practices of Muslims often fall short of Islamic ideals:

Corruption and Injustice: Despite Islam's strong emphasis on justice (*'adl*), corruption is a widespread issue in many Muslim societies. From bribery and nepotism in government institutions to inequitable legal systems, the prevalence of corruption undermines the Qu'ranic principle of fairness:

"And do not consume one another's wealth unjustly or send it [in bribery] to the rulers in order that [they might aid] you to consume a portion of the wealth of the people in sin, while you know [it is unlawful]" (Qu'ran 2:188).

Judicial bias, lack of accountability, and unequal treatment of citizens—whether based on gender, socio-economic status, or ethnicity—stand in stark contrast to the Islamic mandate for impartiality and justice. These failings erode trust in governance and perpetuate cycles of poverty and inequality.

Sectarianism and Intolerance: Islam's call for unity and compassion is often overshadowed by divisions within the Muslim community. Sectarian conflicts between Sunni and Shia groups, and internal disputes among various schools of thought, create divisions that contradict the Qu'ranic exhortation:

"And hold firmly to the rope of Allah all together and do not become divided" (Qu'ran 3:103).

Intolerance extends beyond intra-Muslim conflicts to relations with people of other faiths. Islam advocates peaceful coexistence and respect for diversity, yet instances of discrimination, violence, and exclusion of religious minorities are reported in some Muslim societies. These actions misrepresent Islam's universal message of mercy and respect for all human beings.

Dishonesty and Hypocrisy: The value of honesty (*sidq*) is often compromised in personal, professional, and political domains. In some cases, deceit and corruption are normalized, leading to a loss of trust within communities. This behavior directly opposes the teachings of the Prophet Muhammad, who said:

"The signs of a hypocrite are three: when he speaks, he lies; when he makes a promise, he breaks it; and when he is entrusted, he betrays the trust" (Sahih al-Bukhari, Hadith 33).

Dishonesty in trade, manipulation of religious sentiments for personal gain, and the failure to fulfill promises in leadership roles or otherwise are all manifestations of this gap.

Gender Inequality: Islamic teachings advocate the spiritual and moral equality of men and women, with both tasked as stewards (*khalifah*) of the earth. However, in practice, patriarchal customs and cultural norms often overshadow these principles. Issues such as restricted access to education, economic opportunities, and participation in public life are common in some Muslim societies.

In extreme cases, practices like forced marriages, honor-based violence, and denial of inheritance rights occur, contradicting the Qu'ran's clear commands regarding women's rights. These disparities reflect cultural distortions rather than true Islamic values.

Cultural and Tribal Influences: In many Muslim communities, pre-Islamic cultural practices continue to influence societal norms. These include tribalism, favoritism, and the prioritization of cultural customs over Islamic principles. For instance, the Prophet of Islam warned against the dangers of tribalism, stating:

"He is not of us who proclaims the cause of tribal partisanship" (Sunan Abi Dawood, Hadith 5119).

Yet, allegiance to tribal or familial loyalties often takes precedence over Islamic values, perpetuating inequality and injustice.

Materialism: Modern challenges, such as materialism and the pressures of globalization, have led some Muslims to prioritize worldly success over spiritual growth. This shift is contrary to the Qu'ranic directive to balance material pursuits with a focus on the hereafter:

"But seek, through that which Allah has given you, the home of the Hereafter; and [yet], do not forget your share of the world" (Qu'ran 28:77).

The pursuit of wealth, status, and consumerism often overshadows the emphasis on generosity (*infaq*) and modesty promoted in Islam. This misalignment erodes social solidarity and increases inequality.

Lack of Community Accountability: In many instances, there is a failure to hold individuals and leaders accountable for actions that contradict Islamic principles. Whether it is the misuse of religious authority, neglect of the poor, or failure to address systemic corruption, this lack of accountability weakens the moral fabric of societies. The Qu'ran repeatedly emphasizes enjoining good and forbidding evil as a communal duty:

"Let there be a group among you who call others to goodness, and encourage what is good, and forbid what is evil—it is they who will be successful" (Qu'ran 3:104).

When this duty is neglected, societal values drift away from Islamic ideals. The reality of practiced values in many Muslim societies reveals a significant gap between the ideals of Islam and their implementation. This disconnect is not inherent to Islam but stems from historical, cultural, and socio-political factors that distort its teachings. Recognizing these challenges is the first step toward addressing them, enabling Muslims to better align their personal and collective lives with the moral and ethical framework of their faith.

The Reasons for Divergence

The divergence between the ideal and practiced values of Muslims has multiple reasons. A few are discussed below.

Cultural Distortions: Cultural traditions often intertwine with religious practices, leading to distortions in the understanding and application of Islam's core values. In many societies, patriarchal customs are mistakenly presented as Islamic. For instance, restrictions on women's mobility, education, or participation in public life are enforced in ways that contradict Islam's principles of equality and empowerment. Tribal or ethnic affiliations often overshadow Islamic teachings on justice and meritocracy. This can lead to practices like favoritism, nepotism, and exclusion of those outside a specific group, directly contradicting Islamic principles of fairness. Practices such as adhering to un-Islamic rituals, or prioritizing cultural ceremonies over Islamic obligations often stem from pre-Islamic traditions that were not fully abandoned. These cultural influences dilute the universality of Islam's message and perpetuate practices that clash with its ideals.

Lack of Education: A significant gap in religious and general education has left many Muslims unable to differentiate between authentic Islamic teachings and cultural or modern distortions. Many Muslims do not have access to reliable sources of Islamic knowledge. This can lead to reliance on unqualified preachers or misinterpretation of texts.

Islamic education, where available, often emphasizes rituals and jurisprudence while neglecting the ethical and spiritual dimensions of the faith. This creates a mechanical approach to religion, devoid of deeper understanding. Younger generations in some communities lack exposure to authentic Islamic teachings due to gaps in parental knowledge or ineffective religious instruction in schools and mosques. Teachings through sermons and discourses are often limited to one-way communication. Asking questions is generally not encouraged. Educational reform is critical to bridging this gap, ensuring Muslims are well-informed about their faith's holistic approach to life.

Historical Legacies: Historical events, particularly colonialism, have left a lasting impact on Muslim societies, reshaping their social, political, and religious structures. Colonial powers dismantled Islamic systems of governance, education, and law, replacing them with secular or foreign frameworks. These changes disrupted the organic application of Islamic values in society. Many post-colonial Muslim countries struggle with political instability, economic dependency, and identity crises, making it difficult to prioritize the reestablishment of Islamic ethics in governance and daily life. The divide-and-rule strategies employed by colonial regimes fostered sectarianism and ethnic divisions, which continue to undermine unity among Muslims. Addressing these historical legacies requires a deliberate effort to reclaim and contextualize Islamic principles in a modern framework.

Political Exploitation of Religion: Religion is often exploited by political leaders to consolidate power, leading to a disconnect between Islamic ideals and societal governance. Politicians may invoke Islam to gain public support while failing to implement its principles of justice, accountability, and welfare in governance. In some contexts, dissenting voices are silenced under the pretext of protecting religious values, creating an environment where corruption and injustice thrive. Political manipulation of sectarian or ethnic identities exacerbates divisions, undermining the unity and compassion central to Islamic teachings. This exploitation erodes public trust in religious and political institutions, further widening the gap between ideals and practice.

Globalization and Modern Challenges: Globalization and modernity present unique challenges to the practice of Islamic values. The pursuit of wealth, status, and consumer goods often takes precedence over spiritual and ethical growth, contrary to Islam's emphasis on contentment and generosity. The prevalence of misinformation and negative portrayals of Islam in the media can lead to confusion about what Islam truly stands for, especially among younger Muslims. Balancing Islamic principles with the demands and pressures of the modern world requires critical thinking and community-driven solutions.

Weak Religious Leadership: The lack of qualified and effective religious leadership is another major factor contributing to the gap between ideals and practices. Some religious leaders emphasize rituals and legalistic aspects of

Islam while neglecting its ethical, spiritual, and social teachings. Many religious leaders are unprepared to address contemporary challenges, such as mental health, gender equality, or environmental concerns, leaving communities without clear guidance.

Instances of corruption or hypocrisy among religious figures undermine their authority and disillusioned believers. Developing credible, knowledgeable, and empathetic religious leadership is essential to guiding communities toward a balanced and authentic practice of Islam.

Socio-Economic Inequalities: Economic disparities and systemic injustices hinder the ability of Muslims to fully embody Islamic values. Many Muslims struggle to prioritize spiritual growth and ethical behavior when faced with poverty and economic hardship. Survival often takes precedence over idealism. Furthermore, limited access to education, healthcare, and employment prevents individuals from realizing their potential and contributing positively to society.

Bridging the Gap

Bridging the gap between the ideal values of Islam and the actual practices of Muslims requires a holistic and multi-dimensional approach. This involves efforts at the individual, community, and institutional levels. A few strategies to address this divide effectively are:

Enhancing Education and Awareness: Knowledge and awareness are the foundation for aligning behavior with values. Islamic teachings emphasize seeking knowledge as a means to strengthen faith and practice. Additionally, there is a need to revamp Islamic education. For example, curricula in schools and religious institutions should include both traditional Islamic sciences and contemporary subjects. This approach ensures a balanced understanding of Islam's rituals, ethics, and relevance to modern challenges.

Next, religious education should go beyond memorization of texts to emphasize the ethical and spiritual dimensions of Islam. For example, teachings on compassion, honesty, and justice should be integrated into lessons on prayer and fasting. Also, there is a need to change the pedagogy. Teachers should encourage students to ask questions, debate, and discuss issues. The learning culture in schools and the socialization process of children in the family and community should facilitate the development of scientific temper.

Communities should have access to reliable and comprehensive Islamic literature, online platforms, and lectures to counter misinformation and cultural distortions. Community organizations can run campaigns to educate Muslims on core Islamic principles, addressing common misconceptions and encouraging personal reflection.

Promoting Community Accountability: Islam emphasizes collective responsibility in maintaining moral and ethical standards within society. Communities can play a crucial role in ensuring that Islamic values are upheld. Local councils composed of respected leaders, scholars, and professionals can address issues like corruption, domestic violence, and social injustice in alignment with Islamic principles. Organizations and initiatives that advocate for social justice, poverty alleviation, and ethical governance should be supported and integrated into community structures.

Strengthening Religious Leadership: Qualified, knowledgeable, and relatable religious leaders are essential for guiding communities toward the ideal values of Islam. Religious leaders should receive comprehensive training in both Islamic sciences and social sciences and should be able to discuss contemporary issues, such as the psychology of motivation, mental health, environmental sustainability, and interfaith matters.

Community leaders should adopt an inclusive approach, addressing the needs of diverse groups within the community, including women, youth, and minorities. They must embody the values they preach, demonstrating honesty, humility, and integrity to inspire others. Moreover, they should leverage social media and other digital platforms to reach wider audiences and address pressing social issues effectively.

Encouraging Exemplary Role Models: Individuals who embody Islamic ideals in their personal and professional lives can inspire others to follow suit. Publicizing stories of Muslims who practice their faith with integrity, whether as community leaders, entrepreneurs, or philanthropists, can motivate others to emulate them. Established professionals and leaders can mentor young Muslims, guiding them to balance Islamic values with their ambitions and challenges. Also, schools, universities, and community centers can organize events showcasing role models who have achieved success while remaining committed to their faith. There are several individuals and institutions who are doing excellent work for human rights, community development, aid, and welfare in Muslim countries.

Reforming Institutions and Governance: Institutional reform is critical for creating environments where Islamic values can be practiced and promoted. Governments in Muslim countries should prioritize justice, accountability, and transparency in governance, aligning policies with Islamic principles. They should also undertake economic reforms by addressing income inequality through policies that encourage *zakat* (almsgiving) and *waqf* (endowment) systems. It is also important that legal systems uphold justice for all citizens, ensuring that laws are applied equally without favoritism or corruption. Muslims should be encouraged to participate in governance and public service to contribute positively to societal development.

Balancing Tradition and Modernity: Muslims must learn to navigate modern challenges while remaining rooted in their faith. This requires a balanced approach that respects tradition while embracing beneficial aspects of modernity. Islamic principles should be applied in ways that address contemporary issues, such as environmental degradation, technological advancements, and mental health concerns. It is also important that Muslims should avoid the extremes of rigid conservatism and uncritical adoption of some values, striving instead for a middle path that aligns with Islam's emphasis on moderation. Islamic values can inspire innovation and creativity, particularly in fields like science, technology, and sustainable development.

Fostering Unity and Collaboration: Unity within the Muslim community is essential for bridging the gap between ideals and practice. Islam emphasizes the importance of working together to achieve common goals. Encouraging dialogue between different sects and schools of thought can reduce divisions and foster mutual respect. Working with people of other faiths on shared challenges, such as poverty and climate change, can reinforce Islam's universal values of compassion and cooperation. Also, Muslims around the world should support one another in addressing issues like Islamophobia, economic injustice, and political oppression.

Addressing Socio-Economic Challenges: Socio-economic stability is essential for individuals and communities to focus on spiritual growth and ethical behavior. Providing opportunities for education and employment can empower Muslims to lead productive lives aligned with Islamic values. Also, communities should establish systems to support the underprivileged, ensuring that no one is left behind. Encouraging equitable distribution of wealth through zakat and other Islamic economic principles can reduce inequality and foster solidarity.

Leveraging Technology and Media: Technology and media can play a powerful role in promoting Islamic values and addressing misconceptions. Producing high-quality, engaging content that explains Islamic principles and addresses contemporary issues can reach global audiences. Muslims should actively challenge stereotypes and misconceptions about Islam through positive media representation. Digital platforms can facilitate knowledge-sharing and collaboration among Muslims worldwide.

The ideal values of Islam form a holistic framework aimed at nurturing individuals who are spiritually mindful, ethically upright, and socially responsible. Together, they reflect Islam's mission to establish a just and compassionate society where human dignity and divine accountability are upheld. Bridging the gap between the ideal and actual values of Muslims requires a concerted effort across multiple dimensions. Muslim communities should create environments where Islamic ideals are not only understood but also practiced consistently. These efforts will enable Muslims to better align their personal and collective lives with the timeless values of Islam, contributing to a more just, compassionate, and harmonious world.

References

Ali, A. Y. (2000). *The Qur'an: Translation and commentary.* Tahrik Tarsile Qur'an.

Ashton, M. C., Lee, K., Perugini, M., Szarota, P., de Vries, R. E., Di Blas, L., Boies, K., & De Raad, B. (2004). A six-factor structure of personality-descriptive adjectives: Solutions from psycholexical studies in seven languages. *Journal of Personality and Social Psychology, 86*(2), 356–366.

Berry, C. M., Carpenter, N. C., & Barratt, C. L. (2012). Do other-reports of counterproductive work behavior provide an incremental contribution over self-reports? A meta-analytic comparison. *Journal of Applied Psychology, 97*(3), 613-636.

Cohen, T. R., & Morse, L. (2014). Moral character: What it is and what it does. In A. P. Brief & B. M. Staw (Eds.), *Research in organizational behavior.* Elsevier.

Esposito, J. L. (2002). *What everyone needs to know about Islam.* Oxford University Press.

Gino, F., Schweitzer, M. E., Mead, N. L., & Ariely, D. (2011). Unable to resist temptation: How self-control depletion promotes unethical behavior. *Organizational*

Behavior and Human Decision Processes, 115(2), 191-203.

Hadith collections: *Sahih al-Bukhari, Sahih Muslim.*

Hershfield, H. E., Cohen, T. R., & Thompson, L. (2012). Short horizons and tempting situations: Lack of continuity to our future selves leads to unethical decision-making and behavior. *Organizational Behavior and Human Decision Processes, 117*, 298-310.

Lian, H., Brown, D. J., Ferris, D. L., Liang, L. H., Keeping, L. M., & Morrison, R. (2014). Abusive supervision and retaliation: A self-control framework. *Academy of Management Journal, 57*(1), 116-139.

Nasr, S. H. (2002). *The heart of Islam: Enduring values for humanity.* Harper: San Francisco.

Podsakoff, P. M., MacKenzie, S. B., & Organ, D. W. (2006). *Organizational citizenship behavior: Its nature, antecedents, and consequences.* Thousand Oaks, CA: SAGE Publications, Inc.

CHAPTER 11
ECONOMIC DEVELOPMENT

Economic development in Muslim countries faces unique challenges and complex realities shaped by historical, social, political, and geographic factors. These countries vary widely in economic capacity and resources, with some, like the Gulf States, enjoying high levels of wealth due to oil, while others, like Yemen or Somalia, face significant poverty and instability. Below is a detailed account of the main challenges and realities that influence economic development in Muslim nations.

Economic Diversity and Resource Dependence

Muslim countries span diverse geographies and income levels, from oil-rich nations to low-income agrarian economies. This diversity leads to varying economic structures and development trajectories.

Many Muslim countries, particularly in the Middle East and North Africa (MENA) region, rely heavily on oil and gas exports, which makes their economies highly susceptible to fluctuations in global oil prices. For instance, countries like Saudi Arabia, Kuwait, and the UAE derive a substantial portion of their revenue from hydrocarbons. While this dependence has enabled rapid economic growth and modernization, it also creates vulnerability to oil market volatility, which can destabilize public finances and impede diversification efforts.

Efforts to diversify away from oil, such as Saudi Arabia's Vision 2030 initiative, focus on sectors like tourism, finance, and technology. However, these efforts face obstacles, including workforce skills gaps, a dependence on foreign labor, and an economic structure historically built around energy exports.

Some Muslim countries are fundamentally rentier economies. A rentier economy is an economic system in which a significant portion (40% and above) of national revenue comes from renting natural resources or assets to external clients or foreign entities, rather than through productive activities like manufacturing or agriculture. This "rent" typically involves income from oil, gas, minerals, or other natural resources. Middle Eastern oil-rich states like Saudi Arabia, Kuwait, and Qatar are classic examples of rentier economies, as they derive much of their income from exporting oil and gas. Some resource-rich African and Latin American nations also exhibit rentier economic characteristics. The key feature of these countries is that their economy heavily relies on income from resource exports rather than diverse economic activities. Other sectors like industry or services often remain underdeveloped because resource wealth dominates the economy. A significant portion of income flows into the country from abroad, as foreign entities pay for access to resources. The wealth from resource rents often accrues to a small elite or the government, potentially leading to income inequality. Rentier states may have underdeveloped institutions since the government can finance itself through resource rents instead of taxation, reducing accountability to citizens.

Rentier economies are highly vulnerable to fluctuations in global resource prices. The reliance on resource wealth can lead to corruption, political instability, and lack of diversification, hampering long-term economic development. Governments in rentier states may face less pressure to be accountable to their citizens since they rely on resource rents rather than taxes. This is one of the reasons for the absence of democracy in these places.

Kuru (2021) in his report has classified Muslim countries based on their Constitution and the presence or absence of democracy. Out of 50 Muslim countries, 18 have Shariah-based constitutions. These 18 countries have Shariah courts with jurisdiction over family-law matters, including marriage, divorce, and inheritance. Moreover, in many of these cases, Shariah courts also deal with criminal-law matters. All of these countries have laws punishing apostasy and blasphemy, in some cases involving the death penalty. About two-thirds of these countries have rentier states.

The next group of countries with mixed constitutions, rentier and non-rentier economies. These countries recognize Islam as the official religion without referring to Shariah. In these countries, Shariah is only used for family law and interpreted with varying degrees of severity, unlike the countries in the first group. All countries in this group have blasphemy laws, but only half of them have apostasy laws; none of these laws involve the death penalty.

The third group consists of 22 Muslim countries with secular constitutions. Of these countries, 13 have constitutions that define the state (or republic) as "secular. Constitutions of the remaining nine countries do not use the term "secular," but they do not recognize Islam as the official religion either. Thus, they implicitly define their states as secular.

Analysis of all three groups of countries indicates that the religious institution and state alliance is the most institutionalized in countries where the constitution refers to Shariah as a source of legislation. The religious bodies have official legislative and judiciary roles in these cases. In several Muslim countries, this highly institutionalized religion-state alliance is combined with rentier economies. This has made their authoritarian regimes very robust. Kuru concludes that the strong alliance between *Ulema* (Religious scholars) and the State is determinantal to the lack of scientific, entrepreneurial culture and commerce in these countries.

Demographic Pressures and Youth Unemployment

Many Muslim countries have rapidly growing populations, with a significant percentage under the age of 30. This youth demographic presents both an opportunity and a challenge for economic development.

Youth unemployment rates are alarmingly high in many Muslim countries, especially in North Africa and the Middle East. Factors like limited job opportunities, mismatches between educational outcomes and job market needs, and weak private sectors contribute to this challenge. For example, Tunisia, Egypt, and Jordan struggle with high youth unemployment, which fuels economic frustration and social discontent.

In some Gulf countries, reliance on expatriate labor creates gaps between the local workforce and job market needs. In countries like the UAE and Qatar, foreign workers fill most of the private-sector jobs, while nationals often favor public-sector employment due to higher wages and job security. This imbalance complicates workforce localization and economic sustainability efforts.

Educational and Skills Development

Education and skills development are essential for sustainable economic growth, yet many Muslim countries face challenges in aligning educational outcomes with market demands.

While many countries have improved access to education, the quality often remains uneven. In countries like Egypt, Morocco, and Pakistan, education systems suffer from outdated curricula, underqualified teachers, and inadequate resources. This results in graduates who may lack the skills required by modern economies, particularly in STEM fields and critical thinking.

Some countries are working to bridge the skills gap through vocational and technical training programs, as seen in Saudi Arabia's initiatives to prepare locals for private-sector roles. However, vocational education still struggles with societal perceptions, often being viewed as less prestigious than university education, which can deter students.

Gender Inequality and Economic Participation

In many Muslim countries, women face barriers to economic participation, which limits overall economic growth and productivity. Female Labor Force Participation rates vary significantly among Muslim countries. According to the global gender gap report published in 2012 by the World Economic Forum the female labor participation rate was as low as 16% in Afghanistan, 13% in Syria, 24% in Egypt, and 28% in Turkey. On the other hand, it was as high as 57% in Bangladesh, and 51% in Indonesia. These figures are quite old as a lot of geopolitical changes have taken place in the past one and half decades since these data were collected. Yet, it is true that the gender gap exists in not only labor participation rate but in earnings as well (For details please refer to https://en.wikipedia.org/wiki/Female_labor_force_in_the_Muslim_world).

In conservative societies like Saudi Arabia and Afghanistan, cultural norms and legal restrictions have traditionally limited women's economic roles, though some reforms, like Saudi Arabia's increased support for women in the workforce, are underway. Other countries, like Malaysia and Indonesia, have higher rates of female participation in the workforce, often influenced by cultural, economic, and educational factors. In some such countries, legal constraints and social expectations restrict women's ability to work or own businesses. Challenges such as limited access to financial resources, workplace discrimination, and gender-specific regulations can hinder women's economic empowerment, reducing overall economic productivity. It would be wrong to simply attribute religion as the factor responsible for the low female participation in labor as besides religion, a range of economic and institutional factors tend to differ across time and space. This can explain some of the contradicting results in the literature regarding the effect of religion on economic outcomes (Akyol P, Ökten Ç. 2024).

Political Instability and Governance Issues

Political instability, governance issues, and corruption significantly impact economic development in many Muslim countries. Several such countries face ongoing conflict or political unrest, which disrupts economic activity, destroys infrastructure, and deters foreign investment. Syria, Libya, Iraq, and Yemen have all seen severe economic setbacks due to conflict, with challenges like displaced populations, damaged infrastructure, and weakened governance.

Corruption remains a significant challenge in countries such as Pakistan, Iraq, and Egypt, where bribery, red tape, and nepotism hinder business operations, reduce investor confidence, and increase the cost of public services. These governance issues discourage both local and foreign investment, limiting job creation and growth.

Financial Ecosystem and Capital Access

Access to capital and the development of financial infrastructure are critical for fostering entrepreneurship, investment, and economic growth, but these areas are often underdeveloped in Muslim countries. Many individuals in these countries lack access to formal financial services, particularly in rural areas and among women. This restricts access to savings, credit, and investment opportunities, limiting entrepreneurship and small business growth. In countries like Indonesia and Pakistan, initiatives to promote financial inclusion, such as digital banking and mobile money, are starting to improve access.

Islamic Economics

In recent years there have been lot of publications, conferences, and educational initiatives done across Muslim and non-Muslim countries. Let's take a brief look at this concept. Islamic economics is a system of economics that is based on principles derived from Islamic teachings, particularly the Qu'ran and Hadith. It emphasizes ethical and moral guidelines for economic behavior, promoting social justice, fairness, and equitable distribution of wealth. It aims to create a balance between individual needs and societal welfare.

The strength of Islamic Economics comes in addressing income inequality through zakat, *sadaqah* (voluntary charity), and inheritance laws, ensuring wealth circulation in society. Secondly, it promotes ethical financial practices through the prohibition of exploitative practices such as charging interest (*usury*) to ensure fairness. Instead of charging interest, Islamic banks use profit-sharing models like *Mudarabah*, aligning incentives of borrowers and lenders. This system also promotes economic stability as asset-backed financing reduces speculative bubbles and promotes real economic activity. For example, real estate transactions under Islamic finance require clear ownership and tangible asset exchange. Another benefit of this system is that it encourages risk sharing. By avoiding fixed-interest debt, risk-sharing fosters a partnership mindset and mutual accountability. Finally, Islamic economics emphasizes sustainable and ethical investments that benefit society. Islamic funds focus on projects that align with moral values, avoiding industries like tobacco or gambling.

Nonetheless, scholars have identified some weaknesses as well. First, Islamic economics appears idealistic and often difficult to implement in complex modern economies. For example, adapting financial systems to eliminate interest-based transactions can be logistically and politically challenging. Secondly, risk-sharing models may deter some investors due to shared losses, limiting access to capital. Entrepreneurs may struggle to secure funding from Islamic banks compared to traditional interest-based loans. Also, there are regulatory and standardization issues such as the interpretation of Shariah principles varies across regions, leading to inconsistencies in practice. For example, a financial product considered Shariah-compliant in Malaysia might not be accepted in Saudi Arabia. It is also said that Islamic banks may have lower profitability compared to conventional banks due to profit-sharing and the absence of interest.

Islamic economics provides an ethical framework that promotes social welfare, economic stability, and equitable wealth distribution. While it has strengths like risk-sharing and sustainability, its practical application faces challenges, especially in a globalized and diverse economic environment. To maximize its potential, further standardization, education, and innovation are needed to make Islamic economics more accessible and effective.

Islamic Finance

Islamic finance offers a unique model based on Shariah principles. It is based on core values such as the prohibition of interest (*riba*), risk-sharing, ethical investing, and asset-backed transactions, providing an alternative to conventional finance. While the sector has grown rapidly, especially in the Gulf states, Malaysia, and Indonesia, its adoption remains limited in other parts of the Muslim world. Islamic finance could offer innovative financial products that meet local needs, though regulatory alignment and public awareness are necessary to expand its reach.

Islamic finance has several attractions and therefore getting popular in several Muslim as well as secular nations. Among the reasons for its adoption are:

Financial Inclusion: Islamic finance can increase access to financial services for individuals and businesses who avoid conventional banking due to religious beliefs. By providing Shariah-compliant options, it draws the previously unbanked populations into the formal financial system, fostering economic inclusivity.

Promotion of Ethical Investments: Islamic finance prohibits investments in activities that are considered harmful, such as gambling, alcohol, and arms trading. This ethical approach can potentially attract investors interested in socially responsible investment options and can enhance the overall integrity of financial markets.

Asset-Based Financing and Stability: Islamic financial transactions often require tangible assets and adhere to risk-sharing mechanisms. This asset-backing nature reduces speculative activities, making Islamic financial institutions potentially more stable and resilient in the face of financial crises compared to their conventional counterparts.

Long-Term Growth Focus: With a preference for equity-based and profit-sharing modes of financing, such as *Musharakah* (partnership) and *Mudarabah* (profit-sharing), Islamic finance can encourage entrepreneurial activity and investment in productive assets. This approach supports long-term economic growth and development projects in Muslim nations.

Infrastructure Development: Islamic bonds (*sukuk*) have become increasingly popular as a means of raising capital for infrastructure and development projects. By aligning with Islamic financing principles, governments and corporations in Muslim countries can mobilize funds for projects that drive economic growth, create jobs, and improve infrastructure.

However, there are challenges faced by Islamic finance in economic development. This includes (a) lack of a harmonized regulatory framework across different countries. Variations in interpretations of Shariah principles, coupled with differing legal systems, lead to inconsistencies and limited cross-border cooperation, (b) limited product standardization due to complexities involved in structuring Shariah-compliant financial instruments, (c) the overall market size of Islamic finance remains relatively small compared to global financial markets. The sector's limited penetration in some Muslim countries, due to economic constraints or lack of awareness, limits its overall impact on economic development, (d) scarcity of competent human resources who meet the standard of technical skills and the knowledge of Shariah.

Despite these limitations Islamic finance has proven to be a valuable component of economic development in many Muslim countries, offering ethical, asset-based financing that can promote stability and long-term growth. However, to maximize its impact, there is a need to address regulatory challenges, improve market standardization, enhance cost efficiency, and foster greater awareness and human capital development. By tackling these issues, Islamic finance can become a more robust and inclusive tool for economic progress and poverty reduction in the Muslim world.

Infrastructure and Urbanization

Infrastructure development and urbanization are crucial for economic growth, but many Muslim countries face infrastructure deficits that limit productivity and quality of life.

Poor transportation infrastructure and unreliable energy supply can hinder economic activity. Countries like Pakistan and Bangladesh struggle with frequent power outages and inadequate transportation networks, which increase costs and limit industrial growth. The need for substantial investment in infrastructure is a key priority for these countries.

Rapid urbanization has led to overcrowded cities, inadequate housing, and strained public services in countries like Egypt, Turkey, and Indonesia. While urbanization creates opportunities for economic growth and job creation, it also requires investment in sustainable infrastructure, housing, and public transportation to accommodate growing urban populations.

Environmental Challenges and Resource Scarcity

Environmental challenges such as water scarcity, climate change, and reliance on natural resources present significant obstacles to sustainable development in Muslim countries. Water scarcity is a pressing issue in the MENA region, with countries like Jordan, Yemen, and Saudi Arabia among the world's most water-stressed nations. Limited water availability hampers agriculture and increases dependence on food imports, which can be economically and politically destabilizing. Climate change is another emerging issue. It exacerbates droughts, floods, and extreme temperatures, affecting agriculture, water availability, and public health. Low-income countries like Afghanistan and Sudan are particularly vulnerable, lacking the resources to adapt to climate impacts, while wealthier oil-exporting countries are also starting to recognize the need to address environmental sustainability.

Integration With the Global Economy

While some Muslim countries are well-integrated into the global economy, others face barriers that limit their participation in international trade, investment, and innovation. For resource-poor countries, the lack of diversification and limited access to global markets can stifle economic growth. Non-oil exporting countries like Tunisia and Morocco have made efforts to expand their manufacturing and services sectors, but they often face competition from more industrialized countries, which limits their export potential.

Technological innovation and digitalization are critical for global competitiveness, yet many such countries face challenges in building tech-driven economies. High-tech hubs are emerging in places like the UAE, Egypt, and Malaysia, but limited investment in research and development (R&D), combined with inadequate infrastructure, poses barriers to innovation in other countries.

Social Development and Public Health

Improving social development and public health outcomes is essential for fostering a productive workforce, but public health systems in many Muslim countries face challenges. Public health systems vary widely in quality and access, with wealthier nations like Qatar and the UAE boasting advanced healthcare facilities, while poorer nations like Afghanistan and Somalia struggle with underfunded and understaffed health services. Infectious diseases, malnutrition, and maternal health are significant issues in less developed countries, impacting productivity and economic growth.

Income inequality and poverty remain significant issues, especially in countries with high unemployment and limited social safety nets. Initiatives like cash transfer programs and public health campaigns are being developed in countries like Pakistan and Egypt to improve poverty levels, but these efforts require substantial resources and commitment to have a lasting impact.

Reasons for Economic Under Performance

Timur (2018) has listed several factors related to the economic under performance of Muslim countries. According to him, Islamic finance has a negligible effect on Muslim financial behavior, and low generalized trust depresses Muslim trade. Weak property rights reinforce the private sector's stagnation by driving capital from commerce to rigid waqfs. Waqfs limits economic development through their inflexibility and democratization by keeping civil society embryonic. Parts of the Muslim world conquered by Arab armies are especially undemocratic. States have contributed to the persistence of authoritarianism by treating Islam as an instrument of governance.

In an Opinion Post the former Prime Minister of Malaysia, Abdullah Badawi gave a macro perspective of the issues and challenges facing the Muslim world and made an empathetic plea to act together facing the challenges. His assertions are still relevant even after more than a decade. Here is the summary of what he observed.

"The Muslim world spans a vast and diverse geographical landscape, stretching from Morocco in North

Africa to Mindanao in Southeast Asia. Contrary to common Western perceptions, this region is far from homogeneous. There are countries that are relatively stable, with wealth, good health systems, and educational opportunities for their citizens. Unfortunately, such nations are outnumbered by regions plagued by underdevelopment, poverty, and turmoil. Among the 57 member states of the Organisation of Islamic Cooperation (OIC), 31 are classified as least-developed countries, with several ranking at the bottom of global development indices. High unemployment rates, illiteracy affecting nearly a third of the population, and gender disparities contribute to severe economic and social challenges. Such deprivation serves as fertile ground for radicalization and extremism, as the disaffected are more easily recruited into extremist causes.

Poor governance further exacerbates these challenges in many parts of the Muslim world. Political oppression, human rights abuses, and widespread corruption undermine stability and hinder progress. In some regions, extremism and militancy have taken root, driven by a mix of domestic factors and, at times, external influences. To counter these issues, there must be a unified commitment to eradicating poverty, reducing illiteracy, and creating jobs within the Muslim world. These pressing socioeconomic challenges pose as great a threat as political strife to both Muslim countries and the broader international community. When individuals have access to economic opportunities and a sense of purpose, they are far less susceptible to extremist ideologies.

The challenges facing the Muslim world are multifaceted, but the gravest threats come from within.

Muslim countries must take ownership of their own development and destiny if they are to secure a position of dignity and respect within the global community. Economic strength, political stability, and social resilience are critical prerequisites for achieving such standing. Without them, Muslim nations will remain marginalized and vulnerable to exploitation, internal divisions, and external domination.

Development must be the top priority for Muslim countries and communities. This goes beyond raising income levels, building good housing, and providing healthcare. It also entails creating a literate, informed society; establishing political systems that give people a meaningful voice; reducing inequalities; ensuring efficient, honest governance; and upholding the rule of law. True development also requires respecting civil rights, empowering women, protecting minority communities, and combating corruption at all levels."

The challenges of economic development in Muslim countries are multifaceted and interlinked, ranging from reliance on natural resources to political instability, youth unemployment, gender inequality, and environmental issues. However, there are also promising realities, including efforts toward economic diversification, increased educational initiatives, and rising innovation in sectors like Islamic finance and technology. Addressing these challenges requires sustained investment in governance, infrastructure, human capital, and inclusive economic policies that enable all citizens to contribute to and benefit from economic growth.

References

Akyol, P., & Ökten, Ç. (2024). The role of religion in female labor supply: Evidence from two Muslim denominations. *Journal of Demographic Economics, 90*(1), 116-153.

Badawi, A.A. (2007, May 28). The real challenge for Muslim nations is economic. *Financial Times, May 28, 2007.*

Chowdhury, A., & Tadjoeddin, M. Z. (2012). Economic activity and achievements in the Muslim world. In S. Hasan (Ed.), *The Muslim world in the 21st century: Space, power, and human development* (pp. 197-223). Springer.

Hanif, M., Chaker, M., & Sabah, A. (2024). Islamic finance and economic growth: Global evidence. *Domes: Digest of Middle Eastern Studies.*
https://doi.org/10.1111/dome.12313

Hasan, R. (2017). Islam and development. In *Religion and development in the global south.* Palgrave Macmillan.
https://doi.org/10.1007/978-3-319-57063-1_2

Kuru, A. T. (2021). The ulema-state alliance: A barrier to democracy and development in the Muslim world. *Tony Blair Institute for Global Change.* Published at https://institute.global/policy/ulema-state-alliancebarrier

Timur, K. (2018). Islam and economic performance. *Journal of Economic Literature, 56*(4), 1292-1359.

CHAPTER 12
MUSLIM YOUTHS: CHALLENGES AND ASPIRATIONS

Muslim youth, representing a significant portion of the global Muslim population, are navigating a rapidly changing world, shaped by advances in technology, shifts in global politics, and evolving cultural norms. Their aspirations are diverse, influenced by the socioeconomic, political, and cultural landscapes of their respective countries and by a desire to balance tradition with modernity. This generation of young Muslims is poised to play a transformative role in their societies, yet they face unique challenges and opportunities as they pursue education, careers, social justice, and cultural expression. This chapter gives a closer look at the aspirations, realities, and evolving identity of Muslim youth in a changing world

Education and Career Development

Education is a central focus for Muslim youth, seen as a gateway to upward mobility, personal growth, and contributing positively to society. While access to education has increased in many Muslim countries, quality and alignment with job market demands vary significantly.

Many young Muslims aspire to attain higher education and vocational skills that will prepare them for competitive job markets. Countries like Malaysia, Turkey, and Indonesia have invested heavily in expanding higher education, creating opportunities for youth in science, technology, engineering, and medicine (STEM), entrepreneurship, and global business sectors. However, young people in countries with under-resourced educational systems, such as Yemen or Somalia, struggle with limited access to quality education.

Job security and economic self-sufficiency are primary concerns. However, youth unemployment remains high in several regions, especially in the Middle East and North Africa, where opportunities in both the public and private sectors are often scarce. Many young people, particularly in countries like Egypt, Tunisia, and Pakistan, seek careers that allow for economic independence, challenging traditional career expectations by pursuing entrepreneurial ventures, freelancing, and online businesses to supplement or replace formal employment.

Social and Political Activism

Many Muslim youths are increasingly vocal about social and political issues affecting their societies, demonstrating a commitment to social justice, good governance, and inclusive policies. This generation is more aware of and affected by global social justice movements. They advocate for better governance, fighting corruption, and equal opportunities in their societies, demanding reforms in education, healthcare, and economic policy. Events like the Arab Spring, for example, highlighted the desire among young Muslims in the MENA region for democratic governance and respect for human rights.

The Arab Spring

The Arab Spring refers to a series of pro-democracy uprisings, protests, and demonstrations that swept across many Arab countries in the Middle East and North Africa starting in late 2010 and early 2011. It marked a significant political and social upheaval in the region. There were several reasons for this uprising. Many Arab countries were ruled by autocratic leaders who had been in power for decades. Secondly, corruption, lack of political freedoms, and nepotism were rampant. There were high unemployment rates, especially among youth in many countries of this region. Also, the rising cost of living, inequality, poverty, and economic mismanagement were other reasons.

A large proportion of the population was young, educated, and technologically connected but frustrated by the lack of opportunities and freedoms. The widespread use of social media platforms like Facebook and Twitter allowed activists to organize, share information, and galvanize support. Satellite channels like Al Jazeera played a role in broadcasting the protests and amplifying their message.

The Catalyst was the self-immolation in December 2010 of a Tunisian street vendor protesting police corruption and mistreatment. It became the spark that ignited widespread protests in Tunisia and beyond. This resulted in few political outcomes. For example, Tunisia transitioned to a democratic system with significant reforms. Egypt saw the fall of President Hosni Mubarak but later experienced a military coup, leading to the rise of Abdel Fattah el-Sisi. The uprising in Libya led to the overthrow and death of Muammar Gaddafi but plunged the country into a prolonged civil war. In Syria protests evolved into a devastating civil war, leading to massive loss of life and displacement. In Yemen, political turmoil escalated into a full-scale conflict with regional and international implications.

The Arab Spring demonstrated the power of collective action and the role of technology in mobilizing grassroots movements. However, it also underscored the challenges of transitioning from authoritarianism to democracy, particularly in fragile states. The outcomes were mixed: while Tunisia stands as a relative success story, many other countries remain mired in conflict, authoritarianism, or instability.

Social media platforms are critical tools for Muslim youth, like youth in general, to express their views, raise awareness, and mobilize support for causes. From fighting climate change and promoting gender equality to supporting Palestinian rights and raising awareness on refugee issues, digital activism has become a powerful outlet for young Muslims who use these platforms to connect with global movements.

Identity and Cultural Expression

Young Muslims face a unique challenge in navigating their identities and balancing their religious beliefs with their aspirations in secular and sometimes culturally diverse environments. Many Muslim youth grapples with how to reconcile traditional values with modern lifestyles, especially when it comes to social norms, relationships, and lifestyle choices. They seek ways to express their cultural heritage without compromising their sense of individuality and global citizenship. This can be seen in the popularity of modest fashion, where young Muslims adapt traditional Islamic dress codes into contemporary and stylish forms, creating a niche within global fashion.

In countries like Pakistan, Iran, and Turkey, young Muslims are using music, film, literature, and visual arts to explore and express their identities. Creative forms of expression enable them to address social issues, share personal experiences, and challenge stereotypes about Islam and Muslims. Online platforms have allowed for a broader dissemination of these creative works, allowing young Muslim artists to connect with international audiences and reshape narratives about their culture.

Gender Equality and Women's Empowerment

Gender equality is a priority for many Muslim youth, particularly as young women increasingly pursue education, careers, and social rights within their communities. Young Muslim women are at the forefront of advocating for gender equality, challenging traditional gender roles and advocating for reforms in education, employment, and political representation. Initiatives for women's empowerment are gaining traction across regions, from Saudi Arabia's recent reforms allowing women to drive and travel independently to grassroots movements advocating for legal reforms in countries like Morocco and Tunisia.

Young Muslim women often face dual expectations—to honor family traditions while pursuing personal aspirations. In some contexts, young women who strive for professional success, independence, or progressive social roles may face resistance from conservative segments of society. However, many have managed to push boundaries, integrating their aspirations with cultural values, often gaining support from family and community members who see the benefits of their contributions.

Spirituality and Faith in the Modern Context

Faith remains an integral part of the identity of many Muslim youths, yet they are reinterpreting what it means to be a practicing Muslim in a rapidly changing world. Many young Muslims emphasize a personal connection to faith rather than strictly adhering to cultural traditions or societal expectations. This includes a greater focus on understanding the principles of Islam, connecting with their spirituality, and advocating for interpretations that are compatible with modern values, such as social justice, compassion, and intellectual freedom.

Movements for progressive interpretations of Islam, such as those focusing on gender equality, environmental sustainability, and inclusivity, resonate with many young Muslims. They seek to apply Islamic principles in ways that align with global human rights frameworks, making their faith relevant in addressing modern social issues.

Muslim youths are at a crossroads between meeting social and family expectations and career needs. Smith-Hefner (2021) studied youths in Egypt, Jordan, Morocco, Iran, and Indonesia and concluded that they are increasingly part of a globalizing youth culture that emphasizes self-actualization and personal fulfillment, yet most have not embraced an ethics that elevates individual desires over family or group interests. Instead, the majority remain keenly aware of and responsive to the role of their families and the broader community in monitoring and evaluating their behaviors and achievements – and granting or denying the recognition of their status as a "good" or "proper" man or woman (Ghannam, 2013). Within the current socio-political context, however, achieving that status has become increasingly difficult for youth in many parts of the Muslim world.

Pedagogy of Religious Discourses

There is a need to look at the way knowledge of Islam is provided to young minds. There is a little element of analysis and discussion and the communication is mostly one way. Most people learn about their religion in fragments, primarily through their family and community. Only a few receive advanced religious education by attending formal religious schools. For the average person, the understanding of religion is shaped by what they hear from others, especially those educated in religious institutions. This knowledge often comes from places of worship during Friday prayers or through invited talks by scholars on special occasions.

Such a learning process holds true for followers of all religions including Islam. Growing up in a Muslim family and community, my understanding of Islam was shaped by these same sources. However, the understanding was superficial at best, as it relied more on passive listening than active discussion. Opportunities to ask questions were rare, and when I did dare to inquire, I was often reprimanded and warned against becoming a deviant. The pressure to conform to family and community norms was strong, which gradually shaped my identity as a Muslim—a sense of belonging I particularly cherished during festive celebrations.

In recent years, social media has emerged as a major source of information and education about religion. Unfortunately, the social media ecosystem is rife with conflicting narratives and heated debates. While it is highly influential, especially among the younger generation, there is a real danger of individuals being swayed by emotionally charged content tied to identity. This can lead to skewed and often harmful perspectives on religion.

Religious educators should strive to offer a balanced perspective, contextualizing teachings and explaining why some values conveyed in traditional stories may need to evolve with the times. They should encourage a mindset of inquiry and objective analysis, enabling individuals to differentiate fact from fiction. In this regard, it is valuable to revisit the insights of Paulo Freire, the celebrated Brazilian educator and philosopher, known for his groundbreaking work *Pedagogy of the Oppressed*. Freire introduced the concepts of "domestication" and "liberation" of the mind.

Domestication of the mind refers to the conditioning of individuals to accept and conform to the status quo, often perpetuated through education, media, or religious systems. This approach stifles critical thinking, creativity, and the ability to question authority or societal norms. In this context, learners are reduced to passive recipients of information—what Freire termed the "banking model of education." In contrast, liberation of the mind involves fostering critical consciousness. It emphasizes dialogue, mutual learning between educators and learners, and the empowerment of individuals as active participants in their own lives. Through liberation, people develop the capacity to challenge inequality and engage in collective action for societal transformation. This process helps individuals recognize oppressive structures and motivates them to work toward social change

There is an urgent need to be aware of this domestication process and support the initiatives for liberation of mind. The pedagogy imparting education and religious discourses should change.

Technology and Innovation

Technology plays a transformative role in the lives of Muslim youth, opening new pathways for education, work, and cultural exchange. Technology has created unprecedented opportunities for young Muslims, particularly in e-commerce, digital marketing, and remote work. Countries like Indonesia and Egypt have seen a rise in digital entrepreneurs and startups led by young people who use social media and digital platforms to reach global markets, create online businesses, and bypass traditional economic barriers.

Online platforms offer access to educational resources, global conversations, and intercultural exchanges that allow young Muslims to broaden their perspectives and gain skills. Digital tools enable them to engage in cross-cultural dialogues, counter misinformation about Islam, and build networks that support their career, educational, and personal development goals.

Environmental Awareness and Sustainability

Environmental sustainability is becoming a pressing issue for many young Muslims, especially those in regions vulnerable to climate change, such as North Africa and South Asia. Many young Muslims advocate for environmental conservation as part of their faith, drawing on Islamic teachings that emphasize stewardship of the Earth (*khalifah*). Youth-led initiatives address issues like deforestation, water scarcity, and pollution, which are particularly acute in countries like Bangladesh and Jordan.

In response to environmental challenges, some young Muslim entrepreneurs are launching green businesses and sustainability projects, from eco-tourism in Turkey to sustainable fashion in the Gulf. These initiatives aim to create environmentally friendly solutions that align with Islamic ethics of sustainability and stewardship.

Navigating Challenges and Building Resilience

Muslim youth in many regions face complex challenges, including political instability, discrimination, and limited economic opportunities. These challenges require resilience and adaptability, as they work to create better futures within and outside of their communities.

Muslim youth living in Western countries or facing anti-Muslim sentiment globally often deal with stereotypes, discrimination, and Islamophobia. They are increasingly engaged in initiatives that promote inclusivity, counter prejudice, and highlight the diversity within the Muslim community.

Many young Muslims cultivate resilience by building strong community networks, both locally and online. These networks provide social support, professional mentorship, and opportunities for collaboration, helping them navigate the pressures of discrimination, economic challenges, and balancing cultural identities.

Muslim youth today stand at a dynamic intersection of tradition and modernity, with aspirations that reflect both their cultural heritage and the global influences shaping their worldviews. They are ambitious, motivated, and increasingly empowered to shape their own paths in areas such as education, technology, activism, and creative expression.

While they face unique challenges, young Muslims are determined to bridge the gap between their religious values and contemporary aspirations, contributing to their societies and the world in ways that are innovative, resilient, and deeply rooted in both faith and global citizenship. Through their efforts, they are reshaping perceptions of Islam and Muslims, challenging stereotypes, and building a future that reflects both their hopes and their heritage.

References

Fady, A. Q. (2009). Understanding our Muslim youth: Problems and solutions. In *AMJA/Naif Imams, Workshop Houston, TX February.*

Freire, P. (2000). *Pedagogy of the oppressed* (M. B. Ramos, Trans.). Continuum.

Ghannam, F. (2013). *Live and die like a man: Gender dynamics in urban Egypt.* Stanford University Press.

Herrera, L., & Asef, B. (2010). *Being young and Muslim: New cultural politics in the global South and North.* Oxford Academics.

Smith-Hefner, N. J. (2021). Muslim youth and contemporary challenges. In R. Lukens-Bull & M. Woodward (Eds.), *Handbook of contemporary Islam and Muslim lives* (pp. 199-214). Springer, Cham.

CHAPTER 13
INTERFAITH DIALOGUE AND CO-EXISTENCE

Interfaith relationships and cooperation are essential aspects of social cohesion and peace-building within diverse societies, and they play a prominent role in Muslim countries and communities worldwide. Pluralism—valuing diversity and fostering mutual respect among different faiths—is integral to peaceful coexistence, yet its acceptance and implementation vary across Muslim societies. Factors such as cultural context, political stability, historical interactions with other faiths, and societal attitudes all influence the dynamics of interfaith relationships and pluralism. Here is a closer examination of the status of interfaith relationships, cooperation, and the impact of pluralism within Muslim societies and beyond.

Historical Foundations of Interfaith Relations in Islam

Islamic teachings provide a basis for interfaith tolerance and respect, evidenced by numerous historical examples where Muslims coexisted peacefully with people of other faiths. The Qu'ran encourages respectful relationships with non-Muslims and acknowledges religious diversity as part of God's design. Verses such as, "To you be your religion, and to me my religion" (Qu'ran 109:6) and "There shall be no compulsion in religion" (Qu'ran 2:256) highlight principles of religious freedom and respect.

From the early days of Islam, there were notable examples of pluralism, such as the Constitution of Medina, where Prophet Muhammad established an agreement allowing Muslims, Jews, and other groups to coexist under shared civic responsibility. Likewise, in Al-Andalus (medieval Muslim Spain), a relatively tolerant society allowed Muslims, Christians, and Jews to live together, fostering a golden age of intellectual and cultural exchange.

Contemporary Interfaith Initiatives and Cooperation

In modern times, Muslim countries and communities continue to engage in various interfaith initiatives aimed at building understanding and cooperation among different faith groups. Several Muslim nations promote interfaith harmony through government initiatives. For example, the United Arab Emirates established the Ministry of Tolerance and Coexistence and the Abrahamic Family House, which includes a mosque, church, and synagogue within the same complex. These projects aim to symbolize religious inclusivity and promote interfaith dialogue.

Numerous grassroots organizations across Muslim communities work to build interfaith understanding. In countries like Indonesia, Malaysia, and India, where religious diversity is pronounced, NGOs often lead community projects, dialogues, and workshops that bring Muslims together with people of other faiths to address common social issues such as poverty, education, and environmental sustainability.

Muslim scholars, leaders, and activists participate in interfaith dialogues through international forums like the Parliament of the World's Religions and the Alliance of Civilizations. These platforms allow for discussions on peace, social justice, and climate change, emphasizing shared values and goals across faith traditions.

Challenges to Interfaith Relations and Pluralism

Despite efforts toward cooperation, several challenges complicate interfaith relationships in Muslim societies, often stemming from political, social, or ideological tensions. Extremist groups in certain regions have fueled tensions and conflicts that undermine interfaith harmony. For instance, in countries like Iraq, Syria, and Nigeria, extremist ideologies have exacerbated sectarian violence, leading to strained relations with other faith communities. These events have damaged perceptions of Islam, creating barriers to interfaith trust and cooperation.

In some cases, political actors exploit religious identities to consolidate power or marginalize specific groups, resulting in discrimination or conflict. For example, political rhetoric that casts minority faith groups as outsiders or threats can exacerbate communal tensions, as seen in some areas of the Middle East as well as in Muslim minority countries such as Myanmar and India.

In some Muslim countries, laws and social norms may restrict the rights of minority faith communities, impacting their freedom to practice, build places of worship, or participate in public life. These restrictions can strain interfaith relations, as seen with the non-Muslims in Saudi Arabia, the Ahmadiyya and Shia minorities in Pakistan, or Christian minorities in Egypt and Indonesia, where societal attitudes or legal limitations may affect interfaith coexistence.

Positive Examples of Pluralism and Interfaith Cohesion

Despite challenges, there are numerous examples where Muslim societies have successfully fostered interfaith pluralism, creating models for peaceful coexistence and cooperation. Indonesia, the world's most populous Muslim nation, has adopted "Pancasila," a national ideology that emphasizes religious pluralism and coexistence among the nation's major religions. Interfaith groups in Indonesia engage in frequent dialogues, collaborative projects, and peacebuilding efforts, especially in regions with a history of interreligious conflict. Lebanon has a unique power-sharing model based on its diverse religious population, where different political offices are allocated to specific religious communities. Although the system is not without its challenges, it exemplifies an attempt to balance representation among various faith groups and ensure that each has a stake in governance. Senegal has a Muslim population, but its Sufi traditions emphasize tolerance and peace, resulting in a high level of religious harmony with the country's Christian minority. Interfaith events, such as annual gatherings that bring together religious leaders from different communities, reflect the spirit of mutual respect and cooperation.

Interfaith Relationships among Muslim Diaspora Communities

In Western countries, where Muslims are part of religiously diverse societies, interfaith initiatives are often led by youth and community leaders who seek to bridge gaps and counter stereotypes. In places like the United States, Canada, and the UK, Muslim youth actively participate in interfaith dialogues, advocacy groups, and service projects. These initiatives aim to foster a shared sense of community, address Islamophobia, and build alliances with other faith groups on social justice issues like refugee support, racial equity, and environmental action.

Muslim diaspora communities in multicultural societies often emphasize cultural exchange as a means of fostering mutual respect. Events such as mosque open days, interfaith dinners, and panel discussions on faith and cultural values encourage interaction and understanding between Muslims and non-Muslims, helping dispel misconceptions and build trust.

Many Muslim organizations in the West partner with churches, synagogues, and civic institutions to create educational programs that promote interfaith literacy. These collaborations help individuals learn about each other's beliefs and practices, promoting tolerance and reducing prejudice.

Dealing with Islamophobia

Islamophobia, the prejudice against and fear of Islam and Muslims, is a significant issue at the global level, often fueled by stereotypes, negative media portrayals, and the actions of extremist groups falsely representing the faith. This pervasive bias manifests in discrimination, hate crimes, and marginalization of Muslim communities worldwide. Post-9/11 geopolitics, terrorist attacks in various parts of the world, the Israel-Palestine issue, and political rhetoric have amplified fears and misconceptions, leading to stricter immigration policies, societal exclusion, and violence against Muslims.

Kumar (2012) explores the historical roots of Islamophobia and its links to Western imperialism and politics. She traces the history of anti-Muslim racism from the early modern era to the "War on Terror." Importantly, Kumar contends that Islamophobia is best understood as racism rather than as religious intolerance. In an innovative analysis of anti-Muslim racism and empire, Kumar argues that empire creates the conditions for anti-Muslim racism, which in turn sustains empire. Kumar in her updated book offered a clear and succinct explanation of how Islamophobia functions in the United States both as a set of coercive policies and as a body of ideas that take various forms: liberal, conservative, and rightwing. The matrix of anti-Muslim racism charts how various institutions—the media, think tanks, the foreign policy establishment, the university, the national security apparatus, and the legal sphere—produce and circulate this particular form of bigotry. Anti-Muslim racism not only has horrific consequences for people in Muslim countries who become the targets of an endless War on Terror but for Muslims and those who "look Muslim" in the West as well.

Sheehi (2011) goes further and examines Islamophobia from a cultural, political, and ideological lens. He examines the rise of anti-Muslim and anti-Arab sentiments in the West following the end of the Cold War. Using "Operation Desert Storm" as a watershed moment, Sheehi examines the increased mainstreaming of Muslim-baiting rhetoric and explicitly racist legislation, police surveillance, witch-trials, and discriminatory policies towards Muslims in North America and abroad. Sheehi focuses on the various genres and modalities of Islamophobia from the works of rogue academics to the commentary by mainstream journalists, to campaigns by political hacks and special interest groups.

In response, many Muslims across the globe are working tirelessly to build a more inclusive society through diverse initiatives aimed at fostering mutual respect and understanding. Islamic organizations often engage in interfaith dialogue, creating platforms where religious leaders and followers from different backgrounds can share perspectives and address common challenges. Educational campaigns dispelling myths about Islam and emphasizing its true tenets—peace, compassion, and justice—have been instrumental. Moreover, Muslim youth are increasingly visible in civic leadership, championing social justice, and promoting community service projects that benefit all citizens regardless of their beliefs. Through acts of charity, public engagement, and a commitment to inclusivity, Muslims continue to combat Islamophobia, striving to bridge divides and promote peace and unity within diverse societies. This was seen during the recent pandemic when many Muslim organizations were actively engaged in community welfare programs such as free distribution of food and reaching out to families for help and support irrespective of their faith and background.

In an interconnected world, interfaith engagement significantly influences how Muslims view their role in pluralistic societies and contributes to a broader, more inclusive global Muslim identity. By engaging in interfaith cooperation, Muslims and members of other faiths often discover shared ethical values such as compassion, justice, and respect for human dignity. These values serve as common ground, enabling collaborative responses to global challenges, from humanitarian aid to climate change and peacebuilding.

Active interfaith relationships challenge misconceptions about Islam and Muslims, helping to counter Islamophobia. Positive interfaith interactions, both within Muslim countries and in diaspora communities, create opportunities for people of different faiths to build meaningful relationships and combat negative stereotypes, fostering a more nuanced understanding of Islam. Pluralism and interfaith relationships strengthen community resilience against extremist ideologies by promoting an inclusive view of religion and society. When young Muslims see their faith as part of a pluralistic world where all beliefs are respected, they are more likely to reject divisive ideologies that promote hostility toward others.

The status of interfaith relationships and pluralism in Muslim societies is complex, marked by both achievements and ongoing challenges. While certain regions grapple with ideological and political tensions that hinder interfaith cooperation, other Muslim countries and Muslim communities abroad showcase successful models of pluralism and religious tolerance. These positive examples demonstrate that, with supportive policies, strong community initiatives, and inclusive attitudes, Muslim societies can foster interfaith harmony, embrace pluralism, and contribute to global peace.

In a changing world where religious and cultural diversity is increasingly visible, the role of Muslims in promoting interfaith understanding is crucial. Their efforts not only support social cohesion within their communities but also help to redefine Islam as a faith that values cooperation, compassion, and respect for all people. As interfaith engagement becomes more common, it holds the potential to build bridges across divides, contribute to social harmony, and inspire future generations to pursue a more inclusive vision of the world.

References

Hussain, A. (2016). *Muslims and the making of America.* Baylor University Press.

Inglehart, R. F., & Norris, P. (2009). Muslim integration into Western cultures: Between origins and destinations. *HKS Working Paper No. RWP09-007.* http://dx.doi.org/10.2139/ssrn.1354185

Kumar, D. (2012). *Islamophobia and the politics of empire.* Haymarket Books.

Sheehi, S. (2011). *Islamophobia: The ideological campaign against Muslims.* Clarity Press Inc.

Sachedina, A. (2001). *The Islamic roots of democratic pluralism.* Oxford University Press.

Yvonne, H. (Ed.) (2002). *Muslims in the West: Foundational and contemporary debates.* Oxford University Press.

CHAPTER 14
GLOBALISATION AND FUTURE OF MUSLIM SOCIETIES

The future directions for Muslim societies and the Muslim diaspora will likely be shaped by evolving identities, the transformative role of technology, and expanding cross-cultural collaborations. These three areas interact dynamically, impacting social structures, individual identities, and global perceptions. Here's a closer look at these key directions and the unique opportunities and challenges they present.

Shifting Identities: Navigating Between Past and Present

As Muslim societies and diaspora communities navigate globalization, the evolution of individual and collective identities is central. Many young Muslims are creating hybrid identities that reflect both their cultural and religious backgrounds and their experiences in multicultural, often secular societies. Young Muslims are redefining their identities by incorporating global influences, religious values, and cultural practices into personal narratives. This generation is blending traditional elements, such as modest fashion or Islamic ethics, with global trends, often creating a unique fusion of Eastern and Western values. These hybrid identities allow them to maintain their heritage while adapting to diverse environments, whether in Western diaspora communities or within evolving societies in the Middle East and Asia.

A similar observation has been offered by Duderija and Rane (2018) in their book on *Islam and the West*. They explored the complex and multifaceted relationship between Islamic and Western civilizations. The authors provide a historical overview of Islamic-Western relations, detailing periods of conflict, cooperation, and mutual influence throughout history. They argue that perceptions of Islam and the West have been shaped by colonial legacies, power dynamics, and socio-political developments, and they examine how these perceptions continue to influence policies, media narratives, and public opinion. A key focus of the book is on contemporary challenges, including the rise of Islamophobia, terrorism, and extremist ideologies, as well as Western policies toward Muslim countries. Duderija and Rane emphasize the role of dialogue, education, and intercultural engagement in overcoming misunderstandings and building more harmonious relationships. They critique both Western and Muslim responses that perpetuate polarization and highlight the potential for moderate, reformist, and inclusive Islamic thought to contribute positively to social cohesion. Through case studies and theoretical analyses, they ultimately argue for a rethinking of Muslim identity, integration, and interaction with Western societies, emphasizing shared values, respect for diversity, and collaborative efforts toward peace and mutual understanding.

Writing the editorial of the journal 'Religion' Yucel & Whyte (2023) explored the multifaceted processes through which Muslim identities are shaped within modern contexts. They focused on how Muslims navigate and reconstruct their identities amidst dynamic social, political, and cultural landscapes, often in non-majority settings. Yucel and Whyte examined both individual and collective identity negotiations, touching upon challenges such as religious discrimination, globalization, and secular influences, as well as the role of community practices, religious education, and cultural heritage. They presented case studies and theoretical insights to showcase how Muslim identities are fluid, adaptive, and informed by complex interactions with broader societal norms.

Reflecting on the Muslim identity issue in the global context Khan (2019) examines the evolution of Islamic identity over the past century, marked by the rise and influence of various Islamic revivalist movements. Khan traces how these movements have shaped contemporary Muslim identity and thought, focusing on their social, political, and ideological impacts. He explores the historical context that gave rise to Islamic revivalism, including colonialism, socio-economic struggles, and Western cultural hegemony. Khan discusses how these factors prompted efforts to reclaim and assert Islamic values and practices, often in contrast to perceived external threats and internal challenges. He delves into the diversity within revivalist movements, noting that they range from reformist and modernist approaches to more conservative and politically radical ideologies. Khan emphasizes how revivalist thought has contributed to defining what it means to be a Muslim in modern times. This identity encompasses religious devotion, cultural practices, political activism, and social norms, influenced by historical narratives, religious leaders, and contemporary events. He also discusses the role of globalization, migration, and media in shaping Islamic identity, highlighting how Muslims navigate and adapt their identities in varying contexts. Ultimately, Islam as Identity, Khan argues that while revivalism has empowered many Muslims to assert their identity and engage with modernity on their terms, it has also led to internal debates and conflicts over what constitutes "authentic" Islam. Khan underscores the ongoing negotiation of identity within diverse Muslim communities as they face contemporary challenges and opportunities, aiming to reconcile tradition and modernity.

Hefner (2010) in his scholarly work on religion and modernities within Islam explores the evolution and transformation of Muslim identities and subjectivities in response to the challenges and contexts of modernity. Hefner delves into the plurality of experiences and interpretations within Islam, demonstrating that there is no single or monolithic Muslim response to modernity. He emphasizes how different Muslim societies have grappled with changes brought by colonialism, nationalism, globalization, and sociopolitical dynamics, leading to diverse and contextually rooted expressions of Islam. Hefner argues that the emergence of modern Muslim subjectivities reflects not merely the adaptation to secular modernity but also an active reinterpretation and negotiation of religious traditions and beliefs. By examining case studies across different regions, Hefner illustrates the complex interplay between tradition, reform, and individual agency, showing how Muslims navigate issues such as secular governance, civil society, gender norms, and social change while remaining deeply rooted in Islamic frameworks. Hefner situates these developments within a broader theoretical framework of "multiple modernities," suggesting that modernity itself is a multifaceted and culturally mediated phenomenon, not a homogenous or purely Western-driven process. Overall, Hefner's analysis highlights the diversity and adaptability of Muslim subjectivities, reflecting a dynamic and evolving relationship between religion and contemporary life within Muslim societies and diaspora communities.

Younger generations in Muslim societies increasingly emphasize inclusivity and justice as core aspects of their identity. Many seek a faith-based commitment to social change, prioritizing issues such as gender equality, environmental stewardship, and refugee rights. This focus aligns with Islamic teachings and resonates globally, creating a shared platform for advocacy with peers from other backgrounds.

Many Muslims today seek interpretations of Islam that balance traditional identity with modern outlook, such as gender roles, science, and modern education. This adaptive approach allows for a personalized, spiritually fulfilling practice that still aligns with their broader community's values. In many diaspora contexts, Muslims are leading discussions about integrating Islam into secular societies, aiming to make religious practice relevant, inclusive, and socially engaged.

The Transformational Role of Technology

The digital age is dramatically transforming how Muslims connect, learn, and express their identities. Technology is not only fostering connections within the Muslim community but also enabling greater interaction with the global community.

Social media and online platforms provide spaces for Muslims across the globe to connect, share experiences, and express diverse interpretations of their faith. Influencers, scholars, and activists leverage these platforms to discuss issues ranging from theology to mental health and social justice, democratizing religious discourse and making it accessible. This fosters a sense of global community, bridging cultural differences and creating a platform for diverse voices within the *Ummah* (global Muslim community).

Many young Muslims are using technology to drive innovation, establishing startups that cater to both religious needs and global demands. This includes the development of "halal tech" (e.g., prayer apps, online Islamic education platforms, and halal product marketplaces) as well as ventures focused on social good. An assortment of online courses is now offered on Islamic banking and finance, entrepreneurship, Halal business, humanitarian aid, Islamic fintech, and Islamic management (https://netversity.io/courses). Digital entrepreneurship allows Muslims, particularly in the diaspora, to contribute economically to their societies and promote cultural awareness and understanding.

Technology is increasing access to quality education across Muslim societies, helping close literacy and knowledge gaps in regions with limited traditional infrastructure. Online learning platforms make it possible for students in rural or underserved areas to access international educational resources. Moreover, tech-facilitated education is reshaping the way Islamic studies are approached, with modern interpretations that address contemporary societal issues.

The internet, while a powerful tool for connection, has also contributed to misinformation and Islamophobia. Many Muslims and advocacy organizations use social media to counteract negative stereotypes, raise awareness about Muslim contributions to society, and engage in public discourse. Technology provides a platform for Muslims to represent themselves and combat prejudice through direct, authentic narratives.

Building Alliances and Global Partnerships

As Muslim communities become increasingly interconnected with other cultural and religious groups, there is a growing potential for cross-cultural collaboration in various spheres, including education, business, social justice, and cultural exchange.

Cross-cultural and interfaith initiatives are critical in fostering mutual respect and understanding. Muslim organizations are engaging in partnerships with other faith and cultural groups, participating in community service projects, and advocating for shared values like social justice and environmental responsibility. These collaborations not only bridge cultural gaps but also challenge stereotypes, allowing for positive, humanizing interactions that promote inclusivity.

Many Muslim countries and communities are investing in economic collaborations to address shared challenges. The UAE, Qatar, and Turkey, for instance, are forming economic partnerships focused on innovation, green technology, and infrastructure development. These cross-border initiatives promote job creation, sustainable development, and economic stability, improving conditions for both Muslim societies and their neighbors.

Academic and cultural exchanges enable young Muslims to broaden their worldviews, gain knowledge, and share their unique perspectives on global platforms. Universities in Muslim countries are partnering with Western institutions to create exchange programs, joint research projects, and student internships. By facilitating international learning and engagement, these programs encourage understanding and create future leaders who can bridge cultural and ideological divides.

Muslim societies are increasingly active in addressing global issues such as climate change, refugee crises, and public health. Organizations like Islamic Relief, the Aga Khan Development Network, and the International Federation of Red Cross and Red Crescent Societies lead collaborative projects in disaster relief, healthcare, and environmental sustainability. Muslim countries and communities work with international partners to address these shared issues, contributing positively to global development and stability.

Looking Ahead

While the future holds immense potential, there are challenges that Muslim societies and diaspora communities must address to make the most of these opportunities.

In diaspora settings, Muslims often face pressures to conform to social norms while preserving their heritage. Balancing integration with cultural authenticity is an ongoing challenge, especially amid rising anti-immigrant sentiments in some parts of the world. Nonetheless, many Muslims are finding ways to showcase their identities positively and openly, advocating for social policies that support multiculturalism.

Technology has the potential to equalize opportunities, but disparities in digital access and literacy continue to affect many regions. Bridging the digital divide is essential for empowering young Muslims to access education, entrepreneurial opportunities, and global networks.

Cultural misunderstandings and stereotypes often obstruct collaboration. Initiatives that promote intercultural education, challenge stereotypes and highlight shared values can help dismantle these misconceptions and build bridges.

As Muslim societies seek economic and social development; they must also address issues of sustainability and resource allocation. By prioritizing initiatives that align with Islamic values of stewardship and social justice, Muslim countries can model responsible development that benefits both their communities and the broader world.

Muslim societies and diaspora communities stand at a crossroads, with significant opportunities to shape a future that respects their rich heritage while embracing progress, innovation, and cross-cultural understanding. Through evolving identities, the adoption of technology, and robust cross-cultural collaborations, Muslims have the potential to influence global culture positively, contribute to economic and technological advancements, and promote peace and understanding across societies. In the coming years, these developments will allow Muslim societies and diaspora communities to not only navigate modernity but also to thrive within it, forging a path that values diversity, cultivates interfaith and intercultural respect, and leaves a lasting, positive impact on the world.

References

Darwish, H. (2022). The (in)compatibility of Islam with modernity: (Mis)understanding of secularity/secularism in the Arab and Islamicate worlds. In H. N. Akil & S. Maddanu (Eds.), *Global modernity from coloniality to pandemic* (pp. 103-120). Cambridge University Press.

Duderija, A., & Rane, H. (2018). *Islam and the West*. Palgrave Macmillan Cham. https://doi.org/10.1007/978-3-319-92510-3

Hefner, R. (2010). Modern Muslim subjectivities: Religion and multiple modernities within Islam. In *The New Cambridge History of Islam* (pp. 1035-1050). Cambridge University Press.

Khan, M. A. M. (2019). Islam as identity: After a century of Islamic revivalism. In *Islam and good governance* (pp. 215-232). Palgrave Macmillan, New York.

Martin, R. C. (2010). Hidden bodies in Islam: Secular Muslim identities in modern (and premodern) societies. In G. Marranci (Ed.), *Muslim societies and the challenge of secularization: An interdisciplinary approach* (pp. 47-63). Springer.

Yucel, S., & Whyte, S. (2023). Muslim identity formation in contemporary societies. *Religion, 14*, 1296. https://doi.org/10.3390/rel4101296

CHAPTER 15
ISLAM AND DEMOCRACY

Overview

Just as there are many forms of democracy—making it a "contested concept"—the discussion around Islam and democracy has deeply divided both Muslim and scholarly communities. These debates can be broadly categorized into two main areas. First, there are internal debates within the Muslim world, ongoing for over a century, focusing on governance, the value of democracy, and its compatibility with Islamic principles. These discussions involve a range of perspectives, including religious scholars who either support or critique democratic ideals, politicians who either promote or resist democratization and secular thinkers who argue for or against liberal democracy from diverse ideological viewpoints. Second, there are academic debates, primarily taking place in Western institutions but also increasingly within Muslim countries. These "secondary" debates not only track and assess the primary discussions but often influence them. In some cases, scholarly contributions, such as early Orientalist works, have sparked primary debates. Academic literature also encompasses empirical studies on the status of democracy in specific regions or countries. Over recent years, the output from both sets of debates has expanded significantly, showing notable evolution and, at times, dramatic shifts in participants' positions (Abdelwahab El-Affendi, 2009).

Before proceeding further let us fact-check the status of democracy and socioeconomic development taken together the average of 50 Muslim countries. According to the key criteria used to evaluate a country's degree of democratization[12] and socioeconomic development, Muslim countries score lower than the world average. Although 60

---

[12] The degree of democratization in a country is evaluated using several key criteria, which collectively measure the presence and effectiveness of democratic institutions, practices, and principles. These criteria include:

1. Free and Fair Elections: Regular, transparent, and competitive elections where all eligible citizens can participate without discrimination or intimidation; equal access to voting and candidacy; independent election monitoring to ensure integrity.

2. Political Participation: Broad public involvement in political decision-making, legal frameworks ensuring freedom to form political parties and participate in civil society organizations; absence of barriers based on gender, ethnicity, religion, or other identities.

3. Rule of Law: An independent judiciary that enforces laws impartially, accountability of government officials under the law; protection of human rights, including the rights to life, liberty, and property.

4. Separation of Powers: Clear division of responsibilities among the executive, legislative, and judicial branches of government; checks and balances to prevent the abuse of power by any one branch.

5. Civil Liberties: Protection of freedoms such as speech, press, assembly, religion, and association; legal safeguards against arbitrary arrest, detention, or censorship.

6. Accountability and Transparency: Mechanisms for holding public officials accountable, such as independent anti-corruption bodies and regular audits; transparent decision-making processes accessible to the public.

7. Pluralism and Political Competition: Existence of multiple political parties or movements representing diverse viewpoints; freedom for opposition parties to function and campaign without fear of repression.

8. Media Independence: A free and independent press that can report on government actions without censorship; Access to diverse sources of information for citizens.

9. Minority Rights: Protection of the rights of minorities and marginalized groups; policies that prevent discrimination and promote equality.

10. Public Trust and Civic Engagement: Citizens' confidence in democratic institutions and leaders; active engagement of the population in political processes, such as voting and public consultations.

percent of all countries in the world are electoral democracies, only 14 percent of Muslim countries are. The average gross national income per capita of Muslim countries, despite their substantial oil revenues, is $9,100; the global average is $13,200. The average life expectancy in Muslim countries is 66 years, compared to the world average of 69 years, and Muslim countries also have a higher average child mortality rate (49) than the global average (34). And while the average literacy rate worldwide is 84 percent, with an average of 7.5 years of schooling, Muslim countries have an average literacy rate of 73 percent and an average of 5.8 years of schooling (Kuru (2021).

Assessing the levels of democracy in Muslim-majority countries involves analyzing various indices that measure democratic practices worldwide. One such resource is the 'Democracy Index' published by The Economist Intelligence Unit (EIU), which evaluates countries based on criteria such as electoral process, civil liberties, political participation, and government functioning.

According to the 2022 Democracy Index, Muslim-majority countries exhibit a wide range of democratic practices. For instance, Malaysia is categorized as a "Flawed democracy" with a score of 6.41, ranking 64th globally. In contrast, countries like Afghanistan and Saudi Arabia are classified as "Authoritarian regimes," with scores of 0.32 and 2.52, ranking 167th and 141st, respectively.

Hathout (1995) an Egyptian Physician in his book entitled *Reading the Muslim Mind* explored in length the relationship between Islam and democracy, examining compatibility, historical contexts, and the challenges involved. Hathout maintains that democracy, when understood as a system of governance that promotes justice, accountability, consultation, and the rule of law, can align with Islamic values. He emphasizes the Islamic concept of *shura* (consultation), which he views as a fundamental component of Islamic governance and decision-making. In his view, *shura* reflects a democratic spirit, as it involves collective deliberation and public input. This practice can be seen as a parallel to modern democratic institutions that encourage participation, dialogue, and representation in governance. Furthermore, the author highlights that Islam places a strong emphasis on justice and moral accountability, values that are also central to democratic systems. Islamic teachings call for leaders to be just and accountable to their people, advocating for the rule of law and ethical governance. He argues that Islam's ethical framework promotes equality, fairness, and respect for individual rights, which are compatible with democratic ideals. Hathout contends that Islam is not a rigid or monolithic system; rather, it is adaptable and capable of accommodating different forms of governance, including democratic structures. He points out that Islamic teachings are meant to be interpreted in light of changing societal needs, allowing for diverse political arrangements that uphold core Islamic values.

Despite affirming the compatibility of Islam and democracy, Hathout acknowledges that there are challenges to their integration. These challenges often arise not from the religion itself but from historical, political, and cultural contexts. He criticizes authoritarian regimes that misuse Islam to justify repressive policies, giving the impression that Islam is incompatible with democratic governance.

Hathout calls for a distinction between Islam as a faith and the political practices of certain Muslim states.

Hathout also touches on the importance of religious tolerance and pluralism within Islamic thought. He argues that democratic governance can support religious diversity and protect individual freedoms, aligning with Islam's tradition of tolerance and coexistence with other faiths. This further supports his argument that Islam can coexist with democratic values that prioritize pluralism and human rights.

Hathout concludes that Islam is inherently supportive of democratic principles when they are understood within an ethical framework that emphasizes justice, accountability, and consultation. He argues that any perceived incompatibility stems more from cultural and political contexts than from Islam's core teachings.

There are arguments both in support and opposition on the issue of the compatibility of Islam with democratic principles. Here we look at both sides of the argument.

Islam vs. Democracy: The Great Debate

A significant number of modern Islamic scholars and thinkers, such as Rachid Ghannouchi and Abdurrahman Wahid, have championed the compatibility of Islam with democratic governance. Their work shows that Islamic thought can evolve to embrace democracy while staying true to religious values, emphasizing human rights, political participation, and good governance. Following are arguments suggesting the compatibility of Islam with a democratic system.

Islamic Emphasis on Shura (Consultation): Islam encourages the concept of *shura*, which translates to "consultation." The Qu'ran emphasizes that leaders should consult with their communities when making decisions (Qu'ran 42:38). This concept is similar to democratic governance principles, which involve public participation and collective decision-making. Many scholars argue that *shura* aligns with democratic practices such as parliamentary processes and public debate.

Justice and Accountability as Core Islamic Principles: Islam places great emphasis on justice, equality, and accountability of rulers. For example, the Prophet Muhammad emphasized fairness and just leadership and warned against tyranny. Democratic governance also seeks to promote justice and accountability through systems of checks and balances and equal treatment under the law, suggesting compatibility with Islamic values.

Historical Precedents in Islamic Governance: The early Islamic community, especially during the Rashidun Caliphate, demonstrated elements of democratic principles. Leaders were selected through consultation and consent, reflecting participatory governance and accountability. Although historical contexts differ from modern democracies, this precedent shows that Islamic societies have a tradition of governance that involves collective decision-making.

Compatibility with Human Rights and Pluralism: Many Islamic teachings align with the principles of human dignity, justice, and social welfare, which are central to democratic systems. Islamic ethics emphasize the protection of life, property, religious freedom, and justice. These values are compatible with democratic ideals that promote human rights and protect minority voices.

Flexibility and Adaptability of Islamic Law (Shariah): Shariah, or Islamic law, is not monolithic but varies widely based on interpretation and context. This flexibility allows room for Muslims to integrate democratic principles within the framework of Islamic governance. Many Muslim countries have adopted democratic practices, such as elections and constitutional governance, within an Islamic context.

Separation of Religious and Political Authority in Some Contexts: While not universal, some Islamic traditions advocate for the separation of religious and political authority. This separation allows for political pluralism and democratic governance without state enforcement of religious norms. In countries like Indonesia and Tunisia, democratic practices have been successfully implemented alongside a strong Islamic culture.

Democratic Principles of Consensus-Building and Ijma *(Consensus)*: The principle of *ijma*, or consensus among scholars and the community, is foundational in Islamic jurisprudence. Democratic governance similarly involves building consensus through debate, negotiation, and public participation. This shared commitment to collective decision-making highlights areas of compatibility.

Growing Practice of Democracy in Muslim Countries: Many Muslim countries have incorporated democratic practices such as multiparty elections, constitutions, and civil rights protections. Countries like Malaysia, Indonesia, and Tunisia have demonstrated that Islamic values can coexist with democratic institutions, challenging the narrative that Islam and democracy are inherently incompatible.

Islam's Advocacy for Social Justice and Welfare: Islam emphasizes the importance of social justice, fairness, and the welfare of all members of society, which aligns well with democratic ideals that strive to ensure equality and welfare for citizens. Islamic teachings against oppression and injustice resonate strongly with democratic principles of governance aimed at protecting citizens' rights and promoting social equity.

Here are some arguments identifying the conflict between Islam and democracy.

Islamic Law (Shariah) Supersedes Secular Legislation: Critics argue that Islam's legal framework, known as Shariah, is rooted in divine revelation, making it inflexible and resistant to popular sovereignty. In democratic systems, laws are created, amended, or repealed by the will of the people through elected representatives. In contrast, the divine nature of Islamic law limits the extent to which human beings can make or alter laws, which may clash with democratic norms that place legislative power in the hands of the electorate.

Absence of Separation of Religion and State: A common critique is that Islam lacks a clear separation between religion and state, making it fundamentally at odds with democratic principles that prioritize secular governance. In many interpretations of Islam, religious leaders hold authority over political matters, potentially undermining democratic pluralism and the secular governance structures central to most democracies.

Authority and Sovereignty Belong to Allah, Not the People: In Islamic teachings, ultimate sovereignty belongs to Allah, meaning that no human-made system can fully override divine laws. Democracy, by contrast, is built on the idea that authority derives from the will of the people. This discrepancy is seen as a fundamental incompatibility by some, as Islamic governance often implies that divine rules cannot be modified or repealed by majority decision, thus limiting democratic rule.

Islamic Rejection of Unrestricted Freedom of Speech: Many democratic systems protect the freedom of speech, including criticism of religion and government. In contrast, Islamic norms may impose restrictions on speech, particularly if it is seen as blasphemous or disrespectful to religious figures and principles. This curtailment of free expression and open debate could be seen as incompatible with democratic norms that emphasize individual rights and open discourse. In many countries where Shariah has become a basis of legislation, new laws have been passed to punish blasphemy and apostasy. These laws not only restrict religious freedom and freedom of expression but also punish dissenting religious and political voices (Kuru, 2020).

Role of Gender in Islamic Governance: Critics point out that traditional Islamic teachings often place women in subordinate roles in society and politics, which contradicts democratic principles of equality and equal participation. In some interpretations, women cannot assume leadership roles, which undermines their ability to participate fully in democratic institutions. This gender inequality can present a barrier to the implementation of democratic norms that require the equal treatment of all citizens.

Focus on Collective Duty Rather than Individual Rights: Islam places a strong emphasis on community and collective obligations (e.g., prayer, charity, social behavior).

In contrast, democracy emphasizes individual autonomy and personal rights. Some critics argue that the communal nature of Islamic governance may conflict with democratic ideals that prioritize the individual's freedom and rights over collective religious duties.

Potential for Theocratic Rule and Authoritarian Interpretations: Throughout history, there have been instances where Islamic governance has devolved into authoritarian theocratic rule, with power concentrated in the hands of religious leaders who claim to act on divine authority. This concentration of power can be seen as incompatible with democratic governance, which relies on checks and balances, political pluralism, and limited governmental power.

Lack of Compatibility with Secularism: Democracy often necessitates the accommodation of secular ideologies and values, including a plurality of beliefs and lifestyles. Some interpretations of Islam reject secularism as antithetical to the faith, leading to potential conflict with democratic governance, which must accommodate diverse perspectives, including non-religious and alternative belief systems.

Incompatibility of Some Hudud (Fixed Islamic Punishments) with Democratic Values: The implementation of *hudud* punishments, which include corporal penalties such as flogging or amputation, can be seen as incompatible with democratic values emphasizing human rights, due process, and the prohibition of cruel and unusual punishment. Critics argue that these practices can lead to human rights abuses that would violate international norms upheld by democratic systems.

Potential for Religious Extremism and Suppression of Minority Beliefs: In some contexts, the blending of Islam and governance has led to discrimination or suppression of religious minorities and dissenting beliefs, which is contrary to the inclusivity and protection of minority rights that democracy demands. Critics argue that states guided by strict Islamic law may suppress religious pluralism and impose harsh penalties on apostasy or deviation from orthodoxy, limiting the scope for a truly democratic society.

Rigid Adherence to Tradition versus Democratic Flexibility: Islam, especially in its conservative interpretations, may emphasize the preservation of traditional values and adherence to the past, which can make adapting to new societal needs difficult. In contrast, democracy thrives on adaptability, reform, and the capacity to shift policies based on popular will and evolving societal norms. This rigidity is seen as a point of tension.

These arguments emphasize structural, legal, and cultural aspects of Islam that some critics argue are incompatible with democratic governance. They highlight concerns related to sovereignty, lawmaking, gender equality, religious authority, and human rights, suggesting areas where tension between Islamic principles and democratic norms may arise.

Despite areas of compatibility, there are significant challenges to integrating Islam and democracy. One central issue is the interpretation of Islamic law or *Shariah*. While some view Shariah as immutable and divinely ordained, others interpret it more flexibly and adaptively that allows for democratic governance. Tensions arise when rigid interpretations of *Shariah* conflict with democratic principles, such as freedom of speech, gender equality, and individual rights.

Another challenge lies in political and historical factors rather than religious doctrine itself. Authoritarian regimes, colonial legacies, and external geopolitical pressures have often stifled democratic movements in the Muslim world. Leaders in some Muslim states have leveraged religious rhetoric to suppress dissent and maintain power, thereby creating an impression that Islam is incompatible with democracy. This political use of religion can perpetuate a narrative of conflict between Islamic principles and democratic governance.

Ahmad (2005) presents a nuanced view of how Islam and democracy can coexist while acknowledging the complexities and challenges of aligning democratic practices with Islamic principles in modern contexts. He argues for an "Islamic democracy" model that respects the foundational principles of Islam while incorporating democratic governance elements such as elections, civic participation, and accountability. According to him, Islamic governance places ultimate sovereignty in God's law (Shariah) and requires leaders to act within these moral and legal bounds.

Kuru (2021) in his report "The Ulema-State Alliance: A Barrier to Democracy and Development in the Muslim World", examines how the historical collaboration between religious scholars (ulema) and political authorities has impeded democratic progress and economic development in Muslim countries. He traces the origins of the ulema-state alliance to the mid-11th century when political rulers began to co-opt religious scholars to legitimize their authority. This partnership marginalized independent intellectuals and merchants, leading to intellectual stagnation and economic decline. The alliance promoted a rigid interpretation of Islam, emphasizing conformity and discouraging dissent. By presenting their interpretations as divine commandments, the ulema and political rulers suppressed alternative viewpoints, hindering the development of pluralistic and democratic ideas.

Institutions like madrasas and governmental agencies, such as Egypt's Al-Azhar and Turkey's Directorate of Religious Affairs called Diyanet, became instruments of the ulema-state alliance, propagating state-sanctioned religious interpretations. Financially, the alliance relied on external funding sources, notably oil rents since the 1970s, to sustain its institutions and maintain control over religious and economic life.

Kuru argues that the ulema-state alliance has been a significant barrier to democratization and development in the Muslim world. By suppressing intellectual freedom and maintaining authoritarian governance structures, the alliance has perpetuated underdevelopment and hindered societal progress.

To overcome these challenges, Kuru suggests dismantling the ulema-state alliance by promoting independent scholarship, encouraging economic diversification away from rentier economies, and fostering environments conducive to democratic governance and intellectual pluralism.

Democratization in the Muslim World: The Path Forward

The political history of many Muslim states shows a complex relationship with democracy. During the early years of Islam, the concept of leadership was shaped by the *caliphate*, where leaders were chosen through consensus or community approval among the elites. While not democratic in the modern sense, the notion of public consultation and accountable governance was evident in this system.

In contemporary times, Muslim countries display varying degrees of adherence to democratic norms. Countries such as Indonesia, Turkey, Tunisia, and Malaysia have sought to incorporate democratic practices within their governance frameworks. These cases illustrate how Islamic values can coexist with democratic structures, creating systems that are uniquely shaped by both religious and secular norms.

The path to harmonizing Islam and democracy lies in fostering inclusive political systems that respect religious values while upholding democratic freedoms. Engaging in open, respectful dialogue among religious scholars, political leaders, and civil society is essential to resolving potential conflicts between religious and secular ideals.

Efforts should also focus on education and reform, promoting interpretations of Islamic teachings that emphasize tolerance, pluralism, and equality. Many scholars argue that Islam is inherently dynamic and adaptable, capable of evolving to meet the challenges of modern governance.

Kuru (2021) makes a candid analysis of the democracy in Muslim countries over centuries and offers four recommendations for policymakers and analysts who want to promote democracy and development in Muslim countries. According to him first of all it is important to acknowledge the problem of authoritarianism and underdevelopment that plagues most Muslim countries. It is counterproductive to deny it by hiding behind cultural relativism or other discourses and excuses. Second, it is necessary to cease solely blaming either Islam or Western colonialism. Accusations of Islam as an impediment to development are unfounded; Islam was perfectly compatible with progress in its early history, and the Muslim world continued to produce brilliant thinkers even in later periods. Moreover, the contemporary Muslim world is not an authoritarian and underdeveloped block; it includes some cases of democratisation and development. And while Western colonialism was undoubtedly detrimental to Muslim countries, it did not start their problems. Solely blaming Western imperialism detracts from the domestic problems of Muslim countries. Third, it is crucial to understand how the ulema-state alliance has marginalised intellectuals and economic entrepreneurs in the Muslim world. This does not mean calling for an anti-ulema witch-hunt or seeking stateless anarchy. Instead, it is a call to create open, meritocratic, and competitive systems where the political, religious, intellectual, and economic classes are able to operate autonomously, and none is able to dominate. Such a reform requires the expansion of freedom of thought, by abolishing apostasy and blasphemy laws, and a deeper protection of private properties by preventing the state's seizure of them. The reform also necessitates an institutionalisation of separation between religion and the state. Islam is not inherently opposed to that. There was a certain level of separation between religious and political authorities in early Islamic history. The fourth and final recommendation relates to the economy. Oil rents have funded ulema-state alliances for the past five decades. Soon, these rents may lose their importance with the depletion of reserves, rise of domestic consumption, and/or innovation of alternative energy technologies. Many Muslim countries will need economic restructuring and innovations to be prepared for the challenges of the post-oil era. To maintain long-term stability and prosperity, these countries need to build productive systems that encourage entrepreneurship. Such a reform requires that the ulema-state alliance cease to control sociopolitical life.

A transition towards more open socioeconomic and intellectual systems will create many opportunities for Muslim countries and their Western counterparts, in terms of investment and production. Following failed military and political engagements, some Western countries have tended to disengage from most parts of the Muslim world. Instead, a newly defined partnership between Muslim and Western countries may help reform processes toward democratisation and development. Furthermore, these reforms may provide stronger intellectual and socioeconomic bases for any new engagement between the two.

To sum up, the relationship between Islam and democracy is complex and multifaceted, influenced by historical, cultural, and political factors as well as theological interpretations. While challenges to reconciling Islamic values with democratic governance persist, they are not insurmountable. Through mutual respect, dialogue, and thoughtful adaptation, Islam and democracy can coexist and even complement each other, offering pathways to just, inclusive, and equitable governance for Muslim societies and beyond.

References

Islam, M. N., & Islam, M. S. (2017). Islam and Democracy: Conflicts and Congruence. *Religions,* 8(6), 104-. doi:10.3390/rel8060104

Ahmad, K. (2005). Islam and Democracy: Some Conceptual and Contemporary Dimensions. *Policy Perspectives*, 2(1), 15–32.

Islam, M.N., Islam, M.S. (2020). Islam and Democracy: A Philosophical Debate. In: Islam and Democracy in South Asia. Palgrave Macmillan, Cham.

Abdelwahab El-Affendi (2009). Democracy and Islam. Oxford Bibliographies.

Kalin, M. (2023). Democracy and Islam in the Middle East. In: Maggino, F. (eds) *Encyclopaedia of Quality of Life and Well-Being Research*. Springer, Cham.

Hathout, H. (1995). *Reading the Muslim Mind* (2nd ed.). American Trust Publications.

Kuru A.T. (2021). *The Ulema-State Alliance: A Barrier to Democracy and Development in the Muslim World*. Institute for Global Change.

Kuru, A.T. (2020). "Execution for a Facebook Post? Why Blasphemy is a Capital Offense in Some Muslim Countries", The Conversation, 20 February 2020, https://theconversation.com/

CHAPTER 16
ISLAM AND GENDER EQUITY

Overview

Gender issues in Islam have become a focal point of both internal discourse and external critique, sparking considerable debate over whether Islam promotes or impedes gender equality. This debate is particularly relevant given that Muslim societies encompass a broad spectrum of attitudes toward women's rights, ranging from progressive reforms to deeply conservative practices.

The role and treatment of women in Islam touch upon essential aspects of law, culture, politics, and human rights, making it a significant topic of scholarly and public interest. Critics often raise concerns about practices perceived as discriminatory—such as unequal inheritance laws, male guardianship, restrictions on women's dress, or limitations on their public participation. On the other hand, many Muslims and scholars argue that Islam granted unprecedented rights to women for its time and that contemporary issues often stem from patriarchal cultural practices rather than religious mandates.

Understanding these issues is crucial for promoting informed discussions, challenging stereotypes, and fostering equitable treatment. It also helps highlight the dynamic nature of religious interpretation and the need for dialogue and reform within communities to ensure justice and equality.

The treatment of women in Islam is shaped by various interpretations of Qur'anic verses and Hadith, reflecting differing cultural, social, and historical influences. While core Islamic teachings grant women rights and emphasize dignity and justice, patriarchal customs, misinterpretations, and restrictive social practices can hinder their realization. Efforts to reconcile traditional teachings with modern gender equity often drive ongoing debates and reforms. Following verses from the Qur'an stipulate spiritual and human equality between men and women.

"O mankind, fear your Lord, who created you from one soul and created from it its mate and dispersed from both of them many men and women..." (Qur'an 4:1)

"Indeed, the Muslim men and Muslim women, the believing men and believing women...the patient men and patient women...the remembering men and remembering women – for them, Allah has prepared forgiveness and a great reward." (Qur'an 33:35)

These verses emphasize that men and women are spiritually equal before God and are equally accountable for their deeds. Both genders are promised spiritual rewards based on their actions and faith, highlighting the Qur'an's recognition of their intrinsic worth. Progressive Islamic scholars often cite these verses to assert that any cultural practices that discriminate against women are contrary to the core teachings of Islam. Conservative interpretations may emphasize other verses that delineate gender roles in public and family life, viewing them as a balanced system of *complementary duties rather than strict equality.* Often the following verse from the Qur'an is cited in support of specific gender roles.

> *"Men are the protectors and maintainers of women because Allah has given one more (strength) than the other, and because they support them from their means..."* (Qur'an 4:34)

The Qur'an and Hadith emphasize mutual love, respect, and kindness between spouses. Marriage is depicted as a partnership based on compassion, support, and moral conduct. The verse referring to men as "protectors and maintainers" has been interpreted differently across time and cultures. Traditional interpretations view it as an acknowledgment of men's financial responsibility within a marriage. In some cases, this is cited to justify a male's authority within the household, which, when abused, can lead to patriarchal control over women. Modern interpretations stress mutual responsibility and argue that "protection" should not be equated with dominance but rather as a reminder of familial care and support. The Prophet's encouragement of kind treatment of wives is often cited by reformists as evidence that Islam does not condone domestic abuse or oppressive behavior.

The Treatment of Women: Different Interpretations

Legal Testimony: Qur'anic Basis

> *"...And bring two witnesses from among your men. If there are not two men [available], then a man and two women from those whom you accept as witnesses..."* (Qur'an 2:282).

In financial contracts, the requirement for two female witnesses alongside one male has been subject to debate. Some argue it was context-specific, reflecting a historical period when women generally lacked legal experience.

Critics claim it implies a diminished capacity for women in legal matters. Reformists and modern scholars propose contextual readings, suggesting that the ruling aimed to protect women from societal pressures at the time. Contemporary applications differ, with some legal systems disregarding gender distinctions in witness testimony altogether.

Polygamy: Qur'anic Basis

"...Marry those that please you of [other] women, two, three, or four. But if you fear that you will not be just, then [marry only] one..." (Qur'an 4:3)

The Qur'an permits polygamy under strict conditions, with justice among wives emphasized as a precondition. Critics view this allowance as discriminatory against women, while defenders argue that it provided social welfare benefits for widows and orphans in historical contexts. Today, many Muslim countries either limit or prohibit polygamy in practice, with scholars arguing that true "justice" is difficult to achieve, thus aligning more closely with monogamous marriage.

Inheritance Rights: Qur'anic Basis

"To the male, a portion equal to that of two females..." (Qur'an:11)

The Qur'an grants women inheritance rights, a significant departure from pre-Islamic customs where women were often excluded from inheritance entirely. However, the share allocated to women is often half that of men in equivalent cases, based on the notion that men bear greater financial responsibility within the family. Some critics argue this reflects gender inequality. Defenders claim it reflects a context-based system of financial responsibility and social welfare, where men are required to provide for their families, while women's share is solely for their own use. Modern efforts to address perceptions of inequality include discussions about broader financial fairness, such as sharing responsibilities and emphasizing equitable treatment within inheritance laws in contemporary contexts.

Education and Participation in Society

The Prophet said, "Seeking knowledge is an obligation upon every Muslim." Islam places a high value on education for both men and women. Historical examples include prominent female scholars like Aisha bint Abu Bakr and Fatima al-Fihri. She is credited with founding the al-Qarawiyyin Mosque in 857–859 CE in Morocco. The al-Qarawiyyin Mosque subsequently developed into a teaching institution, which became the modern University of al-Qarawiyyin in 1963. Nonetheless, access to education and public participation for women varies widely across Muslim countries, often shaped by cultural norms rather than purely religious doctrines.

The Prophet often encouraged women to learn and engage in discussions on faith. He established separate teaching sessions for women, recognizing their right to religious education. Female scholars, known as *muhaddithat* (female narrators of hadith), played an essential role in transmitting religious knowledge. Aisha bint Abu Bakr's scholarly influence is among the best-known examples, but hundreds of other women scholars existed during the early centuries of Islam, with their contributions documented in various biographies and historical records.

Economic Rights of Women

Islam granted women rights to own and manage property, a radical change from pre-Islamic customs that often denied such privileges. For example, women retained control over their dowries, could inherit wealth, and had the freedom to conduct business. Historical records indicate that many women in early Islamic society were traders, landowners, and craftswomen. The Prophet's wives, including Khadijah and Zaynab bint Jahsh (a skilled leatherworker), exemplify how women could be financially independent and participate actively in commerce.

Social and Legal Rights

Women in early Islam had the right to accept or reject marriage proposals. They could stipulate conditions in their marriage contracts and retain the right to seek divorce (known as *khula*) if necessary. The Prophet Muhammad spoke against forced marriages, emphasizing the necessity of women's consent.

The Qur'anic reforms introduced a system of inheritance that, for the first time, granted women a legally protected share of family wealth. While the share was often half that of a male counterpart in specific contexts, it was revolutionary compared to previous customs that entirely excluded women from inheritance.

Women in early Islamic society participated in public affairs, including military activities and governance. For instance, Nusaybah binti Ka'ab (Umm Ammarah) was a warrior who defended the Prophet in the Battle of Uhud, demonstrating women's active roles in military efforts when needed. Al-Shifa binti Abdullah was a prominent figure in public administration, as she was appointed by the Caliph Umar ibn al-Khattab to oversee the regulation of markets in Medina, reflecting women's leadership capabilities and public influence.

While some restrictions existed in legal testimony (as in Qur'anic verses regarding financial contracts), women could serve as witnesses in various capacities and testify in court. This reflects a degree of legal agency and participation within judicial processes.

The Qur'an and Hadith promoted the dignity and protection of women, with laws that aimed to eliminate harmful pre-Islamic practices such as female infanticide, coercion, and abuse. The Prophet Muhammad's insistence on kind treatment of women and clear condemnation of their mistreatment laid a moral foundation for gender justice.

The historical practices and examples from early Islamic society reveal that Islam, at its inception, conferred significant rights, responsibilities, and public roles on women, many of which were revolutionary for the era. Women's economic independence, legal rights, and societal influence were upheld by religious teachings, allowing them to make substantial contributions to Islamic society. However, as Islam spread and adapted to various cultures, practices often evolved or were distorted, leading to restrictive interpretations in certain contexts. Modern movements and scholars aim to revive the original ethos of gender justice and equality envisioned during the formative years of Islam, using historical precedents as powerful examples of women's rightful place within the faith. Reformists strongly argue that "if justice is an intrinsic value in Islam, why have women been treated as second-class citizens in Islamic legal tradition." (Ziba Mir-Hosseini, 2022). Now that equality has been established as an essential principle in contemporary conceptions of justice, is it possible to argue for equality between men and women within Islamic tradition? The conservatives argue that the doctrines of Islam emphasize justice, kindness, and the protection of women's rights. Where restrictions exist, they are often balanced with corresponding responsibilities for men and emphasize fairness and ethical treatment.

Cultural Traditions and Practices

As explained before, despite Islam's core teachings on women's rights, many practices within Muslim societies are influenced by local cultural norms rather than religious prescriptions. These norms often reflect patriarchal customs that predate Islam or emerged as Islam interacted with various societies. Practices like honor killings, forced marriages, and female genital mutilation (FGM) have no basis in Islamic doctrine. They are rooted in tribal or cultural beliefs and reflect attempts to control women's behavior. Such practices are condemned by many Islamic scholars as contrary to Islam's emphasis on justice and compassion.

In some communities, women face limitations on their right to education or work outside the home. A recent example comes from Afghanistan where the Taliban government has banned female education beyond primary grades and are not allowed to work. In cases where women are allowed to work, they often face gender-segregated environments and other stringent restrictions. The Taliban claims that these measures align with their interpretation of Islamic law and Afghan traditions. However, many Islamic scholars and Muslim countries have criticized these policies as un-Islamic and detrimental to the country's development. These restrictions are typically cultural rather than religious, as the Prophet Muhammad encouraged education for both men and women. Historically, women in early Islamic societies participated as scholars, merchants, and leaders.

While the Qur'an prescribes modesty for both men and women, how modest dress is interpreted varies widely. In some cultures, women are forced to wear particular clothing styles, such as the burqa, beyond what religious texts stipulate. This imposition is often driven by cultural norms and can lead to debates over autonomy and choice.

Practices such as male guardianship systems in some countries—where women must obtain a male relative's permission for travel, work, or other activities—are influenced more by local tradition than clear Islamic mandates. Although guardianship can be found in classical fiqh (Islamic jurisprudence), many scholars argue that rigid applications contradict Islam's emphasis on women's autonomy and accountability.

Societal Norms and Gender Perceptions

Cultural norms play a significant role in shaping perceptions of gender within Muslim communities, often leading to practices that contradict Islamic principles. Some factors that perpetuate this influence include:

Patriarchal Traditions: Many societies historically emphasize male dominance, affecting family structures, legal interpretations, and social customs. This is reflected in practices that restrict women's mobility, decision-making power, and participation in public life, even when Islamic teachings promote their autonomy.

Colonial Legacies and Legal Systems: The influence of colonial powers on Muslim societies often shaped family laws and gender roles. In some cases, colonial administrations introduced legal structures that reinforced patriarchal norms, distorting indigenous Islamic practices.

Local Interpretations of Islamic Law: Fiqh is subject to human interpretation and has developed differently across regions and historical periods. Scholars, often male-dominated, have historically interpreted Islamic law in ways that can reflect patriarchal biases, leading to cultural practices at odds with broader Islamic ethics.

Economic and Political Factors: In certain contexts, political regimes and social pressures use cultural norms to justify restrictive gender roles, claiming religious legitimacy for political purposes. This can lead to restrictions on women's rights and participation in public life that are not religiously mandated.

Understanding the difference between Islamic doctrines and cultural traditions is crucial for evaluating the treatment of women within Muslim communities. While Islamic teachings emphasize gender justice, equality in spirituality, and balanced roles, cultural practices may distort or undermine these principles. Recognizing these distinctions helps to challenge harmful practices while promoting reform and aligning gender norms more closely with Islam's foundational ethics of justice, dignity, and compassion for all individuals.

Contemporary Reforms

The struggle for gender equality in Muslim societies has gained momentum through various contemporary reform efforts and movements. In a recent publication entitled 'Journeys Towards Gender Equality in Islam' Ziba Mir-Hosseini (2022) explores the evolving interpretation of gender equality within the framework of Islamic thought. As a prominent scholar in Islamic feminism, Mir-Hosseini delves into historical, theological, and socio-political factors influencing gender roles in Muslim societies. She argues for the necessity of reinterpreting Islamic law (fiqh) and traditional norms to align with contemporary ideals of justice and equality. She highlights diverse movements and scholars who have worked to reconcile Islam with gender equality, addressing tensions between conservative interpretations and progressive change. Mir-Hosseini calls for a reinterpretation rooted in the Qur'an's ethical principles while challenging patriarchal practices entrenched over centuries. Through case studies and personal narratives, she presents a dynamic conversation on how Islamic tradition can adapt to foster a more inclusive and equitable society for all genders.

After 9/11, a movement called Progressive Muslims (PM) has emerged. According to Duderija (2016), this movement challenges both traditional and strict Islamic views on topics like modernity, human rights, gender equality, justice, democracy, and the role of religion in society and politics. It also questions Western ways of thinking that are based on Enlightenment values. Progressive Muslims focus on social and gender justice (including Islamic feminism) and believe that every human being has inherent dignity as a reflection of God's spirit. Duderija, & Zonneveld (2021) examine the kinds of issues progressive Muslim organizations have been engaged in and the challenges they have faced in embodying the values and practices they consider to be the ideals and normative teachings of Islam which often are at odds with the mainstream approaches to these teachings.

These initiatives seek to reconcile Islamic principles with modern notions of gender justice, challenge patriarchal traditions, and advocate for equitable treatment of women. Reformers emphasize that gender equality is consistent with the ethical and spiritual essence of Islam while arguing against restrictive cultural practices. Key areas of focus include legal reforms, educational initiatives, and the work of Islamic feminists.

Legal Reforms and Policy Changes

Efforts to improve the legal status of women have taken shape through reforms aimed at protecting women's rights within both secular and Islamic legal frameworks. Some key initiatives include:

(a) Marriage and Divorce Rights. Many Muslim countries have amended family laws to ensure fair treatment for women. For example, Tunisia abolished polygamy entirely in 1956, framing it as incompatible with Islamic values of justice. Morocco reformed its family code (*Moudawana*) in 2004 to grant women greater rights in marriage, divorce, and child custody. The reforms emphasize women's legal agency, restrict unilateral divorce (talaq) by men, and require mutual consent in marriage contracts.

(b) Domestic Violence Laws: Legal measures have been enacted in countries like Jordan, Egypt, and Pakistan to criminalize domestic violence and improve women's access to legal redress and protection.

(c) Inheritance Rights: Efforts to reinterpret Qur'anic inheritance laws have emerged, with reformers advocating for more equitable distribution based on contemporary economic realities. Tunisia, for example, proposed legislation in 2018 to offer equal inheritance rights for women, triggering extensive debate.

(d) Ending Male Guardianship: Saudi Arabia has introduced reforms reducing male guardianship restrictions, allowing women greater autonomy in travel, employment, and public life.

However, such reforms are needed in many other Muslim countries. According to a report published by Human Rights Watch (2023), 15 Muslim countries still apply personal status or family laws that require women to either "obey" their husbands or live with them, and/or deem women disobedient if they leave the marital home or work or travel without their husbands' permission.

Some state universities in Bahrain, Iran, Kuwait, Oman, Qatar, Saudi Arabia, and the United Arab Emirates require women to show they have male guardian permission before they can go on field trips, or stay at or leave campus accommodations or grounds. Social custom in many countries dictates that single women should not live on their own. Women may face discrimination in practice when trying to rent apartments where they are not married or without male guardians' permission.

Most countries in the region allow women to obtain passports without requiring guardian permission. Previously the government had laws requiring women to show their husbands' permission, or even their guardians' permission, to obtain passports, Yet, Iran and Yemen still practice the old requirement. Similarly, while most countries in the region do not require women to have guardian permission *before* they travel it is still needed in Iran and Qatar. Iran's law provides that married women must show their husbands' permission to obtain passports and that their husbands must indicate whether they can travel for single or multiple trips. Even if a husband grants such permission, he can always change his mind and notify the government to prevent her from traveling abroad. Qatar's interior ministry rules require unmarried Qatari women under age 25 to show permission from their male guardian (in person or an exit permit) to travel abroad while allowing Qatari men to travel without such permission from age 18 (Human Rights Watch, 2023).

Despite progress, challenges persist due to opposition from conservative factions that view some reforms as incompatible with Islamic teachings. The success of legal reforms often depends on societal attitudes, political will, and the interpretation of religious doctrine by local religious authorities.

Educational Initiatives

Education has been a focal point for promoting gender equality, with many reform efforts aimed at increasing access to education for girls and enhancing women's literacy, skills, and professional opportunities. Organizations like the *Malala Fund* and numerous grassroots initiatives advocate for universal access to education for girls in Muslim countries. Malala Yousafzai's campaign is particularly prominent, spotlighting challenges to female education in Pakistan and beyond. Some traditional Qur'anic schools (madrasas) have begun incorporating gender equality programs that emphasize women's rights as derived from the

Qur'an and Hadith. These programs aim to counter patriarchal interpretations that often limit women's roles. Women's participation in higher education has increased in many countries. Universities and research centers often host forums and discussions challenging traditional gender roles, fostering new interpretations, and reformist Islamic thought on women's rights.

Islamic Feminism and the Reinterpretation of Texts

Islamic feminists play a vital role in challenging traditional interpretations of the Qur'an and Hadith, advocating for women's rights within an Islamic framework. Unlike secular feminists, Islamic feminists base their arguments on religious texts, using a hermeneutical approach to reveal Islam's progressive stance on gender issues. Some prominent efforts include *hermeneutical and contextual readings of the Qur'an*. It is argued that many patriarchal interpretations of the Qur'an arose from male-dominated scholarly traditions that fail to reflect the egalitarian spirit of Islam. By revisiting original texts and historical contexts, they offer alternative interpretations that emphasize gender equity. For example, Amina Wadud is a leading scholar in Islamic feminism, Wadud advocates for gender-just readings of the Qur'an. Her work, *Qur'an and Woman*, emphasizes that traditional interpretations have been influenced by patriarchal culture and often overlook women's rights. Another prominent name is Asma Barlas. She challenges traditional exegesis (interpretation) of the Qur'an, arguing that the original message of Islam is inherently anti-patriarchal.

In some contexts, women have led mixed-gender prayers and delivered sermons, challenging traditional norms that restrict women's roles in religious leadership. This has been met with varying degrees of acceptance and opposition within different communities.

Groups such as *Musawah* (meaning "equality" in Arabic) work at an international level to promote gender equality through legal reform, research, and advocacy rooted in Islamic principles. Cultural practices often entrench gender disparities, and reformers focus on distinguishing between cultural norms and religious tenets. Many activists work to eliminate harmful cultural practices such as honor killings and forced marriages. They argue that such customs are antithetical to Islam's teachings on justice and human dignity. In some regions, gender segregation in public and educational spaces is more cultural than religious. Reformers emphasize Islam's inclusivity and women's historical roles in public life, such as during the early Islamic period.

Civil society organizations and activists play an essential role in community education, advocating for women's participation in social, political, and economic life. They often emphasize Islam's support for women's rights as a counterpoint to restrictive cultural practices.

Promoting Economic Empowerment

Economic empowerment initiatives focus on enabling women to participate fully in economic life, often highlighting Islamic principles that support women's economic rights. For instance, Organizations like the *Grameen Bank* offer microloans to women, empowering them economically. This approach aligns with Islamic principles of wealth distribution, charity, and justice. Some reformers work to eliminate cultural barriers that restrict women's employment, emphasizing that Islam does not prohibit women from working. Historical examples, such as Khadijah bint Khuwaylid (the Prophet's wife and a successful businesswoman), are often cited.

Social Media and Digital Activism

Digital platforms provide space for Muslim women to share experiences, organize movements, and advocate for reform. Campaigns against gender-based violence, such as #MosqueMeToo, have highlighted the need to address abuse and discrimination within Muslim communities. Also, efforts to reform discriminatory laws, such as those related to child custody or male guardianship, are often championed by women's rights activists within Muslim societies. These campaigns emphasize equality and justice as rooted in Islamic teachings.

Contemporary reform movements aimed at promoting gender equality within Islam address both religious and cultural dimensions. By reinterpreting sacred texts, advocating for legal reforms, and promoting education and economic empowerment, reformers seek to create societies that reflect the original egalitarian spirit of Islam. The efforts of Islamic feminists, educators, policymakers, and activists demonstrate that progress toward gender equality is not only possible but firmly grounded in the principles of justice and dignity central to Islamic teachings.

References

Bowen, J. R. (2018). Gender, Islam, and law. In S. Anderson, L. Beaman, & J.-P. Platteau (Eds.), *Towards gender equity in development* (pp. 225-244). Oxford Academic.

Duderija, A. (2011). Constructing religiously ideal "believer" and "woman" in Islam: Neo-traditional Salafi and progressive Muslims' methods of interpretation. In K. Abou El

Fadl (Ed.), *Palgrave Series in Islamic Theology, Law, and History* (pp. 139-156). New York: Palgrave Macmillan.

Duderija, A. (2016). Progressive Islam and progressive Muslim thought. *Oxford Bibliographies.*

Duderija, A., & Zonneveld, A. O. (2021). Transnational progressive Islam: Theory, networks, and lived experience. In R. Lukens-Bull & M. Woodward (Eds.), *Handbook of contemporary Islam and Muslim lives* (pp. 153-170). Springer, Cham.

Mir-Hosseini, Z. (2022). *Journeys towards gender equality in Islam.* Oneworld Academic.

Trapped: How male guardianship policies restrict women's travel and mobility in the Middle East and North Africa. (2023, July 18). *Human Rights Watch.* https://www.hrw.org/report/2023/07/18/trapped/how-male-guardianship-policies-restrict-womens-travel-and-mobility-in-the-middle-east-and-north-africa

CHAPTER 17
HUMAN DEVELOPMENT IN MUSLIM COUNTRIES

What is HDI?

Human Development Indicator was developed out of the limitation of measuring human well-being from GDP alone. In the 1970s and 80s development debate considered using alternative focuses to go beyond GDP, including putting greater emphasis on employment, followed by redistribution with growth, and then whether people had their basic needs met. These ideas resulted in the human development approach, which is about understanding the richness of human life, rather than simply the richness of the economy in which human beings live. It is an approach that is focused on creating fair opportunities and choices for all people.

United Nations Development Program (UNDP) developed the Human Development Index (HDI) which is a composite index to measure and rank countries' levels of social and economic development. It is published annually by the United Nations Development Programme (UNDP) since 1990. The HDI score provides a broad measure of human development by combining health, education, and income indicators, offering a more comprehensive view of well-being and social progress than economic measures alone. The HDI focuses on three key dimensions of human development, each represented by specific indicators:

Dimensions of HDI

1. Health: Life Expectancy at Birth. This indicator measures the average number of years a newborn is expected to live if current mortality rates continue. It reflects the overall health and longevity of a country's population.

2. Education: This indicator measures the average number of years of education received by people aged 25 years and older in a country. It reflects the educational attainment of the adult population. (ii) Expected Years of Schooling. This measures the total number of years of schooling that a child entering school can expect to receive, assuming that current enrollment rates remain the same throughout the child's schooling years.

3. Standard of Living: This indicator is expressed in terms of constant international dollars using purchasing power parity (PPP) rates. It reflects the average income and wealth available to citizens and their ability to access goods and services.

The HDI is the geometric mean of the normalized indices for each of the three dimensions. It results in a score ranging from 0 to 1, with 1 being the highest possible level of human development. Countries are ranked and grouped into four human development categories based on their HDI scores. They are:

HDI Score, Categories, and Country Ranking

Table 1: HDI levels based on HDI score

HDI Level	HDI Score
Very High	HDI ≥ 0.800
High	HDI from 0.700 to 0.799
Medium	HDI from 0.550 to 0.699
Low	HDI < 0.550

Table 2: Top 10 countries in 2022 based on HDI scores

S.N.	Country	HDI Score
1	Switzerland	0.967
2	Norway	0.966
3	Iceland	0.959
4	Hong Kong, China (SAR)	0.956
5	Denmark	0.952
6	Sweden	0.952
7	Germany	0.950
8	Ireland	0.950
9	Singapore	0.949
10	Australia	0.946

Source: [http://hdr.undp.org] (http://hdr.undp.org)

Table 3: HDI level of selected countries with Muslim population

HDI Category	Countries
Very High (HDI ≥ 0.800)	United Arab Emirates (UAE)
	Qatar
	Saudi Arabia
	Bahrain
	Kuwait
	Brunei Darussalam
High (HDI 0.700 to 0.799)	Malaysia
	Kazakhstan
	Turkey
	Iran
	Oman
	Azerbaijan
Medium (HDI 0.550 to 0.699)	Indonesia
	Morocco
	Egypt
	Pakistan
	Uzbekistan
	Bangladesh
	Algeria
Low (HDI < 0.550)	Yemen
	Sudan
	Afghanistan
	Niger
	Chad
	Somalia

HDI levels of selected countries with Muslim majority populations place UAE, Saudi Arabia, Qatar, Kuwait, Bahrain, and Brunie Darussalam at the top. Malaysia, Kazakhstan, Turkey, Iran, Oman, and Azerbaijan come next. At the middle level are Indonesia, Morrocco, Egypt, Pakistan, Uzbekistan, Bangladesh, and Algeria. Finally, Yemen, Sudan, Afghanistan, Niger, Chad, and Somalia are placed at the lowest rank.

There are several factors that influence the level of HDI in different Muslim countries. Some of them are:

HDI Disparities in Muslim Countries

Disparities in Education: Wealthier countries, such as Qatar, UAE, and Saudi Arabia, have been able to invest significantly in modern education systems, while poorer countries like Niger, Mali, and Afghanistan struggle to provide even basic education infrastructure. Rural areas in many countries often face a lack of schools, inadequate educational materials, and limited availability of trained teachers. In certain regions, social norms and cultural beliefs can restrict female education, though this is gradually changing in many places. Countries like Pakistan and Yemen have faced challenges in ensuring girls' access to education due to traditional practices and social barriers. While Islamic teachings generally encourage the pursuit of knowledge, the implementation of these values varies widely. In some regions, conservative interpretations of gender roles may limit women's access to education. For example, As of January 2025, the educational opportunities for girls and women in Afghanistan remain severely restricted under Taliban rule. Girls are generally prohibited from attending secondary schools (grades 7-12). Women are largely banned from pursuing university education. In December 2022, the Taliban government prohibited university education for females, leading to international condemnation. As of November 2024, some parts of the country have permitted women to attend religious schools to pursue studies in fields like dentistry and nursing. However, these opportunities are limited and do not equate to full access to higher education. Afghanistan remains the only country in the world where secondary and higher education is strictly forbidden to girls and women. This deliberate deprivation has affected approximately 1.4 million Afghan girls, with access to primary education also declining sharply (UNESCO).

Conversely, countries like Indonesia and Malaysia have emphasized educational progress for both genders, reflecting a more inclusive approach to education. The overall situation of education in Muslim lands presents an alarming past as well as a promising present. In an article published in Muslim Mirror, Farooqi (2020) explains it vividly. He quotes historian Donald Quataert[13] who noted that in the early 19th century, literacy rates among Muslims were as low as 2–3%. Even by the mid-20th century, literacy remained limited, with only a few countries like Egypt, Tunisia, Iran, Jordan, Kuwait, Malaysia, Syria, Turkey, and Albania surpassing an average literacy rate of 30%. Muslim-majority regions under Soviet control, however, achieved higher literacy rates.

---

[13] Donald Quataert (1941–2011) was a prominent American historian and scholar specializing in the history of the Ottoman Empire. He was particularly known for his contributions to understanding the socio-economic aspects of the Ottoman world, including labor, industry, and everyday life, rather than focusing solely on the political and military dimensions.

Historian George Sarton[14] described this decline in literacy among Muslims as "puzzling," especially compared to the remarkably high literacy rates during the early Islamic period, which he called "baffling."

Over the last four centuries, Muslims focused on cultural pursuits such as poetry, music, painting, and architecture, while showing limited interest in modern education from Europe. One critical setback was the refusal to adopt the printing press in the 15th century, which hindered the dissemination of knowledge and the scientific revolution that transformed Europe.

In recent decades, the Islamic world has begun to prioritize education, recognizing its role in combating exploitation and fostering progress. Economic resources, particularly from oil-rich countries, have been instrumental in efforts to eradicate illiteracy and poverty. According to John Miller's survey, five Muslim-majority countries—Azerbaijan, Tajikistan, Kazakhstan, Turkmenistan, and Uzbekistan—are among the 25 nations with literacy rates of 100%. Data from the World Bank and UNESCO (2018) shows that 25 Muslim-majority countries now have literacy rates above 90%, including Saudi Arabia (95%), Indonesia (94%), Malaysia (94%), Iran (90%), Jordan (96%), UAE (94%), and Turkey (95%). However, countries like Bangladesh, Pakistan, and Nigeria still lag behind, with literacy rates below 62%. While the global literacy rate in 2017 was 82%, the improvement in literacy across the

---

[14] George Sarton (1884–1956) was a pioneering Belgian-American historian of science, widely regarded as one of the founders of the modern discipline of the history of science. His work laid the foundation for understanding the development of scientific thought and its relationship with broader cultural and historical contexts.

Muslim world—from an average of 30% in 1980 to current levels—is significant.

Encouragingly, the gender gap in literacy has narrowed in many Muslim countries, with 21 nations reporting a male-to-female literacy difference of only 0–7%. However, tertiary education (higher education) still requires substantial development. Research spending has increased in countries like Saudi Arabia, Iran, Qatar, and Turkey, but remains low compared to the West, where tertiary enrollment often exceeds 40%.

Progress is evident in higher education: the *Times Higher Education World University Rankings 2018* listed 96 universities from 18 Muslim-majority countries among the top 1,102 globally. Turkey led with 22 universities, followed by Iran (18), Pakistan (10), Malaysia and Egypt (9 each), and Saudi Arabia (5). Women's participation in higher education is also noteworthy, with several Islamic countries, including Tunisia, Malaysia, Lebanon, Jordan, Bahrain, and Libya, reporting higher female enrollment than male.

Women's achievements in science are also notable. Muslim-majority countries like Bahrain, Brunei, Kyrgyzstan, Lebanon, Qatar, and Turkey surpass the United States in the proportion of women graduating in science fields. Morocco exceeds the U.S. in the percentage of women engineering graduates. The increasing presence of universities from Muslim countries in global rankings and the rise in women's participation in education signal a brighter future for the Islamic world (cf. Farooqi 2020).

Healthcare Disparities: Wealthier nations like the Gulf States have invested heavily in advanced healthcare systems, offering high standards of medical care. In contrast, poorer states often lack basic healthcare infrastructure and medical personnel. Political instability and conflict are yet another factor. Countries affected by conflict, such as Syria, Yemen, and Afghanistan, experience disruptions in healthcare delivery, leading to lower life expectancy and higher mortality rates. Also, cultural and social factors come into play. Healthcare practices can be influenced by religious beliefs, such as views on certain medical interventions or issues surrounding reproductive health. In some conservative settings, access to reproductive healthcare for women may be limited due to cultural norms. However, many Muslim countries are working to balance tradition with modern medical advancements to improve health outcomes.

Several challenges in healthcare remain such as access to healthcare particularly in rural and remote areas, and financial barriers remain significant in low-income nations, where out-of-pocket expenses are high.

In low-income Muslim countries, infectious diseases such as malaria, tuberculosis, and hepatitis remain significant public health concerns. Poor sanitation and water quality exacerbate the spread of these diseases.

Maternal and infant mortality rates remain high in poorer Muslim countries. For instance, countries like Somalia and Afghanistan face alarming maternal mortality rates due to a lack of skilled birth attendants and poor prenatal care.

Countries experiencing conflicts, such as Syria, Yemen, and Libya, face severe disruptions in healthcare services. Hospitals and clinics are often destroyed, and healthcare workers flee, leaving millions without access to basic medical care. Many skilled healthcare professionals from

Muslim countries migrate to Western nations for better opportunities, leading to shortages in their home countries.

Some key statistics suggest that the life expectancy in Muslim countries varies widely, from over 80 years in the Gulf nations to less than 60 in conflict-affected areas like Afghanistan and Somalia. Secondly, wealthy nations like Qatar and UAE allocate over 4% of their GDP to healthcare, whereas low-income countries spend far less. Lastly, the number of doctors per 1,000 people ranges from less than 1 in poorer countries to over 3 in affluent nations like Qatar and UAE.

The future outlook is promising as many Muslim-majority countries are prioritizing healthcare in national development plans, focusing on universal coverage, improving infrastructure, and increasing funding. Efforts to address gender disparities in access to healthcare are growing, with several nations working to improve maternal health and women's access to medical education. Partnerships with global health organizations and donor agencies will continue to play a crucial role in advancing healthcare systems.

Income Disparities: Countries rich in natural resources, particularly oil, have been able to generate high national incomes (e.g., Saudi Arabia and Kuwait). In contrast, nations lacking resource wealth often rely heavily on agriculture or informal economies, contributing to lower income levels and greater poverty rates. Unequal Wealth Distribution is yet another reason. Even within wealthy nations, disparities exist between citizens and non-citizen laborers or marginalized groups, leading to unequal access to economic opportunities. Also, social norms related to gender roles may limit women's participation in the workforce in certain countries, reducing household incomes and economic productivity. However, progressive initiatives in places like Malaysia and Turkey are focused on improving economic inclusivity. Islamic finance principles, which emphasize ethical investment and prohibit interest-based lending, have also shaped economic structures in some regions, creating unique opportunities and challenges for financial development.

Human Rights and Gender Equality: Many Muslim countries face challenges in terms of political freedom, human rights, and gender equity. Discriminatory laws or practices, sometimes rooted in conservative cultural traditions, may hinder social and economic progress for certain groups, particularly women and minorities.

Urban vs. Rural Divide: Disparities between urban and rural areas in terms of access to services, infrastructure, and economic opportunities often impact human development indicators. Cities in many Muslim countries have seen rapid growth, but rural regions frequently remain underdeveloped.

Impact of Conflict and Instability: Civil wars, regional conflicts, and political instability have disrupted development efforts in numerous Muslim countries, leading to a "development gap" compared to more stable regions.

Some cultural, social, and religious practices contribute positively to HDI. In many Muslim societies, charitable giving (Zakat) is a key part of religious practice, providing a social safety net and helping alleviate poverty through community-driven initiatives. Additionally, many Islamic organizations promote literacy and health campaigns aligned with religious teachings on community welfare.

Hasan (2012) in his edited book explores the current state of the Muslim world, focusing on the influence of environment, space, and power on human development. It provides a theoretical framework for studying human development from various perspectives, including social, cultural, economic, environmental, political, and religious. He investigates disparities in education, healthcare, income levels, and other human development indicators within the Muslim world. Hasan discusses the role of cultural, social, and religious practices in either advancing or limiting development efforts. He argues that addressing the developmental challenges of the Muslim world requires a nuanced, context-specific understanding of cultural, economic, and political factors. It also emphasizes the need for more inclusive and sustainable policies that foster human development and equitable growth across diverse Muslim societies. Hasan's work is particularly valuable to anyone interested in understanding the interplay between development and the unique political, historical, and cultural contexts within Muslim societies.

Ahsan (2012) explores the role of women in human development within the Muslim world, comparing Islamic and UNDP's approaches to development. It emphasizes the importance of women's development and the need for coordinated efforts to address gender disparities. Ahsan provides historical context on women's roles and their rights within Islamic teachings, noting how interpretations of Islamic laws and traditions have varied significantly across time and regions. The influence of colonial history, socio-economic conditions, and global political changes is discussed as contributing factors to the diverse experiences of Muslim women.

Ahsan lists several challenges to human development. The major obstacles that women in Muslim countries face include unequal access to education, limited healthcare, economic marginalization, and legal inequalities. Social norms, traditional cultural practices, and patriarchal structures are often cited as significant barriers to women's development.

Ahsan discusses the role of Islamic feminism and reformist movements that seek to reinterpret religious teachings in ways that promote gender equality and women's empowerment. Efforts to align Islamic principles with modern human rights standards, particularly through education, legal reform, and grassroots activism, are highlighted as essential steps toward improving women's human development.

To sum up, the disparities in development indicators within the Muslim world are complex and shaped by multiple, intersecting factors. Balancing cultural and religious values with modern development priorities remains a challenge, but many nations are actively pursuing reforms and initiatives to improve the overall quality of life and social equity for their citizens. Addressing these disparities will require context-sensitive approaches that respect cultural norms while fostering progress in health, education, and economic development.

References

Ahsan, M. (2012). Women and Human Development in the Muslim World. In: *Lovat, T. (eds) Women in Islam*. Springer, Dordrecht. https://doi.org/10.1007/978-94-007-4219-2_4

https://hdr.undp.org

Farooqi, M.I. H (2020). Literacy and Human Development Index in Muslim majority countries, *Muslim Mirror*, December 9, 2020

Hasan, S. (2012). *The Muslim World in the 21st Century*. Springer.

CHAPTER 18
THE GEOPOLITICS: CAUSES AND CONSEQUENCES

Introduction

The geopolitical situation in the Muslim world especially in the Middle East is shaped by a complex interplay of historical, political, socio-economic, and cultural factors. These crises have often led to significant migration flows to the Western world. There are several contributing factors to this situation.

First, many Muslim countries have experienced long periods of political instability, often stemming from authoritarian regimes, lack of democratic governance, and power struggles. For example, civil wars in Syria, Yemen, and Libya; political turmoil in Iraq and Afghanistan. Secondly, dep-rooted sectarian divisions, particularly between Sunni and Shia Muslims, have fueled conflicts in countries like Iraq, Syria, and Yemen. These conflicts are often facilitated by external powers using sectarian divides for geopolitical leverage. Thirdly, military interventions by global powers have disrupted political systems and promoted instability. Examples include the U.S.-led wars in Iraq and Afghanistan and NATO interventions in Libya. Proxy wars, such as in Syria and Yemen, have involved regional powers like Saudi Arabia, Iran, and Turkey. As a result, groups like ISIS, Al-Qaeda, and Boko Haram have exploited political and economic instability to grow, further destabilizing regions and displacing populations. Some other factors, including high unemployment, lack of economic opportunities, and poor governance have contributed to widespread dissatisfaction. Over-reliance on oil and other natural resources has made economies vulnerable to global market fluctuations. Droughts, water shortages, and desertification in parts of the Muslim world have worsened living conditions and triggered competition over resources. Finally, the legacies of colonialism, including arbitrary borders and unresolved territorial disputes, have left deep-seated issues in countries like Palestine, Kashmir, and Sudan.

Muslims Migration

Like migrants as a whole – who gravitate to places that offer safety and better economic conditions – Muslim migrants often leave their birth countries to escape poverty and danger. The most common country of origin for Muslim migrants is Syria, where a war broke out in 2011. Fully 10% of the world's stock of Muslim migrants (8.1 million) were born in Syria. India is the second-most common country of origin among Muslim migrants, with 6.0 million living there. They are much more likely than people in the country's Hindu majority to emigrate. Although India's population is only 15% Muslim, an estimated 33% of all India-born migrants are Muslim. Most Muslim migrants from India live in Muslim countries with job opportunities, including the UAE (1.8 million), Saudi Arabia (1.3 million) and Oman (720,000). Afghanistan is the third-most common origin country for Muslim migrants (5.5 million). A majority of Muslim migrants from Afghanistan live in neighboring Iran (2.7 million) or Pakistan (1.6 million). Migrants from Afghanistan have fled challenging conditions over the decades, including an occupation by the Soviet Union in the 1980s and a U.S.-led invasion in the early 2000s.

Top 10 origins of Muslim migrants

Muslim migrants, by origin

Origin	Count	% of Muslim migrants
1 Syria	8.1M	10%
2 India	6.0M	8
3 Afghanistan	5.5M	7
4 Pakistan	5.3M	7
5 Bangladesh	5.2M	6
6 Indonesia	4.0M	5
7 Palestinian territories	3.9M	5
8 Egypt	3.4M	4
9 Turkey	3.1M	4
10 Morocco	2.5M	3
Top 10 subtotal	**47.1 million**	**59%**
Global Muslim migrants	**80.4 million**	**100%**

Note: Migrants are all adults and children living outside their country of birth, as of 2020, no matter when they moved. Percentages are calculated using unrounded figures.
Source: Data based on migrant counts from the United Nations' "International migrant stock 2020" report and religious composition estimates from Pew Research Center analyses of 270 censuses and surveys.
"The Religious Composition of the World's Migrants"

PEW RESEARCH CENTER

Factors Contributing to Muslims' Migration

Armed conflicts and persecution have forced millions to flee. The Syrian civil war alone has displaced over 13 million people, with many seeking refuge in countries nearby, like Turkey and Lebanon, while some have gone as far as Europe and the U.S. (Kramer & Tong, 2024). Other significant flows include Afghans, Iraqis, and Rohingya Muslims. Many from Muslim countries migrate to

Western nations in search of better economic opportunities, often due to limited prospects in their home countries. Also, the West is a hub for higher education and skilled labor markets, attracting professionals and students from Muslim countries.

The geopolitical crises act as push factors, compelling individuals to seek safety, stability, and opportunity in the West. The West, perceived as a region of prosperity and peace, acts as a pull factor. However, migration has also created tensions within host countries, sparking debates over immigration policies, cultural integration, and the economic impacts of migration.

The involvement of countries like the United States, the United Kingdom, and Israel in the Muslim world has significantly shaped many of its ongoing crises. Their roles have often been motivated by strategic, economic, and ideological interests, sometimes leading to unintended or adverse consequences.

The legacy of British and European colonialism in the Muslim world, including the arbitrary drawing of borders (e.g., the Sykes-Picot Agreement)[15], left unresolved disputes and divided communities. The creation of artificial states, such as Iraq and Syria, without consideration for ethnic and sectarian divisions, sowed the seeds of future conflict.

The establishment of Israel in 1948, supported by the UK and later the US, led to the displacement of hundreds of

---

[15] The **Sykes–Picot Agreement** was a 1916 secret treaty between the United Kingdom and France, with assent from Russia and Italy, to define their mutually agreed spheres of influence and control in an eventual partition of the Ottoman Empire.
(https://en.wikipedia.org/wiki/Sphere_of_influence)

thousands of Palestinians (Nakba), creating a decades-long conflict. The US has consistently supported Israel militarily, economically, and diplomatically, often vetoing UN resolutions critical of Israeli policies, including settlements in occupied territories. Israeli military actions in Gaza, the West Bank, and Lebanon have contributed to instability and fueled resentment in the region.

During the Cold War, the US and UK supported autocratic regimes and armed groups to counter Soviet influence in the Muslim world, often undermining local governance and stability. Example: US support for the Mujahideen in Afghanistan during the 1980s to fight the Soviet Union, which indirectly led to the rise of groups like the Taliban and Al-Qaeda.

The US and UK-led invasion of Iraq (2003), based on false claims of weapons of mass destruction, toppled Saddam Hussein but plunged Iraq into chaos, leading to sectarian violence and the rise of ISIS. In Libya (2011) NATO's intervention, led by the US, UK, and France, removed Muammar Gaddafi but left the country in a state of lawlessness, with competing militias vying for power. In Afghanistan (2001-2021) the prolonged US-led war aimed at dismantling Al-Qaeda and the Taliban resulted in widespread civilian casualties, corruption, and an eventual Taliban resurgence after the US withdrawal.

The US, UK, and their allies have supported authoritarian regimes in the Middle East and North Africa to maintain stability and secure access to oil, often ignoring human rights abuses. Examples: Support for the Saudi monarchy, Egypt's Hosni Mubarak, and Gulf States' rulers. This policy has led to repression, lack of democratic development, and popular uprisings, such as the Arab Spring.

The US and its allies are the largest arms suppliers to the Middle East, fueling conflicts in Yemen, Syria, and beyond. Their arms sales to Saudi Arabia have supported its intervention in Yemen, creating one of the world's worst humanitarian crises.

Western powers have historically exploited the region's resources, particularly oil, often prioritizing their interests over the development of local economies. The examples are the US support for oil-rich Gulf monarchies; and Western-backed coups in Iran (1953) to control oil resources.

The post-9/11 "War on Terror," led by the US, included military actions in multiple Muslim countries, resulting in widespread civilian casualties and displacement. Policies such as drone strikes in Pakistan, Yemen, and Somalia have caused resentment and contributed to anti-Western sentiment. The portrayal of Muslims as potential extremists in Western media and politics has fueled Islamophobia and created tensions both in the Muslim world and in the diaspora.

Role of Israel in Regional Instability

One of the key players in creating trouble and instability is Israel. For the US and its allies, this country has enormous strategic importance for them. It is due to a combination of geopolitical, military, economic, ideological, and domestic political factors.

Israel's actions, including military operations in neighboring countries, annexation of Palestinian lands, and attacks on Iran-linked targets, have contributed to instability.

The US's unwavering support for Israel has alienated many Muslim countries, complicating regional diplomacy. The involvement of the US, UK, some European countries, and Israel in the Muslim world has often prioritized their strategic and economic interests over the stability and well-being of the region's people. While some actions were intended to combat terrorism or promote security, they frequently led to unintended consequences, including political instability, sectarianism, and widespread suffering. These dynamics have driven migration, fueled resentment, and perpetuated cycles of conflict.

Among the factors of strategic value include (a) geopolitical and strategic location of Israel. This country is located in the Middle East, a region critical for global energy resources and trade routes. Its position near the Mediterranean, the Red Sea, and the Suez Canal makes it a strategic partner for controlling regional dynamics, (b) Israel serves as a counterweight to regional rivals such as Iran, Syria, and groups like Hezbollah and Hamas. It aligns with Western efforts to contain anti-Western influences in the region, (c) Israel has one of the most advanced militaries in the world, with cutting-edge technology and a nuclear deterrent, though undeclared. This capability bolsters Western interests in the region. Similarly, Israel's intelligence agencies (e.g., Mossad) are renowned for their capabilities. The US and UK benefit from intelligence-sharing agreements, particularly regarding counterterrorism and monitoring adversaries like Iran. Also, Israel is a major consumer of Western arms, contributing to their defense industries, (d) Israel is seen as a stable, reliable ally in a region often characterized by political upheaval and instability. Unlike many neighboring countries, it has a long-standing democratic system and predictable policies aligned with Western interests, (e), Israel is a global leader in technology and innovation, particularly in cybersecurity, artificial intelligence, and biotechnology. Western countries collaborate with Israel to access these advancements. Moreover, Israel is an important trade partner for both the US and the UK, with strong economic ties in sectors such as defense, technology, and agriculture, (f) another reason is the ideological and religious ties. The UK played a key role in the establishment of Israel through the Balfour Declaration (1917) and subsequent policies. Supporting Israel aligns with its historical commitment. In the US, some evangelical Christian groups view Israel's existence as fulfilling biblical prophecies, influencing American political support for Israel. Western democracies emphasize shared democratic values, framing Israel as a like-minded nation in the Middle East.

In the US and its allies, Jewish communities play a significant role in political, economic, and cultural life. Their support for Israel influences foreign policy. In the US, organizations like the American Israel Public Affairs Committee (AIPAC) wield substantial influence in Congress, ensuring strong support for Israel. A significant portion of the public in both countries views Israel as a key ally, further reinforcing political and military support. Israel plays a pivotal role in Western strategies to counter terrorism and Iranian influence in the Middle East. It has conducted operations against Iranian-linked targets and provides intelligence on Iran's nuclear program.

Though Israel itself is not an oil producer, its strategic position allows the US and UK to monitor and influence regional energy flows. Israel's normalization agreements with Arab states (e.g., UAE, Bahrain) under the Abraham Accords enhance its role as a Western ally facilitating regional diplomacy.

While Israel's strategic importance is clear, its relationship with the Western countries has drawn criticism. Western support for Israel is often criticized for overlooking Palestinian rights and Israeli actions in occupied territories. The recent ongoing situation in Gaza after the October 7, 2023 attack by Hamaz in Israel and the resultant massive military response with active support from the US has led to a massive loss of life civilians, and health workers in the territory. This has drawn worldwide condemnation of Israel and its allies. Support for Israel alienates many Arab and Muslim countries, complicating relations and fueling anti-Western sentiment. Israel's importance to the US and other Western countries stems from its strategic location, military capabilities, technological advancements, and alignment with Western values and goals. However, this relationship also comes with complexities and challenges, particularly regarding the broader Middle Eastern context and global perceptions.

References

Ahmet, A. K., & Kuru, T. (2021). The ulema-state alliance: A barrier to democracy and development in the Muslim world. *Institute for Global Change.* Retrieved from https://institute.global/policy/ulema-state-alliancebarrier

Gu, S., & Fong, E. (2022). Migration from Muslim countries: A tale of two patterns. *Population Research and Policy Review, 41*(5), 1853-1872.

Kramer, S., & Tong, Y. (2024). Muslim migrants around the world. *Pew Research Center.* Retrieved from https://www.pewresearch.org

Qolbi, Y., R, M., Diana, & Sidqi, I. (2024). Geopolitics and Muslim countries: Navigating challenges and opportunities in contemporary international political dynamics. *Metro Islamic Law Review, 3,* 217-235.

United Nations High Commissioner for Refugees (UNHCR). (n.d.). *Middle East and North Africa – Operational regions.* Retrieved from https://reporting.unhcr.org/operational/regions/middle-east-and-north-africa2

UNICEF. (n.d.). *Migrant and refugee crisis in the MENA region.* Retrieved from https://www.unicef.org/mena/topics/migrant-and-refugee-crisis

The Conversation. (2024, March 20). *A year of escalating conflict in the Middle East has ushered in a new era of regional displacement.* Retrieved from https://theconversation.com/a-year-of-escalating-conflict-in-the-middle-east-has-ushered-in-a-new-era-of-regional-displacement-240425

ANNOTATED BIBLIOGRAPHY

Islam and Muslims: From Past to Present

Lapidus, Ira M. A History of Islamic Societies (3rd ed.). Cambridge University Press, 2014.

This comprehensive book provides a detailed history of Islamic societies from their origins to the present day. It covers various aspects such as political, social, and cultural developments, offering a thorough understanding of the evolution of Muslim communities.

Haron, Muhammed, and Aslam Farouk-Alli. Muslims in South Africa: An Annotated Bibliography. University of Cape Town, 1997.

This annotated bibliography compiles research and writings on Islam and Muslims in South Africa, including works by both South African and non-South African scholars. It provides valuable insights into the academic and non-academic contributions to the study of Muslim society in South Africa.

Abdul-Matin, Ibrahim. Green Deen: What Islam Teaches About Protecting the Planet. Berrett-Koehler Publishers, 2010.

This book explores the Islamic perspective on environmental stewardship and sustainability. It highlights how Islamic teachings can contribute to contemporary environmental issues and promote a more sustainable future.

Abe, Satoshi. "Pursuing Moral Dimensions of the Environment: A Study of Islamic Tradition in Contemporary

Iran." Journal for the Study of Religion, Nature and Culture, vol. 15, no. 2, 2021, pp. 151-176.

This article examines the moral dimensions of environmental issues within the context of Islamic tradition in Iran. It provides a nuanced understanding of how Islamic teachings can inform contemporary environmental practices.

Al-Jayyousi, Odeh Rashed. Islam and Sustainable Development: New Worldviews. Gower Publishing, 2012.

This book discusses the relationship between Islam and sustainable development, offering new perspectives on how Islamic principles can contribute to sustainable practices and development goals.

Ahmad, Ali Nobil. "Islamic Water Law as an Antidote for Maintaining Water Quality." University of Denver Water Law Review, vol. 2, no. 2, Spring 1999, pp. 170-188.

This article explores the application of Islamic water law in maintaining water quality, highlighting the relevance of Islamic principles in addressing contemporary environmental challenges.

Wilson, Rasheeda. In Pursuit of New Australian Muslim Stories: An Annotated Bibliography. UN Projects, 2021.

This annotated bibliography explores the diverse experiences of Australian Muslims, addressing issues such as Islamophobia, Orientalism, and the politics of identity within Australian society. Wilson emphasizes the importance of creative writing in reshaping cultural narratives and advocating for the Muslim community.

Caretto, Carla, and Allison McGhee. Bridging Cultures Bookshelf - Muslim Journeys: A Selected Annotated Bibliography. Louisiana Chapter of the ACRL, 2013.

This bibliography is part of the Bridging Cultures - Muslim Journeys grant, which aims to promote understanding between American and Arab culture, history, and society. It includes a collection of books and films organized by themes such as American Stories, Connected Histories, Literary Reflections, Pathways of Faith, Points of View, and Art, Architecture, and Film.

Esposito, John L. Islam: The Straight Path. 5th ed. Oxford UP, 2015.

This book surveys the faith, beliefs, and practices of Muslims from the 7th century to contemporary times. Esposito, a prolific scholar, provides a comprehensive overview of Islam and its global impact.

Murata, Sachiko, and William Chittick. The Vision of Islam. Paragon House, 1994.

This beautifully written work covers the four dimensions of Islam: practice, faith, spirituality, and the Islamic worldview. It offers insights into how Islam transcends cultural and contextual boundaries.

Ghaneabassiri, Kambiz. American Muslims: Globalization and the Politics of Identity. Praeger, 2010.

This book examines the impact of globalization on the identity of American Muslims, exploring how they navigate their cultural and religious identities in a globalized world.

Fischbach, Rahel. *Between God and History: Politics of Modern Muslim Qur'an Hermeneutics.* De Gruyter, 2024.

This volume investigates contemporary Muslim debates on Qur'anic interpretation, focusing on the tension between historical-critical methods and traditional approaches. Fischbach argues that these debates reflect broader societal and ethical concerns, showcasing how scriptural interpretation can serve as a medium for negotiating political and cultural change. The book provides insights into the evolving dynamics of Muslim intellectual thought and bridges the gap between Western and Islamic scholarly traditions.

Aydin, Cemil. *The Idea of the Muslim World: A Global Intellectual History.* Harvard University Press, 2017.

Aydin challenges the notion of a monolithic "Muslim world," instead illustrating how the idea was historically constructed through colonial and political interactions. The book critically examines how identity politics, global power structures, and diverse cultural practices intersect in shaping perceptions of Islam.

Islam – Thought, Culture, and Society" series, De Gruyter.

This interdisciplinary series explores a broad array of topics including Islamic civilization, theology, and culture, with a focus on historical and contemporary contexts. By examining non-Muslim societies and minority Muslim groups, the series highlights the adaptability and diversity of Islamic practices across cultures and eras.

Pew Research Center. *The Future of World Religions: Population Growth Projections, 2015-2060.* Pew Research Center, 2017.

This report provides a data-driven analysis of the growth and distribution of Muslim populations globally. It contextualizes Islam's demographic changes and their implications for cultural and societal integration, particularly in the West. The study also examines factors influencing religious identity and migration.

Ahmed, Akbar. *Journey into Europe: Islam, Immigration, and Identity.* Brookings Institution Press, 2018.

Ahmed explores the challenges of Muslim integration in Europe, delving into issues of identity, pluralism, and cultural clashes. Drawing on fieldwork and interviews, the book highlights the nuanced experiences of Muslims in diverse European settings and proposes pathways for mutual understanding and coexistence.

Muslims in Global Societies Series, Springer (Ongoing since 2013)

This multidisciplinary series focuses on the complexities of Muslim identities across global contexts. Topics include globalization, economic networks, gender, religious pluralism, and Sufism. Notable works explore South Asian American Muslim experiences and Islamic social work. The series is a rich resource for understanding how Muslims navigate cultural and societal transformations in both majority and minority settings.

Green, Nile. *Global Islam: A Very Short Introduction.* Oxford University Press, 2020.

Green examines the global spread and localization of Islam, emphasizing its adaptability and diversity. Using a sociological approach, he critiques the monolithic portrayals of Islam and highlights its role in shaping global history and culture.

Adrian, Melanie. *Religious Freedom at Risk: The EU, French Schools, and Why the Veil was Banned.* Springer, 2016.

This book provides an in-depth analysis of religious freedom in European contexts, particularly the debates surrounding Muslim veils in public spaces. Adrian explores how secular policies affect Muslim identities and integration.

Hoffmann, Thomas & Larsson, Göran. *Muslims and the New Information and Communication Technologies.* Springer, 2013.

This edited volume examines how digital technologies influence Muslim practices, from activism to education. The authors argue that technology reshapes Muslim identities while fostering global connections.

Emerging a Western Islam: Bridging Cultures and Faiths

Duderija, A., Rane, H. (2019). An Emerging Western Islam. In: Islam and Muslims in the West. New Directions in Islam. Palgrave Macmillan, Cham. https://doi.org/10.1007/978-3-319-92510-3_12

This chapter, part of the book *Islam and Muslims in the West: Major Issues and Debates*, explores the emergence of Western Islam and its cultural, religion-philosophical, and socio-political dimensions. It provides an overview of the major issues and debates that have arisen over the last three to four decades surrounding the presence of new Muslim communities residing in Western liberal democracies.

Adis Duderija & Halim Rane (2019). Islam and Muslims in the West: Major Issues and Debates. Springer Link.

This book provides a systematic and broad overview of the major debates affecting Muslims and Islam in the West. It raises a number of issues concerning Western Muslim communities and examines the issue of jurisprudence for Muslim minorities

Islam and Gender Equality

Afkhami, Mahnaz, ed. Faith and Freedom: Women's Human Rights in the Muslim World. Syracuse, NY: Syracuse University Press, 1995.

This book examines patriarchal structures that pit women's human rights against Islam, showing how discrimination and violence result from male theologians' interpretations of religion, diverging legal codes, and gender segregation. It explores how to empower women to redefine their cultures, set priorities, and participate in the political process.

Afkhami, Mahnaz and Friedl, Erika, eds. Muslim Women and the Politics of Participation: Implementing the Beijing Platform. Syracuse, NY: Syracuse University Press, 1997.

This book proposes strategies to implement the Beijing Platform for Action of the 1995 United Nations Fourth World Conference on Women. It offers proposals for Muslim women's empowerment, ranging from critical reading of literature to shape their consciousness to human rights education and collaboration with non-governmental and international organizations.

Ahmadi Khorasani, Noushin. Iranian Women's One Million Signatures Campaign for Equality: The Inside Story. Bethesda, MD: Women's Learning Partnership for Rights, Development and Peace, 2009.

This book details the origins, strategies, and philosophy of a grassroots movement fighting for women's equality in Iran since 2006. It offers a model of citizens surmounting cultural, political, and socio-economic obstacles to advocate for human rights.

AWID, ed. Feminists on the Frontline: AWID Case Studies of Resisting Fundamentalisms. Toronto, Canada: Association for Women's Rights in Development, 2010.

This collection of case studies highlights women worldwide challenging fundamentalisms within different faith traditions. It emphasizes religion's privileged position in defining and potentially denying human rights and the strategies activists adopt to ensure equality and dignity for all.

Tomalin, Emma, ed. Gender, Faith, and Development. Practical Action Publishing Ltd in association with Oxfam GB, 2011.

This book provides valuable evidence of the impact of different gender and faith perspectives on practical development issues. It highlights the complexities and ambiguities of religious influences and advances our understanding of the links between religion, gender, and development in various contexts and cultures.

Islam and Democracy

Ayub, Mohammed. Islam and Good Governance: An Annotated Bibliography. International Institute of Islamic Thought, 2020.

This bibliography explores the relationship between Islamic teachings and good governance, arguing that public policy in Islam should be viewed through the lens of maqasid (objectives of Shariah) rather than just fiqh (Islamic jurisprudence). It provides insights into how Islamic principles can address governance dilemmas.

Adaman, F. & Akbulut, B. "Erdoğan's Three-Pillared Neoliberalism: Authoritarianism, Populism, and Developmentalism." *Geoforum*, 2020.

This article examines the resilience of Turkey's Justice and Development Party (AKP) by analyzing the interplay between authoritarianism, populism, and developmentalism. It highlights how developmentalism is used to legitimize power and gain consent from the populace.

Adetula, V. AO. "Measuring Democracy and Good Governance in Africa: A Critique of Assumptions and Methods." In: Africa in Focus: Governance in the 21st Century. Human Science Research Council, 2011.

This chapter critiques the assumptions and methods used to measure democracy and good governance in Africa, arguing that many reports focus on regime type rather than the nature of the state and its relationship to democratization processes.

Al Din Al Hajjaji, S. "Islam and Reform of Authoritarianism: The Case of Muslim Government."

International Journal of Legislative Drafting and Law Reform, 2019.

This article discusses the connection between Islam, authoritarianism, and totalitarianism in four Muslim countries (Turkey, Saudi Arabia, Egypt, and Morocco). It critiques these regimes for their misinterpretation of Islamic governance and highlights the importance of transparent public participation and good governance.

Hallaq, Wael B. & Little, Donald P., eds. Islamic Studies Presented to Charles J. Adams. Leiden: E. J. Brill, 1991.

This collection of essays presents a comprehensive overview of Islamic studies, including discussions on the relationship between Islam and democracy. It offers valuable insights into the historical and contemporary perspectives on Islamic governance.

Islam and Science

Nasr, Seyyed Hossein. An Annotated Bibliography of Islamic Science. Imperial Iranian Academy of Philosophy, 1985.

This comprehensive bibliography, compiled by Seyyed Hossein Nasr, covers the history of Islamic science from Spain to Eastern Asia over a millennium. It includes works in both Islamic and non-Islamic languages, providing annotations in English and Persian. The bibliography is divided into two volumes, with a total of 4,341 entries.

Nasr, Seyyed Hossein. An Annotated Bibliography of Islamic Science, Volume 2. Imperial Iranian Academy of Philosophy, 1975.

This volume continues Nasr's work on Islamic science, focusing on various scientific disciplines and their development within the Islamic world. It includes entries on individual authors, scientific encyclopedias, cosmology, and more.

Hillenbrand, Robert. Islamic Science and Engineering. Edinburgh University Press, 1993.

This book explores the contributions of Islamic civilization to science and engineering, highlighting the achievements of Muslim scholars in fields such as mathematics, astronomy, and medicine. Hillenbrand provides a detailed analysis of the scientific methods and innovations that emerged during the Islamic Golden Age.

Saliba, George. Islamic Science and the Making of the European Renaissance. MIT Press, 2007.

Saliba examines the influence of Islamic science on the European Renaissance, arguing that many of the scientific advancements attributed to European scholars were actually based on earlier Islamic works. He discusses the transmission of knowledge through translations and the impact of Islamic scholars on European intellectual history.

Ragep, F. Jamil. Islamic Thought and Science: The Case of Ibn al-Haytham. Brill, 2001.

This book focuses on the contributions of Ibn al-Haytham, a prominent Muslim scientist, to the fields of optics and scientific methodology. Ragep explores how Ibn al-Haytham's work influenced both Islamic and Western scientific traditions.

Islamic Attitudes Towards Science: Wikipedia

This Wikipedia article provides an overview of the historical and contemporary perspectives on science within the Islamic world. It discusses contributions from medieval Muslim scholars and the relationship between Islamic teachings and scientific inquiry.

Islamophobia

Gottschalk, Peter, and Gabriel Greenberg. Islamophobia: Making Muslims the Enemy. Rowman & Littlefield, 2008.

This book explores the origins and manifestations of Islamophobia in Western societies. The authors analyze how Muslims have been portrayed as the "other" and the impact of these perceptions on Muslim communities. The book provides a historical context and examines contemporary issues related to Islamophobia.

Kaplan, Jeffrey. "Islamophobia in America? September 11 and Islamophobic Hate Crime." In: Radical Religion and Violence, Routledge, 2015, pp. 292-329.

Kaplan discusses the rise of Islamophobia in the United States following the September 11 attacks. The chapter examines the social and psychological effects of Islamophobic hate crimes on Muslim communities and the broader implications for American society.

Said, Edward W. Orientalism. Pantheon Books, 1978.

Said's seminal work on Orientalism provides a critical analysis of how Western scholarship has historically portrayed the East, including Islamic societies. The book is essential for understanding the roots of contemporary

Islamophobia and the cultural biases that continue to shape perceptions of Islam.

Esposito, John L., and Ibrahim Kalin, eds. Islamophobia: The Challenge of Pluralism in the 21st Century. Oxford University Press, 2011.

This edited volume brings together contributions from various scholars to address the challenges of Islamophobia in a pluralistic world. The book covers topics such as media representation, political discourse, and the impact of Islamophobia on Muslim communities globally.

Cesari, Jocelyne. Why the West Fears Islam: An Exploration of Muslims in Liberal Democracies. Palgrave Macmillan, 2013.

Cesari examines the reasons behind the fear of Islam in Western liberal democracies. The book explores the intersection of religion, politics, and identity, and how these factors contribute to the rise of Islamophobia. It also discusses the experiences of Muslim communities in Western societies.

Western Perceptions and Stereotypes of Muslims

Eid, M. (2014). Perceptions about Muslims in Western Societies. In: Eid, M., Karim, K.H. (eds) Re-Imagining the Other. Palgrave Macmillan, New York. https://doi.org/10.1057/9781137403667_6

This chapter discusses the influence of media on public perceptions of Muslims in Western societies and the tendency to stereotype and frame them negatively.

Pauly, R. J. (2015). Islam in the West: Perceptions vs. Reality [Review of *Securitizing Islam: Identity and the*

Search for Security; Framing Muslims: Stereotyping and Representation After 9/11*, by S. Croft, P. Morey, & A. Yaquin]. *International Studies Review*, *17*(2), 313–317. http://www.jstor.org/stable/24758362

This review explores the gap between perceptions and reality regarding Muslims in Western societies, focusing on the impact of media and significant events like 9/11.

Pauly, R. J. (2015). Islam in the West: Perceptions vs. Reality [Review of *Securitizing Islam: Identity and the Search for Security; Framing Muslims: Stereotyping and Representation After 9/11*, by S. Croft, P. Morey, & A. Yaquin]. *International Studies Review*, *17*(2), 313–317. http://www.jstor.org/stable/24758362

This book by Peter Morey and Amina Yaquin examines how Muslims have been stereotyped and represented in the media post-9/11. It's published by Harvard University Press

Impediments of Economic Development in Muslim Countries

Oweiss, Ibrahim M. "Economic, Demographic and Social Impediments to Development in the Muslim World." Center for Strategic and International Studies, 2003.

This paper analyzes the current state of affairs in low and middle-income Muslim countries, focusing on Bangladesh, Egypt, Iran, and Pakistan. It examines how demographic, economic, and social impediments impact the standard of living and the quest for political and economic reforms.

Kuru, Ahmet T. "The Ulema-State Alliance: A Barrier to Democracy and Development in the Muslim World." Global Institute, 2021.

This report explores the alliance between religious authorities (ulema) and the state as a barrier to democracy and development in Muslim countries. It discusses the historical context and the impact of this alliance on political and economic progress.

Kuran, Timur. "Islam and Underdevelopment: An Old Puzzle Revisited." Journal of Institutional and Theoretical Economics, 1997.

This article revisits the puzzle of underdevelopment in predominantly Muslim countries. It critiques and extends mechanisms proposed as explanations, such as the use of Islam to legitimize vested interests, religious obstacles to free thinking, and communalist norms that dampened capitalist economic institutions.

Pipes, Daniel. "The Muslim Cultures of the World." National Review, 2002.

This article discusses the diversity of Muslim cultures and how cultural factors can impact economic development. It highlights the differences between various Muslim countries and the challenges they face in achieving economic progress.

Oweiss, Ibrahim M. "Economic, Demographic and Social Impediments to Development in the Muslim World." Center for Strategic and International Studies, 2003.

This paper analyzes the current state of affairs in low and middle-income Muslim countries, focusing on

Bangladesh, Egypt, Iran, and Pakistan. It examines how demographic, economic, and social impediments impact the standard of living and the quest for political and economic reforms.

Pipes, Daniel. "The Muslim Cultures of the World." National Review, 2002.

This article discusses the diversity of Muslim cultures and how cultural factors can impact economic development. It highlights the differences between various Muslim countries and the challenges they face in achieving economic progress.

Globalization and the Future of Muslim Societies

Lapidus, Ira M. A History of Islamic Societies (3rd ed.). Cambridge University Press, 2014.

This comprehensive book provides a detailed history of Islamic societies from their origins to the present day. It covers various aspects such as political, social, and cultural developments, offering a thorough understanding of the evolution of Muslim communities in the context of globalization.

Kepel, Gilles. Beyond Terror and Martyrdom: The Future of the Middle East. University of California Press, 2008.

Kepel explores the impact of globalization on the Middle East, focusing on the political, social, and economic changes in the region. He discusses the challenges and opportunities that globalization presents for Muslim societies, including the rise of new political movements and the struggle for democracy.

Esposito, John L. The Future of Islam. Oxford University Press, 2010.

Esposito examines the future of Islam in the context of globalization, addressing issues such as religious reform, political change, and social development. He highlights the diversity within the Muslim world and the various ways in which globalization is shaping the future of Muslim societies.

Khan, Mushtaq H. Globalization and the Muslim World: What's Next? Journal of Muslim Minority Affairs, 2012.

Khan discusses the impact of globalization on Muslim countries, focusing on the economic, social, and political challenges and opportunities. He explores the ways in which globalization is shaping the future of Muslim societies and the potential for positive change.

The Geopolitics of the Muslim World and the Strategic Roles of Western Countries

Guiderdoni, B. A. H. (2019). Transnational religious networks and geopolitics in the Muslim World. Global Discourse, 9(4), 593-614.Transnational Religious Networks and Geopolitics in the Muslim World –

This article in *Global Discourse* explores the interrelationship between religion and geopolitics, particularly the sectarianisation of politics across the Middle East and the Muslim world.

Ahmet, A. K., & Kuru, T. (2021). The Ulema-State Alliance: A Barrier to Democracy and Development in the Muslim World. Institute for Global Change.

The Ulema-State Alliance: A Barrier to Democracy and Development in the Muslim World - This paper discusses how the alliance between Islamic scholars (the ulema) and state authorities has contributed to authoritarianism and underdevelopment in many Muslim countries.

Zelikow, P. (2021). The Wars Within Islam Are Not Over. *Foreign Affairs*, November 4.

The Wars Within Islam Are Not Over - This article in *Foreign Affairs* examines the internal struggles within the Islamic world and their geopolitical implications, particularly since the landmark year of 1979.

Tausch, A. (2019). Migration from the Muslim World to the West: Its Most Recent Trends and Effects. *Jewish Political Studies Review*, 30(1-2), 1-24.

Migration from the Muslim World to the West: Its Most Recent Trends and Effects - This article by Arno Tausch in the *Jewish Political Studies Review* analyzes patterns of global migration, focusing on the recent trends and effects of migration from Muslim countries to Western countries.

Gu, S., & Fong, E. (2022). Migration from Muslim Countries: A Tale of Two Patterns. *Population Research and Policy Review*, 41, 1853-1872.

Muslim Migrants Around the World - This report by the Pew Research Center provides an overview of the religious composition of the world's migrants, with a focus on Muslim migrants.

Kramer, S., & Tong, Y. (2024). *Muslim Migrants Around the World*. Pew Research Center.

Mabon, S., & Wastnidge, E. (2019). Transnational religious networks and geopolitics in the Muslim World. *Global Discourse*, *9*(4), 593-603.

This article discusses the interrelationship between religion and geopolitics, focusing on the sectionalization of politics across the Middle East and Muslim world

Schwartz, A. (2024). Geopolitics of the Middle East. In: Cope, Z. (eds) The Palgrave Handbook of Contemporary Geopolitics. Palgrave Macmillan, Cham. https://doi.org/10.1007/978-3-031-47227-5_20

This chapter explores key geopolitical aspects and trends in the Middle East, including the region's strategic location, the discovery of oil, and the rise of China's influence

Fuller, G.E. (2003). Islamism and Global Geopolitics. In: The Future of Political Islam. Palgrave Macmillan, New York. https://doi.org/10.1057/9781403978608_4

This book chapter examines the dramatic manifestation of political Islam on the Middle Eastern scene and its impact on global geopolitics. It's part of *The Future of Political Islam* by Graham E. Fuller, published in 2003.

Muslim Mindset: Navigating the Conflict Between Tradition and Modernity

Ozalp, Mehmet. Islam Between Tradition and Modernity: An Australian Perspective. Barton Books, 2012.

This book explores the tension between tradition and modernity in the Muslim world, highlighting how Islam can bridge this gap. Ozalp discusses the defining beliefs of Islam and the devotional practices of Muslims, addressing the conflicts and competition with modern popular culture and contemporary liberal values. He emphasizes the importance of constructive dialogue and mutual understanding to avoid a clash of civilizations.

Al-Salimi, Abdulrahman. Arab Philosophical Trends: Responses to Modernity. Oxford Academic, 2024.

This book examines the responses of 20th-century Arab philosophers to Western modernity, secularization, and cultural change. It covers a range of philosophical movements, from Kamal al-Hajj's Equilibriumism to Abderrahmane Badawi's Arab Existentialism, highlighting the ongoing dialogue between tradition and modernity in the Arab world.

Kamal, Yousuf al-Hajj. Al-Taʾāduliyya (Equilibriumism) and al-Naṣlāmiyya (Christislamity). Imperial Iranian Academy of Philosophy, 1985.

This work discusses Kamal al-Hajj's philosophy of Equilibrium and Christislamity, which advocate for a modern renaissance rooted in Arab heritage while engaging with modernity. It provides insights into how Arab intellectuals have navigated the challenges posed by Western ideas of modernization.

Badawi, Abderrahmane. Al-Wujūdiyya al-ʿArabiyya (Arab Existentialism). Imperial Iranian Academy of Philosophy, 1985.

This book delves into Arab Existentialism, exploring how this philosophical movement addresses the conflict between tradition and modernity. Badawi's work emphasizes the importance of maintaining cultural identity while engaging with modern ideas and practices.

Interfaith Dialogue and Co-Existence

Berthrong, John H. Interfaith Dialogue: An Annotated Bibliography. Multifaith Resources, 1993.

This bibliography provides a comprehensive list of resources on interfaith dialogue, covering various approaches and outcomes. It includes works from multiple faith traditions and offers insights into how different religious communities engage in dialogue and co-existence.

Ariarajah, W. The Bible and People of Other Faiths. World Council of Churches, 1985.

This book explores how the Bible can be a resource for interfaith dialogue, emphasizing the importance of understanding and respecting the beliefs of other religious traditions. It provides practical guidance for engaging in meaningful conversations with people of different faiths.

Brown, S. (Ed.) Meeting in Faith. World Council of Churches, 1989.

This collection of essays discusses the challenges and opportunities of interfaith dialogue, highlighting the importance of mutual respect and understanding. It includes contributions from various religious leaders and scholars, offering diverse perspectives on co-existence.

Hick, John. God and the Universe of Faiths. Macmillan, 1973.

Hick's work examines the relationship between different religious traditions and the concept of God. He argues for a pluralistic approach to religion, suggesting that all faiths can contribute to a deeper understanding of the divine.

Panikkar, Raimon. The Intrareligious Dialogue. Paulist Press, 1999.

This book focuses on the dialogue between different religious traditions within the same faith community. Panikkar emphasizes the importance of intra-religious dialogue as a foundation for interfaith co-existence.

Kung, Hans. Declaration of a Global Ethic. SID, 1993.

Kung's declaration outlines a set of ethical principles that can guide interfaith dialogue and co-existence. It emphasizes the need for mutual respect, justice, and peace among different religious communities.

Muslim Identity and Cultural Expression

Hussain, Serena. An Annotated Bibliography of Recent Literature on 'Invisible' Muslim Communities and New Muslim Migrant Communities in Britain. Academia.edu, 2016.

This bibliography focuses on recent literature about 'invisible' Muslim communities and new Muslim migrant communities in Britain. It includes works that explore the cultural practices, identity negotiations, and challenges faced by these communities.

Aly, Ramy MK. Becoming Arab in London: Performativity and the Undoing of Identity. Pluto Press/University of Chicago Press, 2016.

Aly's book provides an autoethnographic account of the contemporary cultural practices of Arab Londoners. It theorizes "Arabness" from the ground up, exploring how young British Arabs negotiate their identity in various social settings.

Lafourcade, Fanny. Europe/Arab World: Identities and Representations in Conflict. Academia.edu, 2016.

This work examines the conflicts and representations of identities between Europe and the Arab world. It discusses how cultural expressions and identity are shaped by geopolitical and social factors.

Ryan, Louise. Imagining the "Arab Other": The Role of the Media in Constructing Islamic Identity. Art Gallery of New South Wales, 2007.

Ryan's paper investigates the role of media in constructing Islamic identity, focusing on museum practices and the representation of Islamic artifacts.

Muslims as a Minority Group: Emerging Issues

Alam, Mohd. Sanjeer. "Muslim Minorities in India: Trapped in Exclusion and Political Populism." In: Minorities and Populism – Critical Perspectives from South Asia and Europe. Springer, 2020.

This chapter examines the socioeconomic exclusion of Muslims in India, the largest religious minority group in the country. Alam discusses how political populism and ethno-majoritarian politics have reinforced exclusion and inequality, making it difficult for Muslims to achieve socioeconomic equality.

Journal of Muslim Minority Affairs

Published by the Institute of Muslim Minority Affairs, this biannual research journal provides a forum for discussing issues related to the life of Muslims in non-Muslim societies. It covers historical, demographic, social, and economic perspectives on Muslim minorities.

Khan, Tabassum Ruhi. Beyond Hybridity and Fundamentalism: Emerging Muslim Identity in Globalized India. Oxford Academic, 2015.

This book explores the emerging Muslim identity in the context of globalized India. Khan discusses the challenges and opportunities faced by Muslim communities as they navigate their cultural and religious identities in a rapidly changing world.

Ahmed, Amina. "The Politics of Literary Postcoloniality." In: Contemporary Postcolonial Theory: A Reader. London: Arnold, 1996.

Ahmed's work examines the political dimensions of postcolonial identity, focusing on how Muslim minorities in India negotiate their cultural and political identities in the postcolonial context.

Islamic Values; Cherished vs Enacted

Mazrui, Ali A. "Islam and the United States: Streams of Convergence, Strands of Divergence." *Third World Quarterly*, vol. 25, no. 5, 2004, pp. 793-820.

This article explores the historical phases of relations between Islam and Western values, highlighting areas of convergence and divergence.

Palmer, Allen W., and Abdullahi A. Gallab. "Islam and Western Culture." *Kennedy Center*, 2010.

This feature discusses the cultural conflicts between Islam and Western societies, focusing on the challenges faced by Muslims in adapting to Western values.

Ozohu-Suleiman, Abdulhamid, and Mohammed Enesi Etudaiye. "Clash of Cultures: The Interface Between Islam and the West." *E-Africa Journal of Humanities*, 2011.

This paper examines the cultural clashes between Islam and Western societies, emphasizing the impact of historical events like the 9/11 attacks.

Haddad, Yvonne. "Islam in the West: Challenges and Opportunities." *Journal of Muslim Minority Affairs*, vol. 11, no. 2, 1991, pp. 3-15.

This article discusses the challenges faced by Muslims in Western societies and the opportunities for cultural adaptation and integration.

Mowlana, Hamid. "Islam and the West: The Dynamics of Cultural Confrontation." *International Communication Gazette*, vol. 58, no. 1, 1996, pp. 178-192.

This paper explores the dynamics of cultural confrontation between Islam and Western societies, focusing on the impact of technological innovations and cultural exchanges.

Koenig, Harold G., and Saad Al Shohaib. "Muslim Beliefs, Practices, and Values." In *Health and Well-Being in Islamic Societies*, edited by Harold G. Koenig and Saad Al Shohaib, Springer, 2014, pp. 27-41.

This chapter examines the beliefs, practices, and values of Muslims, highlighting the discrepancies between Islamic teachings and the actual practices of some Muslims.

www.ingramcontent.com/pod-product-compliance
Lightning Source LLC
LaVergne TN
LVHW091626070526
838199LV00044B/949